Leadership for Environmental Sustainability

Routledge Studies in Business Ethics

1. Rethinking Capitalism
Community and Responsibility
in Business
Rogene Buchholz

2. Organizational Transformation for Sustainability
An Integral Metatheory
Mark G. Edwards

3. Leadership for Environmental Sustainability
Edited by Benjamin W. Redekop

Leadership for Environmental Sustainability

Edited by
Benjamin W. Redekop

First published 2010
by Routledge
270 Madison Avenue, New York, NY 10016

Simultaneously published in the UK
by Routledge
2 Park Square, Milton Park, Abingdon, Oxon OX14 4RN

Routledge is an imprint of the Taylor & Francis Group, an informa business

Typeset in Sabon by IBT Global.

Library of Congress Cataloging-in-Publication Data

Leadership for environmental sustainability / edited by Benjamin W. Redekop.—1st ed.
p. cm.—(Routledge studies in business ethics ; 3)
Includes bibliographical references and index.
1. Sustainable development—Environmental aspects. 2. Leadership. I. Redekop, Benjamin W., 1961–
HC79.E5L394 2010
174—dc22
2010003224

ISBN13: 978-0-415-80650-3 (hbk)
ISBN13: 978-0-203-84699-5 (ebk)

To Katarina, and children like her everywhere: may the world you grew up in endure and flourish in ways that your parents could only imagine.

Contents

Tables

Figures

Acknowledgments

The editor would like to thank the following people for their advice, support, and feedback: Gayle Avery, Joyce Berry, David Blockstein, Bob Colvin, Barbara Crosby, John Gordon, Eugene Hynes, Peter Northouse, and Diana Wall. Special thanks to Paul Steinberg for his detailed and helpful response to the original book proposal. Steven Olson deserves warm thanks for his help in conceptualizing the project and for his friendship and encouragement throughout the entire process. The chapter contributors also merit acknowledgment for their willingness to shape their chapters according to the requirements of this volume. I am grateful for the kind help and support of Routledge editors Laura Stearns and Terry Clague, and editorial assistants Nick Mendoza and Stacy Noto. Thanks to Jennifer Green of the CNU Department of Leadership and American Studies for her cheerful assistance on this project. Finally, I am grateful to my wife, Fran, for her support and encouragement.

Some passages of the Introduction and Chapter 3 have been adapted from Benjamin W. Redekop, "Leading into a Sustainable Future: The Current Challenge," published in Michael Harvey and Nancy Huber (eds.), *Leadership: Impact, Culture, and Sustainability* (College Park: The James MacGregor Burns Academy of Leadership, 2007, pp. 134–46), with the kind permission of the International Leadership Association. Chapter 1 has been adapted with the kind permission of the American Psychological Association. The official citation that should be used in referencing this material is: R. Wielkiewicz & S. Stelzner (2005), "An Ecological Perspective on Leadership Theory, Research, and Practice," *Review of General Psychology*, *9*(4), 326–341. Copyright © 2005 American Psychological Association. The use of this information does not imply the endorsement of the publisher.

Introduction

Connecting Leadership and Sustainability

Benjamin W. Redekop

Achieving environmental sustainability is quickly becoming one of the great leadership challenges of our time. This book is for all those who want to better understand this challenge and are looking for insights, research findings, and stories that will help them to address it. It is becoming painfully clear that there are no "easy" solutions to the environmental problems that we face, and consequently it is going to take deep and sustained reflection, from all viewpoints—technical, biological, social, economic, cultural, historical, and spiritual, among others—if progress is going to be made. This book makes a contribution to the emerging conversation about leadership and sustainability and to the larger discussion about how we are going to ensure our continued flourishing on this planet, not to mention the survival of all the other plant and animal species that we are quickly forcing out of existence.

Rather than spending time cataloging and bemoaning the myriad environmental problems that we face, the authors of this volume seek to understand the leadership dimensions of achieving sustainability. We take it as given that anthropogenic climate change is real, that species are disappearing at such an alarming rate that talk of a "sixth great extinction" is not at all far-fetched, that oceans are becoming acidified garbage dumps increasingly devoid of fish, that ancient forests are disappearing and weather patterns are changing, and that unprecedented population growth is rapidly making everything worse (see Diamond, 2005, pp. 486–496, for a comprehensive accounting of our current planetary ills). We further assume that "sustainability" is a relatively straightforward concept that does not need extensive elaboration. Following the definition provided by the World Commission on the Environment and Development (known as the Brundtland Commission), we take the term to mean "meeting the needs of the present without compromising the ability of future generations to meet their own needs" (United Nations, 1987). Put somewhat more starkly, sustainability entails *living in a way that does not make things worse for future generations, whether they be future generations of polar bears or humans or orchids.* We thus assume that there is a clearly defined problem and a desired future state; what is less clear is how we are going to get there from here.[1]

Readers will find a diverse array of chapters written by scholars and practitioners of leadership who approach the topic of leadership for environmental sustainability from a variety of perspectives. While this book makes a contribution to the scholarly literature on leadership—indeed, it is the first multidisciplinary treatment of environmental leadership—it has been edited for readability and will be of interest to anyone who is concerned about this issue. Chapters are relatively short, and the editor has worked closely with authors to craft rich, thoughtful, and yet accessible treatments of this important topic. Authors approach their subjects from a number of disciplinary backgrounds, including history, philosophy, literature, religion and spirituality, psychology, communication, business, sociology, political science, and the arts. All chapters begin with an introduction that outlines the content of the chapter, and each chapter is also briefly described at the end of this introductory essay. We highly recommend reading all chapters in sequence—readers who do so will find unexpected insights and intriguing parallels, along with diverse approaches and perspectives. The cumulative result is a rich and remarkably coherent set of ideas that helps us to think more deeply not only about leadership for sustainability, but also about the nature and requirements of leadership itself, as we move into the new millennium.

WHY LEADERSHIP FOR ENVIRONMENTAL SUSTAINABILITY?

To answer this question, one might begin with the fact that very little work has been done on this topic in the field of leadership studies. A fairly comprehensive review of recent literature on public leadership, for example, contains only the most fleeting references to sustainability or the natural environment (Kellerman & Webster, 2001). Recent scholarly textbooks on leadership contain scant—if any—mention of the natural environment as a significant context for leadership, or as an "emerging issue" of interest (e.g., Antonakis, Cianciolo, & Sternberg, 2004; Gill, 2006). Books on business leadership that purport to be about meeting future challenges typically contain neither a substantive analysis of the psychology of future orientation nor a sense of the larger systemic constraints on future activities that must be taken into account by leaders. The physical environment, the ultimate constraint on business, is entirely ignored (e.g., James, 1996; Essex & Kusy, 1999; Corbin, 2000). Even prominent works that claim to be "the definitive text" on future leadership, such *The Leader of the Future* (Hesselbein, Goldsmith, & Beckhard, 1996), contain little substantive reflection on the larger systemic constraints on future activity. To be fair, the recently updated edition of this text, *The Leader of the Future 2* (2006), is somewhat improved on this score—Peter Senge's chapter discusses the need for leaders to be involved in systemic change in the face of global constraints, including the constraints posed by the natural environment and global warming (Senge, 2006). In the same collection, Ronald Heifetz's discussion of leadership as a response to "adaptive challenges" goes to the brink of the current environmental abyss, suggesting, "Some realities threaten not only a set of values beyond survival but also the very existence of a society if these realities are not discovered and met early on." Yet although environmental problems like global warming are obviously supreme examples of adaptive challenges, Heifetz seems unwilling to explicitly draw that conclusion, or to clearly identify himself with the "many environmentalists [who believe] our focus on the production of wealth rather than coexistence with nature has led us to neglect fragile factors in our ecosystem" (Heifetz, 2006, pp.82–83). Nevertheless, as will become apparent in a number of chapters in this collection, Heifetz's (1994) theory of "adaptive leadership" provides an important starting point for thinking about leadership for environmental sustainability (this point will be elaborated further in the Conclusion to this volume).

The deficit in taking a serious, long-term perspective on the future—and the looming environmental crisis in particular—in the field of leadership studies reflects both the field's orientation toward the limited time horizons of Anglo/U.S. capitalism, and the general worldview of the first industrial revolution, in which the future was seen to be limitless and constraints on economic and industrial activity were either ignored (as in the case of air and water pollution) or strongly opposed (as in the emergence of organized labor). We are now becoming increasingly aware of the way in which modern industry has been built on the externalization of costs: early on the costs were more social and ethical—slavery and child labor were bound up with early industrialization (Williams, 1961; Mathias, 1969)—but increasingly the environmental costs of industry have taken center stage. The tendency among students of American business leadership to ignore or discount the larger social and environmental contexts in which leadership occurs is simply a reflection of some of the main tenets of American capitalism, as well as the lineaments of the American dream, which stresses the idea that human beings (and by extension, leaders) are free agents who can succeed at whatever they wish to do, if only they work hard enough. Critics have argued for some time that placing too much emphasis on leaders as free agents ignores the fact that "the leader is embedded in a social system, which constrains behavior" (Pfeffer, 1977, p. 107). Three decades later, we must add that leaders are also embedded in a global *environmental* system that also presents a serious constraint on behavior.

While a few very useful books have been written on environmental leadership from the perspective of natural resource management or the management of environmental organizations (e.g., Snow, 1992; Berry & Gordon, 1993; Gordon & Berry, 2006), none has placed the relationship between leadership—as a general construct—and the natural environment at center stage and examined it from diverse viewpoints, as this volume does. Russo (2008) provides an important, comprehensive set of readings on environmental management that touches on nearly every aspect of sustainability, but the leadership angle is left unexplored. Avery (2005) presents a helpful comparison between the leadership model of sustainable "Rhineland/stakeholder capitalism" and unsustainable "Anglo/US shareholder capitalism," while Steinberg (2001) examines how conservation and political leaders in Costa Rica and Bolivia have been able to enact environmental protections and move their nations toward sustainability. Without explicitly mentioning "leadership," Moser and Dilling (2007) provide a comprehensive look at the communication challenges presented by climate change. In a similar fashion, Gunderson, Light, and Holling (1995) provide insights for leaders and managers trying to solve natural resource and other environmental problems. Although not about leadership *per se*, their analysis contains cautionary lessons for those who may think that "managing" nature in a sustainable fashion is a simple proposition; in their view, "sustainable development" is something of an oxymoron.

Books on "responsible leadership" typically contain minimal treatment of the natural environment (e.g., Doh & Stumpf, 2005; Maak & Pless, 2006[2]), as do books on "moral leadership" (e.g., Hoivik, 2002; Ciulla, Price, & Murphy, 2006). Surprisingly, Dunning's landmark collection, *Making Globalization Good: The Moral Challenges of Global Capitalism* (2003) contains very little discussion of the natural environment. On the other hand, Crosby's pathbreaking *Leadership for Global Citizenship* (1999) contains discussion of the natural environment as one pertinent issue among others. Gerzon's *Leading through Conflict* (2006) mentions the natural environment at only a few points, but he tellingly ends his book with a discussion of the looming challenge of achieving sustainability (pp. 233–234).

An important exception to the general lack of attention to this issue in leadership studies is what Simon Western (2008) has characterized as an emerging "eco-leader discourse." Still in its infancy, this discourse (or paradigm) is characterized by "a growing interest in systems thinking, complexity theory, narrative approaches, and also the environment as metaphors for leadership and organizing company structures" (p. 184). Taking an ecological perspective on leadership, the emerging paradigm emphasizes holism, connectivity, spirituality, interdependence, and sustainability as fundamental leadership values. It conceives of leadership as being dispersed, emergent, ethical, and adaptive—able to help groups and organizations adapt themselves to external contingencies like environmental change. Contributions to this discourse, in the form of academic journal articles, include Bolman and Deal (1994), Carlopio (1994), Shrivastava (1994), Allen, Stelzner, and Wielkiewicz (1998), and Egri and Herman (2000). Many of the chapters in the present volume make contributions to this discourse, including the chapter by Western (Chapter 2) that describes the contours of the emerging eco-leader discourse in contrast to previous leadership discourses.

One of the most forceful recent statements on the connection between leadership and sustainability has come from Jim MacNeill, Chair Emeritus of the International Institute for Sustainable Development. MacNeill (2007) argues that powerful individuals in top governmental and private-sector leadership positions will be crucial linchpins in achieving sustainable development: "Institutionalizing sustainable development . . . will not happen, certainly not in any significant way, if the person at the top is not determined to make it happen" (p. 21). In a similar fashion, Thomas Friedman (2008) suggests that in a world that is increasingly becoming "hot, flat, and crowded," leadership from the highest reaches of power down to the state and local levels is essential: "We need leaders who can shape the issues so that people understand why ignoring them is such a threat and *why rising to them is such an opportunity*. We also need leaders who not only understand the importance of dealing with this problem in a systemic way, but who can actually generate the vision and authority to pull that system together" (p. 405; emphasis in original).

Paul Hawken (2007) provides a different view on the role of leadership in confronting ecological crisis. Hawken highlights the "bottom-up" movement for social and environmental justice that, by his estimation, is constituted by over a million local groups and organizations worldwide that have no central leader or ideology. In Hawken's analysis, powerful, ideological leaders have gotten us into this mess, and it is going to take a pragmatic, grassroots approach to get us out of it. Yet he acknowledges the potential lack of "connection, cooperation, and effectiveness" of the diverse, leaderless movement that he describes (Hawken, 2007, p. 19). The tension between Hawken's and Friedman's perspectives on the role of leadership in solving environmental problems highlights an underlying tension within the environmental movement as a whole, between mainstream and more radical approaches. The latter tend to emphasize the role of power and hierarchy in the creation of social and environmental injustice: authoritarian structures have produced the "system" that degrades women, minorities, the poor, and the Earth itself. Consequently, every effort is made to avoid reproducing the offending structures of power and hierarchy in movements and organizations that seek to right the wrongs of the past, and "leadership" itself becomes suspect. While such a view has the merit of logical consistency, in practice it is very difficult to sustain a "leaderless culture," and indeed most environmental groups eventually succumb to some sort of leadership structure, despite their best efforts to the contrary (Chapter 12 in this volume provides a good example of this phenomenon; see also Purkis, 2001; Tranter, 2009).

Despite all of the constraints, limitations, abuses, and diverse understandings of leadership, it is endemic to human (and other primate) societies and unlikely to disappear any time soon (Bass, 1990, pp. 3–20). To say this is not to underestimate the importance of the many grassroots groups and organizations that have led the way in environmental protection, only to acknowledge that even the most antiauthoritarian organizations are dependent, at some level, on leaders and acts of leadership in their formation and effective functioning. The present volume approaches the issue of environmental leadership from all directions and at all levels—we do not assume that leadership necessarily resides in a person or position, but rather is a quality that can be expressed and shared in myriad ways, times, and places. Leaders are both born and made, and leadership positions enable both good and bad leadership; but in itself, leadership is an emergent quality that helps organize and focus groups on achieving substantive goals—such as sustainability—that might otherwise remain elusive.

LEADERSHIP IN CONTEXT

The larger case to be made for the approach taken in this book is a more philosophical one: in a world swiftly heading towards environmental catastrophe, leadership *by definition* entails environmental concern. Why is this so? Because leadership takes place in—and is conditioned by—the two fundamental dimensions of space and time. As to the former, it seems elementary to suggest that context matters when it comes to defining leadership. What counts as "leadership" in any one situation is going to depend at least in part on the needs and constraints presented by that situation. Leader behaviors, values, and tasks will inevitably be shaped by the environment in which leadership is enacted. As stated by Osborn, Hunt, and Jauch (2002), "[Leadership] is socially constructed in and from the context where patterns over time must be considered and where history matters . . . Change the context and leadership changes as does what is sought and whether specific leadership patterns are considered effective" (pp. 797–798). A hunter-gatherer community attempting to find and capture wild game will doubtless require a different form of leadership—and a different skill set—than a modern corporation seeking to shrink its carbon footprint or a local city council that wants to encourage the use of alternative energy in its community.

To make this suggestion is not to argue that there are no fundamental leadership qualities that are widely shared; it is merely to suggest that context—and indeed, culture—matters when it comes to how leadership is understood and practiced (see, for example, Lewis, 2006; Hofstede, 2005; Den Hartog & Dickson, 2004). If our hunter-gatherer community finds itself in a situation in which it is consuming its own food supply faster than it is being regenerated, what counts as leadership will entail a new and likely more complex set of understandings and behaviors. Likewise, the type of leadership shown by western industrial titans of the past few hundred years, premised on the ability to leverage resources regardless of social and environmental consequences, is no longer salient in a world that recognizes universal human rights and is running out of "commons" to exploit. The "industrial paradigm" of leadership—which Rost (1991) characterizes as "good management"—may have counted as "leadership" in the past, but in the present context we may feel compelled to describe it using other, more pejorative terms. As Senge (2006) observes, in complex, interconnected systems, leaders now need to have "systems intelligence," which includes "seeing patterns of interdependency and seeing into the future" (pp. 38–39), if collapse of the whole system is to be averted. Acting on such intelligence may be easier said than done, however, since unlike previous leadership challenges, achieving sustainability is less about promising some new "good" (e.g., rights, justice, prosperity, freedom), than about averting catastrophe.

Secondly, as Senge's remark suggests, leadership has an important temporal dimension—good leaders are those people who help the group navigate its way into a desirable future. Good leaders do not lead their constituents over a cliff, and it would be an odd locution to say that a person "showed leadership" by doing so. There must be some sense of where the group is headed and how it will get there, and it is an act of leadership to have this knowledge and convey it convincingly to one's constituents. Leadership involves, among other things, setting future goals and helping others to meet them, and there is in fact wide agreement among leadership scholars that vision and future orientation are fundamental components of leadership.

Thus James MacGregor Burns, in his classic work on *Leadership*, states: "I define leadership as the leaders inducing followers to act for certain goals that represent the values and the motivations . . . of both leaders and followers" (1978, p. 19; see also Bass, 1990, pp. 14–16; Northouse, 2007, p. 3). Robert Greenleaf's servant leader is more explicitly visionary than Burns's transforming leader: it is not enough to help followers reach their goals, leaders must also have a prophetic vision of the future state into which followers are being led. "Foresight is the 'lead' that the leader has. Once leaders lose this lead and events start to force their hand, they are leaders in name only" (Greenleaf, 2002, p. 40). In Winston and Patterson's (2006) integrative definition of leadership, drawn from a broad survey of the leadership literature, future orientation plays a central role: "The leader achieves . . . influence by humbly conveying a prophetic vision of the future in clear terms that resonates with the follower(s) beliefs and values in such a way that the follower(s) can understand and interpret the future into present-time action steps" (p. 7). In the GLOBE study of leadership and culture in 62 societies, "foresight" and "plans ahead" rank near the very top of "universal leader attributes" (House et al., 2004, p. 677).

Some go so far as to assert that: "Vision is the only characteristic of effective leadership that is universal" (Bolman & Deal, quoted in Harter, 2006, p. 21). The degree of future orientation can be seen as one of the key distinctions between leaders and managers—the higher the organizational position, the greater the emphasis on future orientation (Bass,

1990, pp. 404–406; Kouzes & Posner, 2002, pp. 28–29). This distinction has the merit of also being congruent with everyday language: "to manage" connotes activity in the here and now, while "to lead" suggests forward motion in both space and time. Leaving aside the question of whether vision and future orientation are *absolutely universal* leadership qualities (see Den Hartog & Dickson, 2004, pp. 270–273), there can be no doubt that they are widely held to be crucial leadership attributes, and for good reason. As far back as the writings of Machiavelli, successful leadership has been conceived to include foresight and sustainability: according to Machiavelli, successful princes master *fortuna* by preparing for future challenges, and successful states are those that *endure* (Machiavelli, 1532/1983).

The obvious conclusion to be drawn is that in a situation of diminishing natural resources and growing environmental degradation, "leadership" by definition entails an active concern for the natural environment. We depend on our leaders to respond to time and place in such a way that the group is able to flourish—spiritually, economically, emotionally, and as members of a larger biotic community. Some may want to argue that we do not need a healthy or diverse natural environment to flourish, but such arguments are unconvincing at best and irresponsible at worst. We will at any rate leave that discussion to others; our assumption in this book is that readers are convinced there is a serious problem at hand and wish to do something about it. But where do we begin? What works and what doesn't? Who are the people that we should be paying attention to, and what has contributed to their success as environmental leaders? What kind of systemic changes are needed and how can we as leaders and followers help to bring them about? How does one best convince others to change their ways? How does one collaborate effectively with others to promote change? What kinds of stories should environmental leaders be telling? What is different about "leadership for sustainability" as opposed to other types of leadership? These are the types of questions that the chapters in this volume seek to address, and in the following section I briefly describe the content and argument of each chapter.

CHAPTER DESCRIPTIONS

In Chapter 1, "An Ecological Perspective on Leadership Theory, Research, and Practice," Richard M. Wielkiewicz and Stephen P. Stelzner suggest that current theories of leadership are based mainly on the industrial paradigm, emphasizing the preeminence of positional leaders and the machinelike qualities of organizations. Evolutionary and attributional biases tend to reinforce the industrial paradigm. In response, the authors propose an ecological theory of leadership that makes four important assertions:

Effective leadership processes involve temporary resolutions of a tension between the traditional industrial approach and the neglected ecological approach.
Specific leaders are less important than they appear because the context is more important than what leaders decide to do.
Organizations are more adaptive when there is a diversity of genuine input into decision-making processes.
Leadership itself is an emergent process arising from the human interactions that make up the organization.

The authors suggest that this model is "ecological" in two senses: (a) it approaches organizations as complex systems, and (b) it lays the groundwork for forms of leadership that are more adaptive to external environments, including the natural world.

In Chapter 2, Simon Western continues the discussion by providing an overview of previous dominant leadership "discourses," before describing the origins and contours of the emerging "eco-leader discourse" that is deftly outlined in Chapter 1. While sharing many of the perspectives of Wielkiewicz and Stelzner, Western places organizational eco-leadership in a broad postmodernist framework. Drawing on psychoanalysis and critical theory, and paying attention to issues such as power, social movements, and the homogenization of modern workplaces, Western provides a comprehensive overview of an emerging paradigm of leadership that is more congruent with the current shape and direction of world events than previous paradigms. Like Wielkiewicz and Stelzner, Western argues that an eco-leadership perspective is important not only as a response to environmental crisis, but as a general perspective on the needs and requirements of organizational leadership in a postindustrial era.

Chapter 3, "Challenges and Strategies of Leading for Sustainability," considers some of the specific leadership challenges posed by environmental problems that may not be felt for decades and whose solutions will involve changes in behavior at best, and lifestyle "sacrifices" at worst. In this chapter Benjamin Redekop draws from the field of environmental psychology to understand some of the human, social, and psychological dimensions to the problem of achieving environmental sustainability, and proposes some concrete behaviors and strategies that those wishing to show leadership on this issue may find helpful.

In "Leadership and the Dynamics of Collaboration: Averting the Tragedy of the Commons" (Chapter 4), Robert L. Williams continues the discussion begun in Chapter 3 by exploring the social-psychological dynamics of collaboration aimed at solving environmental problems through three lenses: (a) the attributes of the individual that influence why, when, and how a person collaborates; (b) the attributes of the organization that influence why, when, and how the organization collaborates; and (c) the attributes of the process being used to collaborate that influences why, when, and how the parties collaborate. The conclusions of this chapter are based on surveys and in-depth interviews with environmental and other leaders from a variety of social sectors that have engaged in collaboration. It is through their experiences that we can begin to identify important attributes influencing successes and failures of collaboration, which is a central yet relatively unstudied component of leadership for sustainability.

Martin Melaver, in "Leadership for Sustainability in Business: It's all about the Stories We Tell" (Chapter 5), focuses on environmental leadership in a business context. Melaver, who is CEO of Melaver, Inc., suggests that business leaders are constantly telling stories of one sort or another, and that new stories are needed if we are to move towards sustainability. The chapter includes examples of the kinds of stories that leaders need to start telling, including stories that narrate how we have gotten off-track, as well as those that suggest an alternative future. By telling such stories we can begin to imagine ourselves into a sustainable future, a future that is perhaps not as far-fetched as some might believe.

In Chapter 6, "Green Heroes Reexamined: An Evaluation of Environmental Role Models," Beth Birmingham and Stan LeQuire extend the storytelling theme by suggesting that we need to include stories of lesser-known leaders in our pantheon of "green heroes." Citizen leaders like José Matilde Bonilla, who died in the cause of environmental protection in Honduras, provide leadership role models that deserve to be known alongside more well-known "celebrity activists" like Al Gore and Leonardo DiCaprio. Birmingham and LeQuire compare these two types of environmental role models and provide examples of relatively unknown citizen leaders who young people may find more authentic and inspiring than celebrity activists.

In "Communicating Leadership for Environmental Sustainability: The Rhetorical Strategies of Rachel Carson and Al Gore" (Chapter 7), Denise Stodola brings the discussion back to well-known environmental leaders, demonstrating that despite very different leadership styles, Al Gore and Rachel Carson have been effective communicators with the ability to combine and balance the rhetorical appeals of *ethos*, *pathos*, and *logos* as outlined by Aristotle. Stodola argues that Carson and Gore's blending of these three forms of rhetorical appeal are important factors in their success as environmental leaders, and that their rhetorical strategies are further enhanced by their evocation of the sublime and their status as sociocultural "underdogs." The chapter thus foregrounds successful communication strategies used by environmental leaders that others may want to cultivate.

Chapter 8, "Artists as Transformative Leaders for Sustainability," develops the idea that artists and the arts have an important role to play in environmental leadership. Drawing on their experience collaborating with artists to design a stormwater garden in Duluth, Minnesota, Jill Jacoby and Xia Ji argue that the creativity and diversity of perspectives of civically engaged artists can play a transformative role in the redesign of our cities.

The design *charrette* described in this chapter provides a stimulating example of how artists can play a leadership role in reimagining our landscapes and industrial processes in ways that are both sustainable and aesthetically pleasing. The chapter, like others in this volume, highlights the importance of diversity and collaboration in the leadership process.

In "The Agrarian Mind and Good Leadership: Harvesting Insights from the Literary Field of Wendell Berry" (Chapter 9), Paul Kaak offers the writings of the agrarian writer Wendell Berry as the provider of a postindustrial model of sustainable leadership that is based on agricultural practices and lifestyles. In this model, good leaders and thoughtful agrarians carry the same general objective: nurturing people, places, and products that are sustainable, healthy, and life-giving. In this model leaders and cultivators strive for the development of followers and fields that have the capacity to produce what is good in independent and proper ways. Leaders interested in sustainability therefore may have much to learn from visionary agrarian thinkers like Berry, according to Kaak.

Chapter 10 examines another dimension of agrarian leadership. In "Leadership from Below: Farmers and Sustainable Agriculture in Ethiopia," Ezekiel Gebissa describes how state-sponsored agricultural initiatives—leadership from above—have failed to adequately address the ongoing Ethiopian subsistence crisis. Meanwhile, farmers in the densely populated Harer highlands have shown "leadership from below" by developing environmentally responsible farming practices that have raised local standards of living and been adopted in other parts of the country. Gebissa argues that the Ethiopian subsistence crisis is a classic "adaptive challenge" that cannot be solved under existing food-producing and employment paradigms, and that farmers in the Harer highlands have been better at leading the way towards sustainability than state-sponsored programs administered from above. These farmers responded to food shortages by developing strategies based on indigenous knowledge of the ecosystem, cultural farm management practices, and the ability to quickly respond to external economic opportunities. The chapter thereby contributes to the growing awareness that centralized, command-and-control forms of leadership are often less helpful in the move towards sustainability than more dispersed and emergent forms of leadership.

Chapter 11, "The League of Nations and the Problems of Health and the Environment: Leadership for the Common Good in Historical Perspective," by Michael Callahan, provides an early example of international leadership and cooperation in solving problems of human health and the environment. Although the Covenant of the League of Nations made no direct mention of the natural environment, the League provided the first international framework for addressing problems like air, noise, and water pollution; toxic chemicals; infectious diseases; and unsustainable whaling practices. Callahan demonstrates that a mix of scientists, technical experts, diplomats, businesspeople, League officials, and others collaborated on addressing these and other similar problems, led by figures like Dr. Alice Hamilton, a scientist who was the first woman on the faculty of Harvard Medical School. Callahan concludes that despite significant League failures and setbacks, it provided a model for international cooperation in addressing environmental problems, and leaders like Woodrow Wilson and Alice Hamilton illustrate how Crosby and Bryson's (2005) conceptions of visionary and ethical leadership for the common good are possible in a "shared-power world."

In "Protest, Power, and 'Political Somersaults': Leadership Lessons from the German Green Party" (Chapter 12), Heather R. McDougall suggest that the Greens present an instructive variation of "citizen leaders"—educated and active citizens who emerge when traditional leaders are not acting in the best interests of society. Citizen leaders are often temporary leaders—their intention is not to obtain or retain formal leadership power or to become part of "the system." McDougall suggests that the Greens exemplify the successful crossover—with many bumps in the road along the way—from citizen leadership into formal political leadership, allowing the group to move from "outsider" with limited political impact to "insider" with national legislative authority. Drawing on interviews with Green Party leaders, the chapter examines the ways in which the Greens have adapted themselves to the realities of power politics while leading the way in progressive social and environmental legislation as well as towards inclusion and gender equality within their own party organization.

Chapter 13, "Religion, Leadership, and the Natural Environment: The Case of American Evangelicals," by Calvin Redekop, shifts our focus to the role of religion and religious leadership in achieving environmental sustainability. Redekop provides an overview of the long and complex interplay between religious beliefs and the natural world, noting the particular ideological challenges faced by evangelical leaders when it comes to mobilizing their constituents to embrace environmental causes. He goes on to profile five American evangelical figures who have shown exemplary leadership on environmental issues, highlighting the ways in which such leaders have shown "adaptive leadership" (Heifetz, 1994) in their religious communities. The chapter demonstrates that although evangelical beliefs present particular challenges to developing a fully fledged concern for the natural world, leadership shown by a variety of individuals and groups has resulted in a growing concern for the natural environment within American Evangelicalism. As such, there can be no better example of the importance of leaders and leadership in achieving environmental sustainability.

In "The Turn toward Spirituality and Environmental Leadership" (Chapter 14), Corné Bekker examines the spiritual dimensions of leadership for sustainability. Bekker grounds his discussion in an analysis of three spiritualities that show concern for the natural environment while advocating ethical leadership. These include the medieval nature-mysticism of St. Francis of Assisi, the participatory mutuality of the South African philosophy of Ubuntu, and the "frugal leadership" model of Quaker spirituality. Bekker suggests that environmental leadership can and does emerge from these spiritualities, which can provide a coherent and meaningful basis for leaders' understanding of the world and their place in it.

Chapter 15, "Deep Systems Leadership: A Model for the 21st Century," brings the discussion full circle. Author Rian Satterwhite combines insights from cultural biology, systems thinking, and deep ecology to craft a multidimensional leadership model that provides a philosophical foundation for new and more sustainable forms of leadership. The specter of massive anthropogenic climate change presents a particularly compelling reason to formulate a fundamentally new way of thinking about leadership, one that acknowledges the deep and complex interconnections between human beings and nature. The model that emerges is nonhierarchical, is a capacity rather than a position, and is more of a lifestyle that results from deep contemplation and reflection rather than a skill gained through training. This chapter provides a brief yet rich synthesis and further development of the emerging "eco-leader" paradigm.

Finally, the Conclusion identifies emergent themes and implications for further research and thinking about leadership for sustainability. It suggests that a truly "general theory of leadership" becomes possible when a universally shared context—such as the biosphere—is explicitly identified and made a starting point for theorizing, and that one can in fact begin to see the outlines of such a general theory in this collection. This theory is revealed to have Darwinian underpinnings and to be grounded in the processes and workings of nature itself. It emphasizes adaptation, diversity, decentralization, systems thinking, cooperation/collaboration, creativity, holism, and may ultimately be characterized as a kind of "leadership by design." But readers will doubtless draw their own conclusions, and it is our hope that the present volume stimulates new thinking, insights, and research into a subject that urgently requires our attention.

NOTES

1. That the way forward may involve rethinking how best to reframe this "problem" of sustainability is assumed, and is discussed in some of the chapters in this collection. The point to be made here, however, is that semantic debates over the term "sustainability" are a distraction that often do little to help us move in the desired direction. The basic idea is clear and simple.
2. To be fair, Chapter 15 of Maak and Pless (2006), "Developing Leaders for Sustainable Business" (pp. 227–244), is a useful discussion of efforts by Royal Dutch Shell to "embed" sustainable practices within company culture.

REFERENCES

Allen, K., Stelzner, S., & Wielkiewicz, R. (1998). The Ecology of Leadership: Adapting to the Challenges of a Changing World. *Journal of Leadership Studies*, *5*(2), 62–82.

Antonakis, J., Cianciolo, A., & Sternberg, R. (2004). *The Nature of Leadership*. Thousand Oaks, CA: Sage Publications.

Avery, G. (2005). *Leadership for Sustainable Futures: Achieving Success in a Competitive World*. Cheltenham: Edward Elgar.

Bass, B. (1990). *Bass & Stogdill's Handbook of Leadership: Theory, Research, and Managerial Applications*. New York: The Free Press.

Berry, J., & Gordon, J. (1993). *Environmental Leadership: Developing Effective Skills and Styles*. Washington, DC: Island Press.

Bolman, L., & Deal, T. (1994). Spirited Leadership. *The Leadership Quarterly, 5*(3/4), 309–312.

Burns, J. (1978). *Leadership*. New York: Harper Perennial.

Carlopio, J. (1994). Holism: A Philosophy of Organizational Leadership for the Future. *The Leadership Quarterly, 5*(3/4), 297–307.

Ciulla, J., Price, T., & Murphy, S. (2006). *The Quest for Moral Leaders: Essays on Leadership Ethics*. Northampton, MA: Edward Elgar.

Corbin, C. (2000). *Great Leaders See the Future First: Taking your Organization to the Top in Five Revolutionary Steps*. Chicago: Dearborn.

Crosby, B. (1999). *Leadership for Global Citizenship: Building Transnational Community*. Thousand Oaks, CA: Sage Publications.

Crosby, B., & Bryson, J. (2005). *Leadership for the Common Good: Tackling Public Problems in a Shared-Power World*. San Francisco: Jossey-Bass.

Den Hartog, D., & Dickson, M. (2004). Leadership and Culture. In J. Antonakis, A. Cianciolo, & R. Sterbnerg (Eds.), *The Nature of Leadership* (pp. 249–278). Thousand Oaks, CA: Sage Publications.

Diamond, J. (2005). *Collapse: How Societies Choose to Fail or Succeed*. New York: Viking.

Doh, J., & Stumpf, S. (2005). *Handbook on Responsible Leadership and Governance in Global Business*. Cheltenham: Edward Elgar.

Dunning, J. (2003). *Making Globalization Good: The Moral Challenges of Global Capitalism*. Oxford: Oxford University Press.

Egri, C., & Herman, S. (2000). Leadership in the North American Environmenta Sector: Values, Leadership Styles, and Contexts of Environmental Leaders and Their Organizations. *Academy of Management Journal, 43*(4), 571–604.

Essex, L., & Kusy, M. (1999). *Fast-Forward Leadership: How to Exchange Outmoded Practices Quickly by Forward-Looking Leadership Today*. Edinburgh: Financial Times/Prentice Hall.

Friedman, T. (2008). *Hot, Flat, and Crowded: Why We Need a Green Revolution—And How It Can Renew America*. New York: Farrar, Straus and Giroux.

Gerzon, M. (2006). *Leading through Conflict: How Successful Leaders Transform Differences into Opportunities*. Boston: Harvard Business School Press.

Gill, R. (2006). *Theory and Practice of Leadership*. Thousand Oaks, CA: Sage Publications.

Gordon, J., & Berry, J. (2006). *Environmental Leadership Equals Essential Leadership: Redefining Who Leads and How*. New Haven & London: Yale University Press.

Greenleaf, R. (2002). *Servant Leadership: A Journey into the Nature of Legitimate Power and Greatness*. New York: Paulist Press.

Gunderson, L., Light, S., & Holling, C. (1995). *Barriers and Bridges to the Renewal of Ecosystems and Institutions*. New York: Columbia University Press.

Harter, N. (2006). A Signpost at the Crossroads: Hermeneutics in Leadership Studies. In S. Huber & M. Harvey (Eds.), *Leadership at the Crossroads* (pp. 14–27). College Park: The James MacGregor Burns Academy of Leadership.

Hawken, P. (2007). *Blessed Unrest: How the Largest Movement in the World Came into Being and Why No One Saw It Coming*. New York: Viking.

Heifetz, R. (1994). *Leadership without Easy Answers*. Cambridge, MA: Harvard University Press.

Heifetz, R. (2006). Anchoring Leadership in the Work of Adaptive Progress. In F. Hesselbein & M. Goldsmith (Eds.), *The Leader of the Future 2* (pp. 73–84). San Francisco: Jossey-Bass.

Hesselbein, F., & Goldsmith, M. (2006). *The Leader of the Future 2*. San Francisco: Jossey-Bass.

Hesselbein, F., Goldsmith, M., & Beckhard, R. (1996). *The Leader of the Future: New Visions, Strategies, and Practices for the Next Era*. San Francisco: Jossey-Bass.

Hofstede, G. (2005). *Cultures and Organizations: Software of the Mind*. New York: McGraw-Hill.

Hoivik, H. (2002). *Moral Leadership in Action: Building and Sustaining Moral Competence in European Organizations*. Cheltenham: Edward Elgar.

House, R., Hanger, P., Javidan, M., Dorfman, P., & Gupta, V. (2004). *Culture, Leadership, and Organizations: The GLOBE Study of 62 Societies*. Thousand Oaks, CA: Sage Publications.

James, J. (1996). *Thinking in the Future Tense*. New York: Simon and Schuster.

Kellerman, B., & Webster, S. (2001). The Recent Literature on Public Leadership Reviewed and Considered. *The Leadership Quarterly, 12*(4), 485–514.

Kouzes, J., & Posner, B. (2002). *The Leadership Challenge*. San Francisco: Jossey-Bass.

Lewis, R. (2006). *When Cultures Collide: Leading across Cultures*. Boston: Nicholas Brealey.

Maak, T., & Pless, N. (2006). *Responsible Leadership*. London & New York: Routledge.

Machiavelli, N. (1532/1983). *The Prince*. New York: Penguin Classics.

MacNeill, J. (2007). Leadership for Sustainable Development. In *Institutionalizing Sustainable Development* 9(pp. 19–23). Paris: Organisation for Economic Cooperation and Development.

Mathias, P. (1969). *The First Industrial Nation: An Economic History of Britain 1700–1914*. New York: Scribners.

Moser, S., & Dilling, L. (2007). *Creating a Climate for Change: Communicating Climate Change and Facilitating Social Change*. Cambridge: Cambridge University Press.

Northouse, P. (2007). *Leadership: Theory and Practice*. Thousand Oaks, CA: Sage Publications.

Osborn, R., Hunt, J., & Jauch, L. (2002). Toward a Contextual Theory of Leadership. *The Leadership Quarterly, 13*(6), 797–837.

Pfeffer, J. (1977). The Ambiguity of Leadership. *Academy of Management Review, 2*(1), 104–112.

Purkis, J. (2001). Leaderless Cultures: The Problem of Authority in a Radical Environmental Group. In C. Barker, A. Johnson, & M. Lavalette (Eds.), *Leadership and Social Movements* (pp. 160–177). Manchester: Manchester University Press.

Rost, J. (1991). *Leadership for the Twenty-First Century*. New York: Praeger.

Russo, M. (2008). *Environmental Management: Readings and Cases*. Thousand Oaks, CA: Sage Publications.

Senge, P. (2006). Systems Citizenship: The Leadership Mandate for this Millennium. In F. Hesselbein & M. Goldsmith (Eds.), *The Leader of the Future 2* (pp. 31–46). San Francisco: Jossey-Bass.

Shrivastava, P. (1994). Ecocentric Leadership in the 21st Century. *The Leadership Quarterly, 5*(3/4), 223–226.

Snow, Donald. (1992). *Inside the Environmental Movement: Meeting the Leadership Challenge*. Washington, DC: Island Press.

Steinberg, P. (2001). *Environmental Leadership in Developing Countries: Transnational Relations and Biodiversity Policy in Costa Rica and Bolivia*. Cambridge, MA: MIT Press.

Tranter, B. (2009). Leadership and Change in the Tasmanian Environment Movement. *The Leadership Quarterly, 20*(5), 708–724.

United Nations. (1987). *Report of the World Commission on Environment and Development* (General Assembly Resolution 42/187, 11 December 1987). Retrieved from http://www.un.org/documents/ga/res/42/ares42–187.htm

Western, S. (2008). *Leadership: A Critical Text*. Thousand Oaks, CA: Sage Publications.

Williams, E. (1961). *Capitalism and Slavery*. New York: Russell and Russell.

Winston, B., & Patterson, K. (2006). An Integrative Definition of Leadership. *International Journal of Leadership Studies, 1*(2), 6–66.

1 An Ecological Perspective on Leadership Theory, Research, and Practice

Richard M. Wielkiewicz and Stephen P. Stelzner

INTRODUCTION

For those who care about environmental issues, it can be deeply frustrating to observe leadership processes resulting in decisions that ignore the environment. It often seems as though the environmental perspective is completely absent, and the result is a constant stream of decisions and policies that undermine society's sustainability. Historically, it has been easy for leaders in positions of authority to reject or ignore the need to focus on sustainability. One reason is that traditional theories of leadership (and resulting practice) are based mainly upon the industrial paradigm emphasizing the preeminence of positional leaders and the machinelike qualities of organizations (e.g., Zaccaro, 2001). These theories focus on "positional leaders" (presidents, members of congress, CEOs, directors, executives, managers, military officers, chairpersons, etc.), and according to this theoretical perspective, positional leaders are directly responsible for organizational success and adaptation. This represents an industrial approach to leadership. With this emphasis, it is easy for leaders in positions of authority to reject or ignore the advice and counsel of organizational experts, including those who represent the perspective that organizations need to focus on sustainability.

We propose a theory of leadership based upon the same ecological principles that drive the environmental movement. This leadership theory makes four important assertions:

1. Effective leadership processes involve temporary resolutions of a tension between the traditional "industrial approach" and the neglected "ecological approach" to leadership.
2. Specific leaders are less important than they appear because the ecological context (defined later) is more important than what leaders decide to do.
3. Organizations are more adaptive when there is a diversity of genuine input into decision-making processes.

4. Leadership itself is an *emergent* process arising from the human interactions that make up the organization.

The ecological side of the tension sees organizations as complex *systems* in which an infinite number of variables, including positional leader behaviors, influence adaptation. This ecological–industrial tension exists in every organization. An implication is that organizations strengthening the role of ecological principles in leadership processes will enhance their adaptive characteristics and their long-term sustainability. Our theory suggests that the key to effective leadership is that all perspectives, especially those advocating for our environment, need to be fairly represented in leadership processes. On the other hand, absence of such diversity, consistent with overemphasis of the industrial side of the tension, threatens the long-term adaptability of the organization. This chapter describes our theory in detail and points the way toward a more sustainable model of leadership.

DEVELOPING AN ECOLOGICAL PERSPECTIVE ON LEADERSHIP

The history of leadership studies has generally been written from the perspective of what Rost (1997) calls the "industrial paradigm," a perspective that emphasizes the preeminence of leaders and the machinelike qualities of organizations. Our main contention is that the dominance of the traditional industrial paradigm in leadership research and practice is not healthy. Instead, we see leadership processes as involving a tension between the traditional *industrial* approach and the more neglected *ecological* approach.

Ecology and Leadership

In the context of biology, ecology is the study of the habitats in which organisms live. Many psychologists have applied an ecological framework to psychology. Among the most prominent have been Bronfenbrenner (1986) and Kelly (1979). We are particularly indebted to Kelly for applying traditional ecological principles to social settings (e.g., Kelly, Ryan, Altman, & Stelzner, 2000). Borrowing from Kelly's ecological paradigm, Allen, Stelzner, and Wielkiewicz (1998) elaborated on four ecological principles that are critical to understanding leadership and organizations.

Interdependence

Both biological and social systems consist of interdependent components that have bidirectional influences on each other. The networks that generate leadership are interdependent systems, which consist of families, organizations, subgroups within organizations, communities, the natural environment, the economy, and so on. Any attempt to understand the complexities of an organization by focusing on its leader is incomplete. We cannot understand leadership in isolation from the rest of the organization or larger environment.

Open Systems and Feedback Loops

Any organization is completely dependent upon inflows of material, information, and other resources. These organizational systems are, themselves, part of larger open systems (economic, political, social, and environmental). Treating organizations as closed systems does not reflect the human enterprise that is the organization (Katz & Kahn, 1978). Furthermore, organizations that attempt to cut off various feedback loops place the organization at risk because its ability to adapt declines. If we are to understand leadership, we must understand it from an open systems perspective, including the interdependent nature of those systems and the dependence of all organizations upon a healthy environment.

Cycling of Resources

Biological systems use resources in multiple ways. Waste material from one organism becomes nutrients for another in a sustainable cycle. Organizations that take in resources must cycle them to the environment in a benign way, rather than compounding environmental problems with pollution. Similarly, leadership processes need to take advantage of the multitude of talent or capacities that exist within the organization. As a result, leadership is developed on an ongoing, long-term basis, rejecting the notion that positional leaders should dominate leadership processes. This does not preclude one individual initiating key action at a particular point in time, but it does suggest that demanding or expecting that a single individual act as *the leadership* is unrealistic and inefficient.

Adaptation

Biological systems are adaptive through evolutionary processes. A change in climate, for example, causes characteristics adaptive to the change to become more dominant among the organisms in the system. The greater the adaptive learning that takes place within an organizational ecosystem, the greater the ability to respond to the adaptive challenges that the organization, community, or larger society encounters. Structures and processes for learning must be developed throughout an organization so that the system is capable of adaptation to changes in technology, social structures, or economies. This is similar to what Senge (1990) and others (Levitt & March, 1988) refer to as a "learning organization."

We have integrated these principles of ecology into a theoretical model of leadership. A challenge in developing such a theory is the difficulty of shifting the focus *away* from positional leaders. Attributional processes and evolutionary influences create a bias to view leaders as having an exaggerated role in organizational events. For example, observers from western cultures seeking to explain the behavior of another person are likely to *over*estimate the importance of personality factors and *under*estimate the importance of situational factors, a tendency called the fundamental attribution error (Harvey & Weary, 1984). The many contexts in which positional leaders can be observed (speeches, media events, public appearances, etc.) engender a tendency to attribute their behavior to an internal characteristic, leadership, as opposed to the situational context and organizational history.

Gemmill and Oakley (1992) argued leadership is a "social myth" that allows individuals to attribute blame for societal problems. Furthermore, our anxieties and fears are projected onto positional leaders, which cause us to withdraw from our own responsibilities for making the world a better place. They call this process "deskilling" or taking away our personal skills and ability to influence the world, with two important consequences. First, positional leaders who reinforce this perspective will be able to enhance their "charismatic" characteristics and influence subordinates or followers to adopt their vision for the organization. If these leaders lack luck or insight, groupthink and decisions based upon incomplete information may take the organization on a self-destructive, unsustainable path. The second consequence is that positional leaders will experience difficulty influencing a greater proportion of members to participate in leadership processes because other members have been "de-skilled" by these attributional biases.

Evolutionary and genetic factors also play a role in the way people view leadership. Cosmides and Tooby (1992) argue that humans have evolved context-specific cognitive mechanisms for detecting inequities or cheaters in social interactions involving exchanges of resources. A key variable in such exchanges is variability in the food supply. High variability causes some individuals to have stretches when they cannot hunt or gather sufficient food and thus some form of communal sharing is likely. If variance is low and resources are abundant, more authoritarian and hierarchical societies were likely to emerge because survival is not so dependent upon equitable social exchanges. Industrialized societies, characterized by the appearance of an incredible abundance of resources, would reinforce individualistic tendencies rather than collectivism and lead to hierarchical organizations in which individuals tend to hoard their individual resources. This has taken us down an unsustainable path.

For example, it is common knowledge that the effects of industrialization are leading to shortages of clean air, clean water, and a healthy environment (Oskamp, 2000). Since we have the *appearance* of abundant resources, society is structured hierarchically with elite members of society hoarding vast amounts of resources while consumption and hoarding of resources continues at an unsustainable pace. We must apply more of our evolved cognitive ability to understand and cope with these problems. Hedrick-Wong (1998) concludes that evolutionary ideas must be accounted for in the solution to our emerging environmental crisis. Appeals to individuals must be based upon the original motives for the evolution of nation-states: preservation of one's descendants from the ravages of a crippled environment or other organizations. This kind of appeal creates a picture of limited resources that would tend to be associated with more cooperation. If we continue to compete for resources at both the individual and organizational level, we may enter into a series of commons tragedies that we do not identify because the perception of abundant resources remains strong.

Thus, our evolutionary bias seems to direct us toward the industrial perspective for several reasons. First, the dominance and aggression displayed by positional leaders is an inherited adaptation. We can also speculate that a certain degree of cooperation and deference toward successful leaders of hunting and gathering groups was adaptive because recognizing success at these endeavors would enhance reproductive potential and survival. Second, the apparent and illusory abundance of resources in western cultures tends to favor hierarchy and accumulation of resources over cooperation. Third, the evolution of groups also encourages competition because the groups evolved in a context of providing protection from other groups. These evolved characteristics seem to be predominant in organizations today and contribute to making the industrial perspective embedded into our views of organizations.

THE ECOLOGY OF LEADERSHIP

The ecological perspective of leadership is based upon ecological principles (Bronfenbrenner, 1986; Capra, 1996; Colarelli, 1998; Katz & Kahn, 1978; Kelly, 1979). The theory suggests if we are to understand leadership, we must do so in the context of *ecological systems*. The theory was first described by Allen et al. (1998). The six premises of our current version are discussed in the following.

Premise 1: Leadership is an Emergent Process

Although cognitive and evolved biases may make it *appear* as though positional leaders are directing and controlling organizational adaptation, it is far too limiting to define leadership as the activities of positional leaders. Our definition is that leadership is an *emergent process*, that is, it emerges from the interactions and actions of individuals within an ecological system. An empirical implication is that correlations between positional leader behavior and organizational performance should always be moderated by contextual variables (e.g., Haleblian & Finkelstein, 1993). Others who have implicitly or explicitly viewed leadership as a process include Day (2001), Kelly et al. (2000), and Yukl (2002). A process view of leadership encourages focus on decision-making processes and suggests that a key question is to discover to what extent the ability to influence decisions is distributed among organization members.

However, we are going beyond a simple process view of leadership to say that leadership is actually an *emergent* process. *Emergence* is defined as properties of a system that "arise from the interactions and relationships among the parts" (Capra, 1996, p. 29). A good example of such a process is intelligence, which emerges from the interactions among the tissues, cells, and structures that make up the human brain. When we define leadership as an emergent process, we mean that leadership does not consist of the actions of individuals. Instead, leadership emerges from the interactions *among* individuals. Then, this emergent process is translated into adaptive decisions and executive processes. The emergent processes that result in either improvements or declines in the adaptiveness of the organization are defined as its leadership. Adaptiveness can then be operationalized in terms of profitability, growth, competitiveness, stock price, efficiency, sustainability, program effectiveness, and other concepts. The key is to focus on the degree to which the organization is able to adapt to changes in the surrounding ecology.

This definition does not deny the importance of positional leaders. In fact, positional leaders can be a beneficial focus of organizational studies. In contrast to traditional views, we argue that the focus should not be upon positional leader decisions and their impact, but upon the *way* that decisions emerge from the interactions of positional leaders with all other members of the organization. Two key markers are the existence of participatory structures and the genuineness of participation in these processes by both positional leaders and other organization members. We would also expect to see that measures reflecting member development and training would relate to the adaptiveness of the organization.

A positional leader who has control over the distribution of organizational resources has considerable control over the adaptability of the organization. Yet, even the most powerful positional leader is completely dependent upon other organization members to carry out decisions and upon the surrounding ecology to respond in the way that the leader predicts. Ecological theory predicts that the long-term adaptability of an organization will be associated with finding an appropriate balance between vesting power and control in the positional leader versus having a diverse sample of organization members influence leadership processes. Thus, organizational performance should be related to member, as well as positional leader behavior.

In an ecological context, the role of positional leaders is to assist organizations in developing processes that make them more adaptive. According to Schein (1992), the role of the leader is to develop an intimate understanding of the organizational culture and then use various mechanisms to promote needed change. Colarelli (1998, 2003), writing from an evolutionary perspective, suggested that organizations are "loosely coupled" and that they are an emergent property of the specific components. Relationships among the parts are "loose" or weakly associated so that it is not possible to predict the precise impact of a particular intervention or change. The implication is that organizations should be structured for maximum flexibility and adaptiveness, rather than to accomplish a specific purpose. Then, organization learning will occur as various social technologies and procedures are discarded or retained because of their functionality. Thus, an ecological perspective encourages positional leaders to assist in the emergence of leadership rather than creating change through executive orders and decisions.

Premise 2: The Cognitive Task of Organization Members is to Optimize the Tension between the "Old School"/Industrial Perspective and the "New School"/Ecological Perspective

This premise argues that a balance between the industrial perspective and the ecological perspective is necessary for effective adaptation. Kelly et al. (2000) state that too much structure can inhibit adaptation, whereas a focus on "process" to the exclusion of structure or hierarchy can cause disintegration. The more skill a positional leader brings to the task of balancing the *tension* between industrial and ecological processes, which implies that both the industrial and ecological dimensions should be strong, the more effective the organization will be. If either perspective guides leadership processes at the expense of the other perspective the more likely it is that the organization will disintegrate.

Similar ideas are embodied in the "competing values model" (e.g., Buenger, Daft, Conlon, & Austin, 1996; Quinn & Rohrbaugh, 1983). The basic principle is that the more an organization adheres to one side of an organizational value, while excluding the other side, the greater the danger that the organization will fail to adapt. According to Quinn and Rohrbaugh, organizational failure often results from the inability to balance competing values, a task made very complex by the fact that successful pursuit of only one side of the competing values eventually becomes a failing strategy as the context changes. Many contrasting sets of competing values appear in the leadership literature: transactional versus transformational leadership (Pearce & Sims, 2002); democratic versus autocratic leadership (Gastil, 1994); loose versus tight styles of positional leadership (Sagie, 1997); organic versus mechanistic systems (Courtright, Fairhurst, & Rogers, 1989); exploration versus exploitation (March, 1991); the individual versus relationship orientation (Rost, 1997); open versus closed leadership processes (Allen et al., 1998); and the paradoxical roles of organizational culture as both stabilizing force and a force for change (Schein, 1992). Many public corporations continue to pursue profit at the expense of the environment. However, the context has radically shifted and all organizations need to decrease their environmental impact or society and these organizations are at risk.

Premise 3: Leadership Occurs in a Web of Interdependent Social and Biological Systems

According to Heifetz (1994; Sparks, 2002), organizations face two kinds of problems: those that can be solved with "authoritative expertise" and those that create *adaptive challenges* for the organization. Adaptive challenges require fundamental shifts in organizational expertise and the development of new, untried, experimental ways of adapting to a fundamentally changing environment. These concepts parallel the industrial–ecological tension. Solving problems with "authoritative expertise" represents the industrial side of the tension, whereas adaptive challenges require more emphasis on an ecological approach. Allen et al. (1998) identified five universal adaptive challenges that frame the context of organizational adaptation: (a) the need to develop an increasingly global perspective in life and work (Mays, Rubin, Sabourin, & Walker, 1996); (b) the need to live within the limits of our natural environment (Oskamp, 2000); (c) the need to convert the increasing flow of new information into useful knowledge (Wurman, 1989); (d) coping with scientific and technological advances in a way that enhances rather than destroys humanity (Kaku, 1997); and (e) coping with a fast-changing and fluid social ecology (Clark, 1985). In addition to these universal adaptive challenges, organizations must also adapt to local challenges including local and national regulation, competition, economic factors, finding trained workers, and so on.

The implications of these adaptive challenges for leadership theory and the need for a sustainable society are profound. These universal and local adaptive challenges are interactive, so it is difficult to consider any one in isolation from the others. For example, the increasing availability and volume of information applies to each of the other adaptive challenges, which increase the difficulty of understanding their implications. Each adaptive challenge tends to multiply the complexity and uncertainty generated by the other adaptive challenges; thus, sustainability issues occur in a context of economic and social issues, increasing their complexity. Leadership theorizing needs to provide strategies that enable leaders and others to respond in a flexible manner to this dynamic environment. This requires developing a deeper understanding of the interdependent systems context within which organizations exist. The complexity of the ecological context creates a tension between devoting resources to thoroughly understanding this context versus being more action-oriented, which means making timely and effective decisions based upon an admittedly incomplete understanding of the context. This idea is elaborated in Premise 4.

Premise 4: Adaptability is Determined by the Richness and Variability of Feedback Loops Allowed to Influence Leadership Processes

Sustainability is an excellent organizational example of a feedback loop. Ignoring environmental feedback loops is harmful to organizations in many ways. For example, unsustainable harvesting of a renewable resource such as ocean fish or forests eventually will result in declining harvests, exhaustion of the resource, and the end of an income stream, if not the end of the entire organization. If an organization "externalizes" its costs by dumping harmful pollutants into the environment, the effects may be more subtle and take longer to become evident, but anything that negatively affects human health is likely to harm an organization. Customers may be lost or find other, more sustainable, sources from which to obtain the same products or services. Feedback loops are the mechanism through which adaptation occurs. An organization that identifies and responds to its relevant feedback loops will be the most adaptive. For-profit corporations are an organizational form that may be compelled to operate unsustainably because of the "best interests of the shareholder" principle that demands that the profit feedback loop be given priority above all other considerations (Bakan, 2004). Unfortunately, this can lead to decisions that are unsustainable such as the unchecked use of natural resources and dumping of dangerous chemicals into our environment.

How does an organization identify "relevant" feedback loops? There are no guaranteed routes to success. Too much dependence on positional leaders can cause the organization to focus on a limited number of feedback loops, thereby missing a key feedback loop or adaptive challenge, such as developing technology. By themselves, positional leaders may be unable to understand the implications of a new technology or an emerging environmental feedback loop. Instead, individuals with relevant knowledge may be at any level of the organization. The key is to keep the industrial–ecological tension active. Too much attention to the ecological complexity of an adaptive challenge may prevent the organization from making a decision and taking action. On the other hand, if the amount of information and knowledge brought to bear on the adaptive challenge is too limited, the organization risks going forward with an inadequate understanding of the problem, which may lead to ineffective decisions and a decline in adaptiveness. The *tension* must remain active.

Premise 4 predicts that employee empowerment increases organizational adaptation (e.g., Kirkman & Rosen, 1999). Forms of empowerment such as "high involvement work processes" (Vandenberg, Richardson, & Eastman, 1999); organizational citizenship (Sivadas & Dwyer, 2000); and democratic, shared, or participative leadership styles (Gastil, 1994; Pearce & Sims, 2002; Van de Ven, Hudson, & Schroeder, 1984) would encourage the broadest contributions to leadership processes and have been empirically demonstrated to make positive contributions to organizational adaptiveness. In sum, there is ample evidence that all organization members can beneficially contribute to identifying relevant organizational feedback loops.

In contrast, constricting feedback loops, which would be associated with overemphasis of the industrial side of the tension, interferes with adaptation. Barker and Mone (1998) studied the relationship of the "mechanistic shift" to several organizational variables in 29 manufacturing firms in decline. The mechanistic shift is a tendency for organizations undergoing decline to become more organizationally rigid with centralization of organizational decisions, increasing use of rules and formalized procedures, decreased meetings and communication across the organization, and less time spent by managers in analyzing key data and decisions (Barker & Mone, 1998). Barker and Mone described the potential impact of the mechanistic shift as follows:

> Mechanistic firms may have more difficulty changing their strategic orientation in response to decline, as authority is consolidated with people who interact less directly with the environment, top managers receive or develop fewer alternatives due to less vertical communication, and formalization of procedures blocks the generation of innovative solutions. (p. 1228)

Barker and Mone's main finding was that as the degree of mechanistic shift increased, the probability of actions likely to bring the company to a successful turnaround declined. The most powerful predictors of a failure in strategic reorientation were more centralized and less participative decision processes. Thus, restricted flow of communication and overdependence upon hierarchical leadership, both characteristic of overemphasizing the industrial side of the tension, inhibit adaptability.

Premise 4 implies that group decision processes are advantageous for an organization because they maximize the number of feedback loops influencing leadership processes. However, some caution is necessary to avoid unfavorable processes such as groupthink (Janis, 1982). Lerner and Tetlock (1999) reviewed related literature on outcome versus process accountability. Process accountability means having to justify the *process* of making a decision, as opposed to allowing the *outcome* to be the measure of accountability. Outcome accountability has detrimental effects, such as over-commitment to a strategy and poorer performance, because it does not ensure that alternative strategies and ideas have been thoroughly and objectively evaluated. Furthermore, strategies that are compatible with ideology, mission, and existing projects of the organization are likely to be evaluated more favorably. On the other hand, process accountability is an opportunity to build a thorough examination of all alternatives into the decision process. Thus, process accountability may attenuate problems such as stereotyping, groupthink, social loafing in group tasks, and concurrence seeking in group discussions, and ensure that the information brought to bear on a problem or issue is diverse and representative of all perspectives. This has particular importance for environmental issues because organizations may need to make a radical shift in priorities in order to integrate environmentally sustainable policies and procedures into the organizational culture.

Other ways of improving group processes include: the use of "methodical decision-making procedures" (Moorhead, Neck, & West, 1998, p. 346), open, participative leadership processes, and interaction with the environment outside the decision-making team's normal boundaries via membership turnover or having members be on several teams (Moorhead et al., 1998); devil's advocacy, introducing information about the base rate of success, searching for examples of failure (as opposed to resting arguments on small numbers of successful cases), and discussing why key variables may be out of the control of the team (Houghton, Simon, Aquino, & Goldberg, 2000); following brainstorming protocols and having group members complete some brainstorming in private before the group meets to evaluate ideas (McCauley, 1998); and positional leaders who encourage disagreement and participation, emphasize that reaching a wise decision is important, encourage divergent opinions, and avoid strongly stating an opinion at the beginning of the process (Chen, Lawson, Gordon, & McIntosh, 1996; Leana, 1985; Neck & Moorhead, 1995; Schafer & Crichlow, 1996).

A key principle of an ecological theory of leadership concerns the importance of diversity and feedback loops. As Capra (1996) has stated, "[A] diverse community will be able to survive and reorganize itself . . . In other words, the more complex its pattern of interconnections, the more resilient it will be" (p. 303). Thus, a key to effective organizational action is to recognize that any decision is made in the context of many systems, such as competing organizations, the environment, the economy, local and world communities, and families, all interacting in highly complex, interdependent ways. Organizations that incorporate as many feedback loops as possible from these systems into leadership processes are most likely to generate effective responses to their challenges. This requires an organizational structure that creates multiple opportunities for organization members to influence leadership processes, and it must be combined with awareness that too much emphasis on process (the ecological side of the tension) can interfere with timely and effective decision-making. Thus, it is important to keep a tension between process and decision-making active.

Premise 5: A Tension Exists between a Need for Human and Social Diversity within the Organization versus Single-Minded Pursuit of Common Goals and Objectives

Diverse groups of organization members contribute to organizational adaptability (Bantel & Jackson, 1989; Krishnan, Miller, & Judge, 1997;

Mai-Dalton, 1993; Nemeth, 1995; Ng & Van Dyne, 2001; Paulus, 2000). This idea comes directly from ecological principles (Capra, 1996; Klingsporn, 1973). The more diversity within a system, the more adaptable it will be, because variability enhances the ability of the system to generate a wide range of adaptive strategies. One implication is that positional leaders need some degree of belief in the idea that they are essentially equal to other members. The idea that they are a talented and elite corps deserving of privilege is inappropriate. Such views can lead to mistreatment of members, loss of focus on their development, and their exclusion from participation in leadership processes.

When individuals perceive they are supported by the organization, they tend to reciprocate with increased commitment and performance (Eisenberger, Armeli, Rexwinkel, Lynch, & Rhoades, 2001) which enhances the diversity of ideas applied to leadership processes. Miller and Lee (2001) performed an interesting study of this phenomenon in a sample of Korean companies. They began with the argument that assiduous environmental scanning (i.e., searching for relevant feedback loops) should be useful for many companies because it could reveal "important customer needs, market threats and opportunities, as well as areas of strategy requiring improvement" (p. 168). They hypothesized that the *quality* of scanning activity would be related to the degree of genuine commitment shown toward employees, which would "minimize parochial politics and facilitate effective collaboration" (p. 170). Consistent with these predictions, they found that the effects of information processing, collaboration, and initiative on financial performance were enhanced by genuine commitment to employees.

Elron (1997) showed that cultural heterogeneity among top management teams enhanced organizational performance. This occurred despite evidence that cultural heterogeneity was associated with higher issue-based conflict within the team, which, itself, was related to the *perception* that team performance was weakened by such conflict. However, the overall effect of cultural heterogeneity on objective performance was positive. The inference was that cultural heterogeneity enabled the teams to integrate both local and global knowledge to enhance performance. The perception that issue-based conflict negatively influenced team performance was not surprising and suggested a need for training in conflict management and resolution (e.g., Robbins, 2003, p. 92). Elron also suggested that increased cultural diversity would be an asset at all organizational levels. Hambrick, Cho, and Chen (1996) found that top management team diversity contributed to profits and market share of airline companies. There is also substantial empirical evidence that gender diversity enhances organizational performance (Bass & Avolio, 1994; Neubert, 1999). Finally, the effects of diversity appear to be enhanced when the organization has a collectivistic as opposed to individualist culture (Chatman, Polzer, Barsade, & Neale, 1998).

We have emphasized the ecological side of the tension because we believe that leadership studies and practices have been dominated by the industrial perspective. An organization's human resources generate the strategies needed for adaptation to a challenging, rapidly changing, and sometimes hostile environment. The more diversity in an organization's human resources, the more able the organization will be to generate adaptive strategies. However, with definite limits on the number of such strategies that can actually be implemented and time constraints on developing strategies, the industrial side of the tension must be acknowledged so the organization can focus personnel and resources upon strategies it believes will increase adaptation. Homogeneous organization cultures are likely to keep the organization focused on successful adaptive strategies, but at the expense of failing to detect environmental shifts to which the organization needs to adjust. Strong hierarchical structures, with most decision powers vested in positional leaders, may dramatically decrease the diversity of thinking applied to adaptive challenges. Furthermore, hierarchical organizational structures are likely to contribute to "organizational silence," which can be demoralizing and detrimental to the organization (Morrison & Milliken, 2000). Maintaining the diversity needed for success is a critical function of positional leaders.

Premise 6: Leadership Processes Need to be Evaluated in Terms of How Adaptively an Organization Responds to its Long-term Challenges

Hannan and Freeman (1984, 1989) used evolutionary principles to describe organizational adaptation. They argued that the inertial forces to which organizations are subject prevent them from making the radical changes needed for adapting to environmental threats. High levels of structural inertia are the result of sunk costs, relationships with other organizations, a need for accountability and reliability, and legal barriers, all working against radical change. Starbuck (1983) reached a similar conclusion, arguing that organizations often become locked into "action patterns" that prevent successful adaptation to a changing environment. Thus, most organizations are faced with conditions that favor inertia and resistance to change. When the environment changes radically, these organizations are more likely to fail and be replaced. An ecological perspective suggests that organizations with mechanisms to detect the emerging adaptive challenges are more likely to adapt successfully. On the other hand, an organization devoting all its resources to exploring the environment for such trends may fail to execute its adaptive strategies. Thus, a tension between the two extremes remains the only constant for an adaptive organization.

We chose the word "ecological" to describe this theory both for its ability to convey a set of important principles *and* its implications for our environmental future. One of the most important feedback loops that is being suppressed and ignored concerns our natural environment. Organizations that ignore the environmental feedback loops may be undermining their own adaptability and that of the larger communities to which we all belong (Oskamp, 2000). We rarely see the immediate and direct impact of unsustainable behaviors on our environment. These effects accumulate over time and concerns about them can be easily outweighed by short-term considerations such as the drive for profit (Bakan, 2004). Adaptability requires that organizations develop sensitivity to feedback loops that provide information about the environmental sustainability of their practices. Andersson and Bateman (2000) found that frequent environmental scanning was an important component of moving companies toward addressing environmental issues. They also found that the nature of the organization, particularly whether the organization had a strong "environmental paradigm," was associated with the success of environmental initiatives. Qualitative analysis indicated that moving an organization toward addressing environmental issues was most successful when the financial advantages of doing so were emphasized.

Emphasis on the financial benefits of addressing environmental issues is congruent with McWilliams and Siegel's (2001) theory of corporate social responsibility. We must learn how to identify and activate the tensions that enable organizations to examine critically their impact on humanity's long-term environmental future. There seems to be an absence of such a tension in many public corporations (Bakan, 2004; Simon, 2000; Terry, 1995). An ecological leadership perspective predicts that causing harm to the natural environment can generate long-term feedback loops that can eventually harm the organization. To put this more bluntly, any activity that may eventually harm customers (e.g., pollution, global climate change, unsustainable use of resources, etc.) will eventually harm the organization itself. Thus, more organizations need to be responding to the neglected ecological side of the industrial–ecological tension. The absence of a dynamic tension related to environmental and other issues will leave far too many organizations without the knowledge and diversity of ideas they need to respond to the adaptive challenges of the present and future.

CONCLUSION: LEADERSHIP THEORY FOR THE FUTURE

Our theory uses ecological systems as its basic organizational metaphor, the same metaphor that is the core of the environmental movement. An ecological theory of leadership allows one to see the complexity of organizational systems and the adaptive challenges to which each must respond. The ecological metaphor also stands as a reminder of the environmental challenges faced by the entire human race and the need for each organization to face those challenges effectively. Since many environmental challenges are new and have never been confronted by humankind, they require new and untried strategies to address them. This means that the diversity required for adaptation must consist of much more than one person who argues for sustainability. It will take a multitude of such voices, each with unique expertise, to generate successful adaptive strategies.

Leadership, as we view it, is an *emergent* process that can be detached from positional leaders. Our model for understanding organizational processes is to focus on the processes involved in adapting to the ecosystem. These processes emerge from the interactions among members of the organization. Thus, the focus is upon the style and substance of these interactions throughout the organization, instead of the personality and actions of positional leaders alone. An understanding of organizational processes emerges from observing the patterns of interactions. However, the appearance of a *stable* pattern of interaction may be a signal that the organization needs to beware of environmental shifts that could make the current adaptation obsolete.

The ideal organization has a clear vision of the industrial versus ecological tension and has introduced mechanisms into leadership processes that counter the attributional biases that cause some to see leadership as "owned" by positional leaders. The presence of a high degree of "cooperative competency" (Sivadas & Dwyer, 2000) and democratic or participative processes would be two indicators that an organization is leaning in the right direction. Giving weight to a long-term perspective leads the organization to implement environmentally friendly practices, emphasize human development, avoid exploitation of workers or customers, control costs within the organization rather than externalizing them, and keep positional leader compensation at reasonable levels.

In our view, most organizations need to decrease dependence upon positional leaders, increase input from organizational experts, involve the entire organization in environmental scanning, subject decisions to review and criticism by organizational members, enhance organizational diversity, and ensure that sustainability has a strong multifaceted voice. The role of a consultant is to assist the organization in moving in these directions while helping it to avoid groupthink and other faulty decision-making processes. This will require careful intervention, especially if the organization or group has a history of downsizing or petty tyranny (Ashforth, 1994). In such contexts, obtaining genuine input into leadership processes and breaking down systemic barriers that create "organizational silence" (Morrison & Milliken, 2000) may be difficult as employees may view the invitations as feigned rather than genuine (Harlos, 2001).

Unfortunately, we believe voices representing the push toward a sustainable society may find themselves in a context where the desire for their input is not genuine. Instead, organizations will desire to put a token effort in sustainability initiatives rather than the genuine efforts that are needed. Our theory points toward a couple of useful strategies for these situations. First, energy issues and associated CO_2 emissions can often be approached as cost-reduction strategies, a feedback loop to which most organizations will respond. Second, there are environmental feedback loops that are near or past their tipping points. Leadership processes need to take these feedback loops into account. Finally, the superabundance that characterizes our society is an illusion. Clean air, clean and abundant freshwater, a stable and predictable climate, biological diversity, natural resources, and many other critical components of our ecology are in danger. These feedback loops have the potential to change society for the worse. Our survival depends upon our ability to integrate these feedback loops into leadership processes.

REFERENCES

Allen, K. E., Stelzner, S., & Wielkiewicz, R. (1998). The Ecology of Leadership: Adapting to the Challenges of a Changing World. *Journal of Leadership Studies, 5*(2), 62–82.

Andersson, L., & Bateman, T. (2000). Individual Environmental Initiative: Championing Natural Environmental Issues in U.S. Business Organizations. *Academy of Management Journal, 43*(4), 548–570.

Ashforth, B. (1994). Petty Tyranny in Organizations. *Human Relations, 47*(7), 755–778.

Bakan, J. (2004). *The Corporation: The Pathological Pursuit of Profit and Power.* New York: Free Press.

Bantel, K., & Jackson, S. (1989). Top Management and Innovations in Banking: Does the Composition of the Top Team Make a Difference? [Special Issue: Strategic Leaders and Leadership]. *Strategic Management Journal, 10*(Summer), 107–124.

Barker, V., & Mone, M. (1998). The Mechanistic Structure Shift and Strategic Reorientation in Declining Firms Attempting Turnarounds. *Human Relations, 51*(10), 1227–1258.

Bass, B., & Avolio, B. (1994). Shatter the Glass Ceiling: Women May Make Better Managers. *Human Resource Management, 33*(4), 549–560.

Bronfenbrenner, U. (1986). Ecology of the Family as a Context for Human Development: Research Perspectives. *Developmental Psychology, 22*(6), 723–742.

Buenger, V., Daft, R., Conlon, E., & Austin, J. (1996). Competing Values in Organizations: Contextual Influences and Structural Consequences. *Organization Science, 7*(5), 557–576.

Capra, F. (1996). *The Web of Life.* New York: Anchor Books.

Chatman, J., Polzer, J., Barsade, S., & Neale, M. (1998). Being Different Yet Feeling Similar: The Influence of Demographic Composition and Organizational Culture on Work Processes and Outcomes. *Administrative Science Quarterly, 43*(4), 749–780.

Chen, Z., Lawson, R., Gordon, L., & McIntosh, B. (1996). Groupthink: Deciding with the Leader and the Devil. *The Psychological Record,* 46(4), 581–590.

Clark, D. (1985). Emerging Paradigms in Organizational Theory and Research. In Y. Lincoln (Ed.), *Organizational Theory and Inquiry: The Paradigm Revolution* (pp. 43–78). Beverly Hills, CA: Sage Publications.

Colarelli, S. (1998). Psychological Interventions in Organizations: An Evolutionary Perspective. *American Psychologist,* 53(9), 1044–1056.

Colarelli, S. (2003). *No Best Way: An Evolutionary Perspective on Human Resource Management.* Westport, CT: Praeger.

Cosmides, L., & Tooby, J. (1992). Cognitive Adaptations for Social Exchange. In J. Barkow, L. Cosmides, & J. Tooby (Eds.), *The Adapted Mind: Evolutionary Psychology and the Generation of Culture* (pp. 163–228). New York: Oxford University Press.

Courtright, J., Fairhurst, G., & Rogers, L. (1989). Interaction Patterns in Organic and Mechanistic Systems. *Academy of Management Journal, 32*(4), 773–802.

Day, D. (2001). Leadership Development: A Review in Context. *The Leadership Quarterly, 11*, 581–613.

Eisenberger, R., Armeli, S., Rexwinkel, B., Lynch, P., & Rhoades, L. (2001). Reciprocation of Perceived Organizational Support. *Journal of Applied Psychology, 86*(1), 42–51.

Elron, E. (1997). Top Management Teams within Multinational Corporations: Effects of Cultural Heterogeneity. *The Leadership Quarterly*, 8(4), 393–412.

Gastil, J. (1994). A Meta-Analytic Review of the Productivity and Satisfaction of Democratic and Autocratic Leadership. *Small Group Research, 25*(3), 384–410.

Gemmill, G., & Oakley, J. (1992). Leadership: An Alienating Social Myth. *Human Relations, 45*(2), 113–129.

Haleblian, J., & Finkelstein, S. (1993). Top Management Team Size, CEO Dominance, and Firm Performance: The Moderating Roles of Environmental Turbulence and Discretion. *Academy of Management Journal, 36*(4), 844–863.

Hambrick, D., Cho, T., & Chen, M. (1996). The Influence of Top Management Team Heterogeneity on Firms' Competitive Moves. *Administrative Science Quarterly, 41*(4), 659–684.

Hannan, M., & Freeman, J. (1984). Structural Inertia and Organizational Change. *American Sociological Review, 49*(2), 149–164.

Hannan, M., & Freeman, J. (1989). *Organizational Ecology*. Cambridge, MA: Harvard University Press.

Harlos, K. (2001). When Organizational Voice Systems Fail: More on the Deaf-Ear Syndrome and Frustration Effects. *The Journal of Applied Behavioral Science*, 37(3), 324–342.

Harvey, J., & Weary, G. (1984). Current Issues in Attribution Theory. *Annual Review of Psychology, 35*, 427–459.

Hedrick-Wong, Y. (1998). The Global Environmental Crisis and State Behavior: An Evolutionary Perspective. In C. Crawford & D. Krebs (Eds.), *Handbook of Evolutionary Psychology: Ideas, Issues, and Applications* (pp. 573–594). Mahwah, NJ: Lawrence Erlbaum Associates.

Heifetz, R. (1994). *Leadership without Easy Answers*. Cambridge, MA: Harvard University Press.

Houghton, S., Simon, M., Aquino, K., & Goldberg, C. B. (2000). No Safety in Numbers: Persistence of Biases and Their Effects on Team Risk Perception and Team Decision Making. *Group and Organization Management,* 25(4), 325–353.

Janis, I. (1982). *Groupthink* (2nd ed.). Boston: Houghton Mifflin.

Kaku, M. (1997). *Visions: How Science Will Revolutionize the 21st Century*. New York: Doubleday.

Katz, D., & Kahn, R. (1978). *The Social Psychology of Organizations* (2nd ed.). New York: Wiley.

Kelly, J. (1979). 'Tain't What You Do, It's the Way You Do It. *American Journal of Community Psychology,* 7(3), 244–261.

Kelly, J., Ryan, A., Altman, B., & Stelzner, S. (2000). Understanding and Changing Social Systems: An Ecological View. In J. Rappaport & E. Seidman (Eds.), *Handbook of Community Psychology* (pp. 133–159). New York: Plenum.

Kirkman, B., & Rosen, B. (1999). Beyond Self-Management: Antecedents and Consequences of Team Empowerment. *Academy of Management Journal, 42*(1), 58–74.

Klingsporn, M. (1973). The Significance of Variability. *Behavioral Science, 18*(6), 441–447.

Krishnan, H., Miller, A., & Judge, W. (1997). Diversification and Top Management Team Complementarity: Is Performance Improved by Merging Similar or Dissimilar Teams? *Strategic Management Journal, 18*(5), 361–374.

Leana, C. (1985). A Partial Test of Janis' Groupthink Model: Effects of Group Cohesiveness and Leader Behavior on Defective Decision Making. *Journal of Management, 11*(1), 5–17.

Lerner, J., & Tetlock, P. (1999). Accounting for the Effects of Accountability. *Psychological Bulletin, 125*(2), 255–275.

Levitt, B., & March, J. (1988). Organizational Learning. *Annual Review of Sociology, 14*, 319–340.

Mai-Dalton, R. (1993). *Managing Cultural Diversity on the Individual, Group, and Organizational Levels.* In M. Chemers & R. Ayman (Eds.), *Leadership Theory and Research* (pp. 189–215). San Diego: Academic Press.

March, J. (1991). Exploration and Exploitation in Organizational Learning. *Organization Science, 2*(1), 71–87.

Mays, V., Rubin, J., Sabourin, M., & Walker, L. (1996). Moving Toward a Global Psychology: Changing Theories and Practice to Meet the Needs of a Changing World. *American Psychologist,* 51(5), 485–487.

McCauley, C. (1998). Group Dynamics in Janis's Theory of Groupthink: Backward and Forward. *Organizational Behavior and Human Dynamics, 73*(2/3), 142–162.

McWilliams, A., & Siegel, D. (2001). Corporate Social Responsibility: A Theory of the Firm Perspective. *Academy of Management Review, 26*(1), 117–127.

Miller, D., & Lee, J. (2001). The People Make the Process: Commitment to Employees, Decision Making and Performance. *Journal of Management, 27*(2), 163–189.

Moorhead, G., Neck, C., & West, M. (1998). The Tendency toward Defective Decision Making within Self-Managing Teams: The Relevance of Groupthink for the 21st Century. *Organizational Behavior and Human Decision Processes, 73*(2/3), 327–351.

Morrison, E., & Milliken, F. (2000). Organizational Silence: A Barrier to Change and Development in a Pluralistic World. *Academy of Management Review, 25*(4), 706–725.

Neck, C., & Moorhead, G. (1995). Groupthink Remodeled: The Importance of Leadership, Time Pressure, and Methodical Decision-Making Procedures. *Human Relations, 48*(5), 537–557.

Nemeth, C. (1995). Dissent as Driving Cognition, Attitudes, and Judgments. *Social Cognition, 13*(3), 273–291.

Neubert, M. (1999). Too Much of a Good Thing or The More the Merrier? Exploring the Dispersion and Gender Composition of Informal Leadership in Manufacturing Teams. *Small Group Research, 30*(5), 635–646.

Ng, K., & Van Dyne, L. (2001). Individualism-Collectivism as a Boundary Condition for Effectiveness of Minority Influence in Decision Making. *Organizational Behavior and Human Decision Processes, 84*(2), 198–225.

Oskamp, S. (2000). A Sustainable Future for Humanity? How Can Psychology Help? *American Psychologist, 55*(5), 496–508.

Paulus, P. (2000). Groups, Teams, and Creativity: The Creative Potential of Idea-Generating Groups. *Applied Psychology: An International Review, 49*(2), 237–262.

Pearce, C., & Sims, H. (2002). Vertical Versus Shared Leadership as Predictors of the Effectiveness of Change Management Teams: An Examination of Aversive, Directive, Transactional, Transformational, and Empowering Leader Behaviors. *Group Dynamics: Theory, Research, and Practice*, 6(2), 172–197.

Quinn, R., & Rohrbaugh, J. (1983). A Spatial Model of Effectiveness Criteria: Towards a Competing Values Approach to Organizational Analysis. *Management Science, 29*, 363–377.

Robbins, S. (2003). *Essentials of Organizational Behavior* (7th ed.). Upper Saddle River, NJ: Pearson Education.

Rost, J. (1997). Moving from Individual to Relationship: A Postindustrial Paradigm of Leadership. *Journal of Leadership Studies, 4*(4), 3–16.

Sagie, A. (1997). Leader Direction and Employee Participation in Decision Making: Contradictory or Compatible Practices. *Applied Psychology: An International Review,* 46(4), 387–452.

Schafer, M., & Crichlow, S. (1996). Antecedents of Groupthink: A Quantitative Study. *Journal of Conflict Resolution, 40*(3), 415–435.

Schein, E. H. (1992). *Organizational Culture and Leadership* (2nd ed.). San Francisco: Jossey-Bass.

Senge, P. M. (1990). *The Fifth Discipline: The Art and Practice of the Learning Organization*. New York: Doubleday Currency.

Simon, D. R. (2000). Corporate Environmental Crimes and Social Inequality: New Directions for Environmental Justice Research. *American Behavioral Scientist, 43*(4), 633–645.

Sivadas, E., & Dwyer, F. (2000). An Examination of Organizational Factors Influencing New Product Success in Internal and Alliance-Based Processes. *Journal of Marketing, 64*(1), 31–49.

Sparks, D. (2002). Bringing the Spirit of Invention to Leadership (An Interview with Ronald Heifetz). *Journal of Staff Development, 23*(2), 44–46.

Starbuck, W. (1983). Organizations as Action Generators. *American Sociological Review, 48*(1), 91–102.

Terry, L. (1995). The Leadership–Management Distinction: The Domination and Displacement of Mechanistic and Organismic Theories. *The Leadership Quarterly,* 6(4), 515–527.

Van de Ven, A., Hudson, R., & Schroeder, D. (1984). Designing New Business Startups: Entrepreneurial, Organizational, and Ecological Considerations. *Journal of Management, 10*(1), 87–107.

Vandenberg, R., Richardson, H., & Eastman, L. (1999). The Impact of High Involvement Work Processes on Organizational Effectiveness: A Second-Order Latent Variable Approach. *Group and Organization Management, 24*(3), 300–339.

Wurman, W. S. (1989). *Information Anxiety*. New York: Doubleday.

Yukl, G. (2002). *Leadership in Organizations* (5th ed.). Upper Saddle River, NJ: Prentice Hall.

Zaccaro, S. J. (2001). The Nature of Executive Leadership: A Conceptual and Empirical Analysis of Success. Washington, DC: American Psychological Association.

2 Eco-Leadership

Towards the Development of a New Paradigm

Simon Western

INTRODUCTION

This chapter discusses a new paradigm of emerging leadership in organizational life that I call "eco-leadership" (Western, 2008b). To be clear from the outset, eco-leadership is not focused on a leader who defines themselves through environmental concerns, although this plays a part. Instead, eco-leadership implies leadership in relation to the ecosystems in which we live and work. Eco-leadership conceptualizes leaders as being agents distributed throughout organizations (of all kinds) taking a holistic, systemic, and ethical stance. Eco-leadership works in organizations that are conceptualized as "ecosystems within ecosystems." This contrasts with the normative 20th-century idea of organizations as stable and boundaried systems that operate with leaders at the top of clear hierarchies. Eco-leadership shifts the focus from individual leaders to leadership, asking of an organization "how can leadership flourish in this environment?"

Leadership is too often reduced to the heroic individual, when leadership is about much more. Leadership includes individual leaders as well as collective groups and teams taking leadership, for example, boards of directors, senior management teams, and self-organized activist teams taking a lead at a demonstration. Nation-states can take a leadership role, and leadership can be seen in processes and cultures. The first task of eco-leadership is to make leadership generative, broadening the common reductionism that restricts it to elite individuals at the top of an organization.

Leadership was interpreted in the 19th and 20th centuries as manifesting and controlling the environment—a leader created change—whereas with eco-leadership the focus is on a reciprocal relationship between leadership and its environment. It decenters individuals and challenges centralized power, claiming that by creating the right culture and conditions, leadership will emerge in plural forms and unexpected places. When we limit leadership potential to a few individuals the environment becomes elitist and linear, reducing diversity. Governments and businesses around the world reflect this tendency and are dominated by homogenous groups of male leaders dressed in suits of a certain age and disposition.

The emergent eco-leadership discourse follows a century of leadership discourses that were forged in the heat of western modernity. By a discourse I mean the unconscious and normative assumptions that trap us into a particular way of thinking, speaking, and doing. The 20th-century leadership discourses, which I call the Controller, the Therapist, and the Messiah discourses,[1] still dominate organizational thinking, but in the past decade a new eco-leadership discourse has been emerging. This chapter will first situate eco-leadership in relation to the three discourses of the past century in order to understand how leadership and organizations have evolved, where they are now, and the direction in which we are traveling. It will then discuss eco-leadership in relation to the changing social, organizational, and environmental conditions of the 21st century.

LEADERSHIP DISCOURSES: A META-ANALYSIS OF LEADERSHIP CULTURES 1900–2000

Four discourses of leadership have dominated westernized organizations over the past century (Western, 2005, 2008b). They remain present today and are easily recognized across diverse contexts. These discourses, emerging from a meta-analysis of leadership from historical, social/political, and economic perspectives, show how organizational leadership has been constructed and enacted over the past century. The majority of the literature on leadership during this time did not relate leadership changes in the workplace with external social, historical, and economic changes. It was as if business schools, corporations, and consultancies lived in a bubble, researching and practicing leadership from their citadels, feeding off each other, but paying little attention to the social-political-natural world, except when it had an impact on business interests. This helps explains the compartmentalized mentality within organizations, and how little social or environmental responsibility or engagement has taken place in the past.

A discourse is a linguistic and cultural set of normative assumptions, an institutional way of thinking (Foucault, 1972). A discourse defines what we take for granted and how we think about something. Judith Butler (1990) claims that we are trapped by discourses and cannot easily think or act outside of them, citing gender as an example. Critical theory attempts to identify normative discourses, so that once revealed they can be critiqued. It is this approach I take with leadership, to define the discourses that dominate leadership thinking, so we can "untrap" ourselves and see which leadership discourses are being "performed" within ourselves, our teams, and our organizations. This enables us to change what we previously took for granted and to explore new possibilities.

The leadership discourses I set out (see Figure 2.1) all have merits and weaknesses; they are not right or wrong, they simply exist within wider social phenomena.

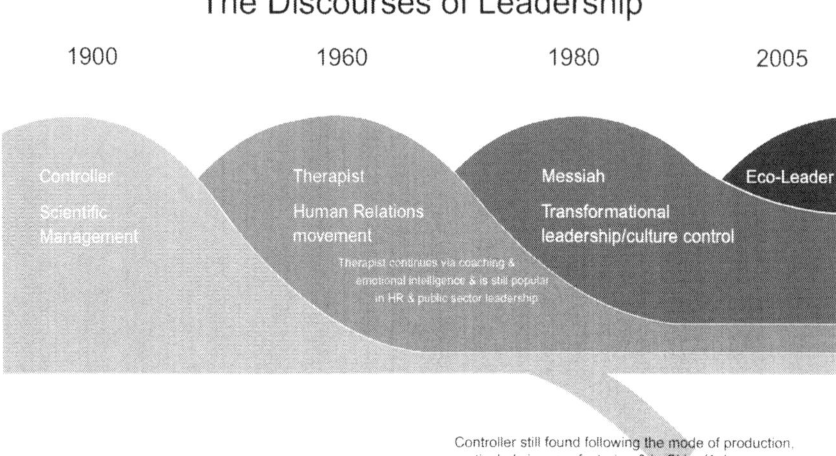

Figure 2.1 The discourses of leadership. Source: Western (2008b).

I argue later that these discourses should be tempered and only partially enacted within the eco-leadership discourse. In what follows, I will briefly describe and summarize the first three discourses of leadership before articulating the new emergent discourse of eco-leadership.[2]

THE CONTROLLER DISCOURSE

Control Resources to Maximize Efficiency

The Controller leadership discourse emerged at the turn of the 20th century, gaining credence from the cultural belief in modernism and scientific rationalism that grew in the wake of the European Enlightenment. The Industrial Revolution paved the way for urbanization, and new organizations such as the industrial factory emerged, alongside new ways of working and new forms of leadership. The Controller discourse was epitomized by what Frederick Taylor called "scientific management" and the "efficiency craze" (Taylor, 1911/1997). Taylor's ideas informed the teaching of the Harvard Business School in the early part of the 20th century and paved the way for Fordism and the factory production line. Increasing efficiency, the division of labor, and time and motion studies had a profound impact, increasing salaries and production, which led to mass consumption and the modernization of society.

However, the shadow side of this discourse is its dehumanizing consequences. Employees become functional, replaceable human resources, people become cogs in the wheel of the efficient machine. The Controller leadership discourse remains with us, particularly in manufacturing. Recent attempts to "modernize" public and private sectors have seen a reversion to the Controller discourse with a focus on measurements, targets, and audits to achieve greater efficiency and outputs. Automobile manufacturing methods are pushed by consultants to change public-sector organizations such as hospitals, creating a deeply worrying ethical trend where people/patients become units of productivity. In this discourse, the leaders of organizations believe that controlling resources (including humans) to maximize efficiency is their key task. The Controller leadership discourse was always critiqued for being inhuman, but it was after the Second World War that people began questioning the central tenets that science and rationality would always lead to progress since, as Karen Armstrong put it, "The Nazi Holocaust revealed that a concentration camp could exist in the same vicinity as a great university" (Armstrong, 2000, p. 200). Post-WWII society reviewed what science and rationality meant and the Controller leadership discourse slipped slowly into a decline but it did not disappear.

THE THERAPIST DISCOURSE

Happy Workers are More Productive Workers

The Therapist leadership discourse focuses on human relations, and in particular individual and team motivation. This discourse emerged in the postwar period as a more democratic society was sought. Workers returning from the Second World War wanted a "life fit for heroes" and the Controller discourse was no longer fitting for this (although it continued into the 1950s and 1960s and is still present today). Politicians and employers also feared a return to right-wing dictatorships or socialist reactions if poor treatment of workers continued, so they aimed to democratize society and the workplace.

The Therapist leadership discourse works on the principle that "happy workers are more productive workers" and this leadership discourse produced many years of successful growth, combining production with personal satisfaction. Workers no longer simply brought their labor to work, but also their identities. The United States dominated the economic market during this period and its business schools influenced organizations worldwide. The human relations movement began in the 1920s and 1930s with Elton Mayo's Hawthorne experiments and continued later with the work of Lewin, Maslow, and the Tavistock Institute, which dealt a blow to classic management theory.

Postwar American culture privileged individualism and this was further advanced in the 1960s with the rise of the personal growth movement epitomized by Carl Rogers's (1951) "client-centered therapy." Phillip Rieff

(1966) calls this social period "the triumph of the therapeutic" and personnel departments were established in workplaces to achieve therapeutic goals. The leadership task was now to encourage workers to self-actualize through work, engaging workers to increase motivation and commitment (Rose, 1990).

This discourse remains very popular in the public and not-for-profit sector and "people-focused" organizations. Much current leadership education is dominated by the Therapist discourse, often focusing on developing the individual and high-potential leaders by attempting to modify their behavior to fit the company's desired universal leadership competency framework. The Therapist discourse was a great leap forward in terms of engaging employees, yet it has limits. Firstly, it focuses on individuals rather than collective culture, reflecting a western bias. Secondly, it can be manipulative, using psychological techniques to shape individuals to fit company norms. The Therapist discourse remains strong today through, for example coaching, psychometrics, and emotional intelligence; however, in the late 1970s a new discourse arose and became dominant.

THE MESSIAH DISCOURSE

Visionary Leaders and Strong Conformist Cultures

The Messiah leadership discourse arose in the late 1970s and early 1980s following an economic slump in the United States and the surprise of the Asian tiger economies that began outperforming the U.S. in key production areas. This new covenantal leadership style emerged with the aim to create strong, dynamic organizational cultures under the vision and charisma of a transformational leader (Burns, 1978; Bass, 1990). It drew on the lessons of the collective cultures of Japan, which harnessed loyalty and commitment within teams and linked personal success to company success. The Messiah leadership discourse leveraged the collective culture to influence individuals rather than focus on individual psychology.

In *Leadership: A Critical Text* (2008), I argue that the rise of Christian fundamentalism in the U.S. happened at the same time as the rise of the transformational leadership literature, and that the two are inextricably linked at an unconscious cultural level. America was seeking in the economic and sociopolitical sphere a form of "Messiah Leadership" to reaffirm its status as the leading world power and to reaffirm a collective sense of what it was to be an American. The business schools, consultancies, and multinational corporations acted with vigor selling the new leadership discourse of a transformational (Messiah) leader who could offer vision and passionate leadership to an inspired, loyal, and committed workforce.

These prophetic leaders initially were heralded as creating entrepreneurial and dynamic companies, yet they also created highly conformist cultures. Peters and Waterman's (1982) best-selling book, *In Search of Excellence*, described the most successful companies as having cult-like cultures, and the organization was rethought of as a community (Kunda, 1992). Organizational control was no longer achieved through hierarchical power or coercion but through peer and self-surveillance. Individuals and teams worked because they believed in the company vision, and those who didn't were soon expelled.

The long-term results of this discourse can create a totalizing mind-set and company monoculture that resists critical reflection and excludes difference. Transformational leaders attempt to "engineer culture" (Kunda, 1992) and create "designer employees" (Casey, 1995). Carol Axtell Ray (1986) argues that transformational leaders seek devotion from employees with the aim of getting them to love the firm and its goals. Individuals find themselves capitulated to the firm without the capability to critically reflect on their position. The Messiah leadership discourse dominated leadership thinking firstly in the private then public sphere between the late 1970s and 2000. It then fell into decline as it wasn't delivering the promised land, and the hubris of evangelical leaders and their vision statements were seen to be a façade.

Before I move into a discussion of eco-leadership, it is important to restate that these discourses are not neatly time-bound, one ending and another beginning. They all remain with us, and contemporary organizations can still be dominated by any one of them. This outline simply reveals very briefly how they emerged and when they dominated. Parts of organizations will also be more closely aligned to a particular discourse: for example, human resources departments may try to assert the Therapist leadership discourse in a company that operates under the Messiah or Controller discourse, leading to tensions between HR and the senior management team. In mergers, one of the biggest flaws is how each separate company will often operate under different discourses without recognizing the difference. They all talk about leadership as if they mean the same thing, and this leads to constant misunderstandings. The foregoing discussion helps to clarify alternative discourses of leadership as they have developed over time and as they exist in organizations.

THE EMERGENCE OF THE ECO-LEADERSHIP DISCOURSE

And so we arrive at the 21st century, facing climate change and the realization that our natural resources are finite and fast disappearing, a financial and economic crash, a scientific and technological revolution, a growing population, and an economic and international power shift. The rise of the "BRIC" countries—Brazil, Russia, India, and China—brings positive change, redistributing power from the west and bringing many out of poverty, but as these countries with huge populations become increasingly wealthy, consume more, and use more fossil fuels, the pressures on the environment and climate increase too. The power shift is also away from the nation-state to the transnational corporation, bringing new challenges as to how they can be regulated.

The old ways are passing, and as Yeats wrote in *The Second Coming* (1919), "Things fall apart; the centre cannot hold." Our challenge today is to finally understand that in a globalized world the "center can *never* hold." When humans assume omnipotence over each other and over nature, and try to control things from the center, they always (sooner or later) fall apart. This is the lesson for the 21st century, and it lies at the heart of eco-leadership. Eco-leadership redistributes leadership and power from the center to the edges, recognizing the impossibility of "going it alone" when we are interdependent on each other and on planet Earth. There are no isolationist policies anymore, no exceptions; we are all connected and interdependent at micro-local levels and at macro-global levels.

This new eco-leadership discourse has risen to mainstream status since the turn of the 21st century, firstly as a reaction to economic decline as the Messiah leadership discourse failed to deliver on its hyperbole, the promised kingdom never arrived and people became disenchanted with overpaid CEOs and vision statements that were not aligned to their experience in the company. At the same time a new zeitgeist was emerging, brought on by three converging intellectual and social changes:

1. *Quantum physics and new science* challenged our dualistic and binary view of the world. Fritjof Capra writes: "The new concepts in physics have brought about profound change in our worldview; from the mechanistic worldview of Descartes and Newton to [a more] holistic and ecological view" (1996, p. 5; see also Wheatley, 2006).
2. *Globalization and technological advances* continually make the world "smaller"; we struggle with the new reality of globalization and what it means to us whether through business, politics or even terrorism. Technology also transforms our personal and social worlds via artificial intelligence, discovery of the human genome, biogenetics, and advances in information and nanotechnology, among others.
3. *The environmental social movement* has raised awareness of finite natural resources, the imminent dangers of climate change, and the increasing loss of biodiversity. Once the province of a minority of activists, around the turn of the millennium (signified by the demonstrations at the 1999 World Trade Organization [WTO] meeting in Seattle) the world seemed to awake to the looming environmental challenges that it is facing.

Eco-leadership is the incorporation of this zeitgeist and while I focus on organizational and business leadership, it is equally relevant to social and political leadership.

While traditional historical teaching points to the "great man" theory of leadership, it is the marginalized, grassroots social movements that often lead and innovate change, and so it is with eco-leadership, which emerges from environmental social activism. The environmental movement has had three major social impacts that are now being taken seriously by the business community and organizations. Firstly, it has raised awareness of our limited natural resources and an imminent environmental catastrophe. Secondly, it reflected back to mainstream society its drift towards "destruction" in relation to the project of modernity. Material wealth and growth have produced many benefits, including (among others) material comforts, ease of travel, education, health care advances, and longevity, but these have been countered by a century of war, climate change, social injustice in the south and alienation, individualism, narcissism, and breakdown of community in the north (Lasch, 1979, Putnam, 2000). Thirdly, along with other new social movements, the eco-movement offers new democratized ways of organizing with emergent and distributed forms of leadership, utilizing social networks and harnessing new technology. For example, Iranians today use YouTube and Twitter to organize and publicize antigovernment demonstrations.

The environmental movement was considered countercultural until around 2000 when the world awoke from its slumber and the other factors listed earlier added to the new zeitgeist. The Seattle demonstration was a radical moment in history: the WTO, a transnational global body, was confronted by a transnational global movement. *USA Today* reported that with the new media "the whole world was watching" a new coalition of diverse groups come together: "At least in the economic sphere, an expansive new dissident consensus seems to have developed—bridging the political divide of right and left—something utterly unthinkable in the Vietnam war era" (Meddis, 1999). This social movement had organized in new ways using "the wired society" to challenge the hegemony of corporate power aligned with transnational organizations such as the WTO.

Seattle protestors challenged more than environmental damage, they were challenging the underlying logic of late capitalism itself. The new millennium helped focus people and we are finally seeing eco-leadership as an emergent new discourse in corporate and public-sector organizational life. Business leaders and politicians can no longer ignore what has become obvious; we have reached the limits of inherited modes of existence.

While eco-leadership emerges from environmental social activism it is not a woolly, feel-good approach to leadership; it is rather a serious and radical approach that challenges the very coordinates of current theory and practice, and includes a critique of power relations. Structure, power, and authority *do not* disappear in some utopian dream when we move towards eco-leadership, environmental awareness, and social responsibility. One of the deficits in current systems theory, complexity theory, and environmental thinking about organizations is a lack of critical theory particularly in relation to power. Coopey (1995) claims, for example, that Peter Senge's work idealizes community and overplays the importance of dialogue without adequately addressing power.

Central power and control do exist but they have a fragile existence, resilient but also fluid and changeable. Power is also much more distributed than we usually recognize in our narratives about how "the social" functions (Latour, 2004; Law, 1991; Western, 2008a). One of today's biggest challenges is to change mind-sets and discourses, not towards a retrospective romanticism where we become happy peasants in a technology-free world, but where we think beyond the short-term, binary, linear solutions and machine metaphors. Organizational leaders are called to address a key emotional and psychological task that recognizes the limits of our ability to control things. We mistakenly recognize power at the center as strength, and power at the margins as a structural weakness when neither is the case. Eco-leadership shifts the focus from individual leaders to leadership—a radically distributed leadership—in an attempt to harness the energy and creativity in a whole system. Learning from new social movements, it recognizes that new forms of organizing will only be possible if spaces are created for leadership to emerge from within, and this cannot be planned. Ecosystems can be nurtured but not controlled.

FORM AND FUNCTION

Eco-leadership challenges the central modernist slogan *form follows function*, which remains dominant today in our conscious and subconscious minds. This ethos focuses on functionality, rationality, linear thinking, and utilitarianism. We design buildings, structures, and organizations that are "fit for purpose" to carry out their utilitarian function. This seems an obvious truism, until we realize that the opposite statement is equally true: *function also follows form*. Modernity traps us in "forms" that limit us; urban worlds of production lines, shopping malls, traffic jams, square boxes to live in, square screens, and public spaces colonized by mass advertising that we internalize (Klein, 2000). Our inner human desires become distorted towards consumerist goods that can never satisfy us, and this "unfulfilled desire" provides the basic logic of late capitalism.

External landscapes shape our internal landscapes, influencing how we think, feel, and perceive the world and ourselves in it. In natural or creative urban environments we become creative ourselves, our imagination is unleashed. As humans we imagine ourselves as the creators but we are also the created, constructed by a world around us that limits our individual and collective potential. This is especially true of many workplaces. I recently worked as a consultant within a major bank in London and the experience of getting to the meeting awoke me once again to the totalizing nature of contemporary workplaces. I traveled on the underground, stepped onto an moving walkway, then traveled up an escalator, walked through a glass-covered shopping arcade, arrived at security and was "screened," took the elevator to the 30th floor, finally to arrive in a huge open-plan office with 300 uniform desks. I was transported to my destination by moving stairways, in linear lines: I was being efficiently "processed" as if on a production line, with thousands of other commuters and finance workers. When I arrived I experienced "sameness," monotonous rows of linear chairs and desks. There were explicit rules that no one must have any object on their desk above a certain height to maintain uniformity, along with implicit rules, maintained by peer and self-surveillance, for how long you stayed at the desk, how loud you could speak, and so on. There was nowhere to hide in this open-plan panopticon. The room reminded me of a large Victorian factory, except the weaving machines had become computers, and a sterile cleanliness and white noise replaced the commotion and dirt of the old. I found the experience dislocating and totalizing. I recalled other corporations I had worked in, and like the business hotels I stayed in, they are conformist, modern, glass buildings, minimalist, utilitarian, white walls, open-plan offices with occasional grandiose spaces signifying power.

How can employees bring a creative self to work in this anonymous, uniform office that eliminates any diversity, stripping people of their individuality? When I asked the staff at the bank about diversity, they proudly repeated the "politically correct" mantras of the company, mostly unaware of what Casey (1995) calls the "corporatised self":

> The new corporatisation of the self is more than a process of assault, discipline and defeat against which employees defend themselves. It is a process of colonisation in which, in its completion assault and defeat are no longer recognised. Overt displays of employee resistance and opposition are virtually eliminated. Corporatised selves become sufficiently repressed to effectively weaken and dissolve the capacity for serious criticism or dissent. (p. 150)

The challenge is to break into a new paradigm, where functionality and a utilitarian approach no longer determine us, and where we can imagine and create new forms that liberate rather than constrain us. In 1930, Max Weber prophetically wrote:

> his order is now so bound to the technical and economic conditions of machine production . . . perhaps it will so determine them until the last ton of fossilized coal is burnt. In Baxter's view the care for external goods should only lie on the shoulders of 'the saint like a light cloak, which can be thrown aside at any moment'. But fate decreed that the cloak should become like an iron cage. (p. 123)

Weber's "iron cage" remark is often quoted, but without the reference to the last ton of coal. The finite resources of carbon fuel and the implications of climate change are such that perhaps we are now, for the first time since we ensnared ourselves, able to free ourselves from this iron cage of materialism, unending growth, and devotion to the market. Market trading is one thing, but when the market colonizes our emotional and social lives and determines all of our interactions with each other and with nature, it has become a perverse social form of organizing.

The primary task of eco-leadership is to dismantle the modernist hegemony. The three earlier leadership discourses have their place: we need some leadership control over our use of resources, some motivational and psychological support, and some transformative vision, but they must operate within the *zeitgeist*, acknowledging that we live in a fragile ecosystem and are all part of the "web of life."

NEW ORGANIZATIONAL FORMS: HARMONY NOT CONFORMITY

Eco-leadership is about reframing the "form of the organization" and "the purpose of organizations." The organization is no longer—and perhaps never was—a bounded, fixed entity, but is reimagined as an ecosystem within other ecosystems. Within each organization, microcultures exist and continually interact, creating a macroculture we call an organization or company. When one part of the company expands another part contracts, one part makes things, another sells things, and yet these "separate" functions are interrelated and between them auxiliary functions work across the whole. Organizations do not function like machines as the organizational charts and business schools teach. In spite of a move towards systems theory in business schools, most continue to peddle outdated modes of thinking, producing MBAs with a pedagogy dating back to the war years. They do not, in other words, teach managers how to be leaders in a manner appropriate to present conditions (see Mintzberg, 2004; Parker, 2002).

Today's organizations are more fluid and operate in a more organic way than in the past. Parker (2002, p. 73) suggests they are more like communities (in a loose sense of that term), while John Law, in *Organizing Modernity* (1993), conceptualizes organizations as actor-networks, theorizing from his ethnographic observations that networks do not have clear boundaries, but rather are found where we look for them. Law claims that an organization is a network going through a period of relative stability, created by actors with enough agency working towards this end. However, I think the most apt metaphor for an organization is an ecosystem set within other ecosystems. This metaphor immediately evokes the notion of interdependence and sustainability based on balance and biodiversity. I claim these attributes are essential not only for a sustainable natural environment but also for organizational success.

Eco-leadership is about "reading" organizations from a systemic perspective. For example: when it appears that a particular department is working with a "silo mentality" the usual response is to get managers or consultants to try to "fix it." However, the reality is often more nuanced, with different systemic resistances and patterns occurring. As an organizational consultant I work using a psychoanalytic-systemic methodology and we observe that in any system, one department will "act out" emotions or behaviors on behalf of other departments or the whole system. I recently worked with a senior management team who wanted me to align a finance department with the rest of the company culture because it was underperforming and "continually resisting change." We asked the following systemic questions:

1. "What is the finance department carrying on behalf of the whole system?"
2. "What emotions, projections, and data get put into the finance team from the rest of the system?"
3. "What does their resistance mean?"

Working on the assumption that any part operates interdependently in relation to the whole, we discovered a general anxiety in the organization about it expanding too fast, which was held by others but not openly acknowledged. Psychoanalytic insights teach us that when things are unacknowledged—hidden in the unconscious—they become split off and projected onto others.

In this case, the anxiety relating to growing too quickly and hence making the company vulnerable is projected onto the finance team. They resist change because they experience the tensions of the other departments and of the outside world (banks, clients, debtors, etc.). They intuit that a period of stability is needed to "get the house in order" to build a more solid base, to get structures in place to manage the growth sustainably. Their resistance is merely a symptom of a wider systemic problem. Therefore to align the finance culture to the hyper-growth culture of rest of the company, fueled by bonuses, would be a huge mistake. Our approach was to help the senior management team take an eco-leadership perspective and to start to utilize the knowledge held in different parts of the "system" rather than to try and push top-down solutions and create a one-size-fits-all culture.

WORKPLACE BIODIVERSITY: RESISTING MONOCULTURES

Contemporary leadership wisdom advises aligning values and cultures; however, this encourages leaders to think that monocultures create company success. In spite of claims to value diversity, organizations strive to align their cultures without recognizing the resulting tensions. There is an uncritical belief that employees should be highly engaged and support the company's vision and values. Peters and Waterman claim that successful corporations have leaders and employees who are "fanatic centralists around core values, as one analyst argues, 'the brainwashed members of an extreme political sect are no more conformist in their central beliefs'" (Peters & Waterman, 1982, pp. 15–16).

However, it must be remembered that homogenized organizations with monocultures become very dangerous. Fundamentalist religions and cults spring to mind: an employee engagement survey administered to a religious cult would produce fantastic results, but who would argue this is a healthy place to be? Ecosystems are healthy when they have biodiversity, but as soon as monocultures occur in the natural world—as when humans plant acres and acres of a single crop—problems soon occur. Difference is vital to promote creativity, as Florida (2003) suggests:

> Creativity defies race, gender and ethnicity. It knows no race, it knows no ethnicity, it knows no gender, it knows no age, it knows no income-level, it knows nothing about appearance, it knows nothing about sexual orientation. Every single human being is creative, and we don't know where that creativity will come from. (p. 28)

Working together on agreed tasks with shared values is important, but this means developing solidarity, not conformity. Companies need engaged employees, but not with a passive acceptance. They must not become dependent followers but active leaders themselves, retaining their autonomy and creativity. Habermas (1984) uses the phrase the "colonization of the life-world" to describe how the individual subject is penetrated by bureaucracy and the ideology of efficiency and rationality, claiming we become colonized and unable to think outside of this ideology. Eco-leadership involves helping individuals and organizations to become decolonized. It works towards harmonization so that each individual, each part, contributes to the health of the whole system; and to achieve this they must retain their diversity and autonomy.

SPATIAL LEADERSHIP AND ORGANIZATIONAL ARCHITECTURES

A key role for eco-leaders is to be an organizational architect, taking a spatial leadership approach. New organizational forms are evolving and as organizational forms change, new business models emerge and new leadership is sought that mirrors the form of the organization. Eco-leadership means focusing on the spaces as much as the people, machines, and buildings that occupy them. This requires a radical shift in leadership thinking. The concept of space is essential to eco-leadership, refocusing our attention on the spaces within ourselves, our organizations, and in our social networks where the emergent capability lies. Business changes so quickly these days that the adaptive companies with capability for change are the winners. When training eco-leadership, we work on the idea of creating "thinking spaces" within individuals and in their teams and their organizations, where thinking and knowledge exchange can take place. Nodal points in a network are identified so that a crossover point between knowledge carriers happens, and where diverse people meet, from which unplanned strategies emerge. Eco-leadership focuses on designing, shaping, influencing, and creating spaces and structures to enable the self-organizing and self-regulating systems of an organization to work.

Organizations' internal structures and cultures commonly mirror the physical architectures of organizations. A skyscraper bank has a hierarchical structure and culture mimicking its building, with a CEO in the top office and power relationships that are vertical like the building. Likewise, the size of a church mimics the power of the post holder, the Vatican representing the power of the Pope. The Amish people have a much flatter hierarchy, their bishops remain local and independent of an extensive church power structure, and in sympathy they have no church "buildings." Instead they hold rotating Sunday services in different family homes, reflecting their belief system of humility and a plain, simple lifestyle. Quakers also have a flat structure without any clergy or hierarchy. For 350 years they have survived with an organizational architecture of spiritual consensus, "a priesthood of all believers" whereby anybody can "minister" in their meetinghouses and where big decisions are taken at an annual gathering where all members are present and all have a voice. Their meetinghouse architecture mimics this: small, simple buildings without steeples, inside are a circle of chairs or wooden benches in a plain room without any ornamentation or religious symbols. Eco-leadership in contemporary organizations must learn from new social movements as well as diverse organizations and faith groups like the Quakers and Amish who have managed to create unusual organizational forms that enable them to operate in nonlinear, nonhierarchical, or specifically sustainable lifestyles. An important lesson is that superficial change doesn't work. The architecture of an organization means its buildings, its people, its processes; all have to be in harmony for successful sustainability.

ECO-LEADERSHIP AND SYSTEMIC ETHICS

Eco-leadership relies on "leadership spirit," which means drawing on a deeper source, a unifying source. It might be a religious or spiritual belief, or the idea of holism with the natural world, or perhaps a compassion for justice and the human capacity for good. Whatever underpins the deeper source, eco-leadership demands an ethical approach that stands firmly against the ethic of Milton Friedman that dominated much of the last century. Friedman (1962) claimed that businesses serve society only if they focus on profit: "The executive is an agent serving the interests of his principle to serve the stockholders and thus there is only one social responsibility of business—to use its resources and engage in activities designed to increase its profits" (pp. 132–133). This ethic has led us to climate crisis, war, division between rich and poor, and individual alienation. A new ethic is needed in business and public-sector organizations, one that subverts the logic of the market. To achieve this we have to reconnect ourselves with nature and with the idea that diversity and interdependence are at the heart of human survival. Gary Snyder (1990) puts it this way:

> When an ecosystem is fully functioning, all the members are present at the assembly. To speak of wilderness is to speak of wholeness. Human beings came out of that wholeness and to consider the possibility of reactivating membership in the Assembly of All Beings is in no way regressive. (p. 121)

We are all called to rejoin the assembly and collectively we must find adaptive structures and processes to accommodate the idea that nature and the human "other" are vital to our survival, and more than this, vital for a civilized and creative future. This is a philosophical task, an ethical task, and a practical task. Much of the leadership literature seeking an ethical stance unfortunately oversimplifies the challenge, and by doing so contributes to the problem. Servant leadership (Greenleaf, 1977), transformational leadership (Bass & Riggio, 2006), and post-heroic leadership (Binney, Wilke, & Williams, 2004) all promote individualistic approaches to leadership: they define the leader as an individual, and argue for ethical approaches from individuals. Bass (1998), for example, argues:

> Leaders are authentically transformational when they increase awareness of what is right, good, important and beautiful, when they help to elevate followers needs for achievement and self-actualisation, when they foster in followers higher moral maturity and when they move followers to go beyond their self interests for the good of their group, organisation or society. (p. 171)

While this is an important point, it unfortunately does nothing to question the structural power imbalances that take place. A new ethics is required that extends the systemic stance of eco-leadership to its ethics. Slavoj Zizek (2008) differentiates systemic and subjective violence. He claims that subjective violence (interpersonal violence) can indicate and also be caused by the much greater evil, systemic violence. News reports are "fascinated by the lure" of subjective violence, the murder of a youth or the abduction of a child, for example. Systemic violence, on the other hand, is invisible: it is the unseen and disowned violence that inhabits bureaucracies, institutions, and governing structures. It is the violence of poverty that kills infants in the thousands, the violence of oppression where immigrant workers get low pay, poor health care, and suffer accordingly. It is the violence that surrounds us but becomes "normal" and ignored.

Likewise with ethics, one cannot donate to charity and consider oneself ethical if leading an organization that is involved in dumping toxic waste in Africa, legal or not. Knowing that increased productivity contributes to global warming, causing systemic violence to those in Bangladesh and other peoples facing catastrophic consequences of climate change requires a new ethical response from business and political leaders. Systemic ethics means to take into account the impact of your organization on others and on the natural world, to account for the externalities, the toxic waste, the use of carbon fuel, the social justice to workers in the developing world who work for your supply chain. Eco-leadership situates ethics as part of an overall systemic approach, asking questions about the primary purpose of an organization, how it serves society, and its impact on the natural world, before jumping to immediate assumptions about profit, output, and growth.

CONCLUSION: DEVELOPING CREATIVE AND GENERATIVE LEADERS

I have been working in the leadership field with leaders and managers in private, public, and not-for-profit sectors as a coach and organizational consultant and as an academic, teaching eco-leadership. The interest and practical engagement from leaders in all sectors has taught me that the eco-leadership discourse, in spite of inherent tensions in the workplace for productivity, growth, and profit, has come of age. It is happening and at the same time is emergent: we are learning as we go.

What is absolutely clear is an urgent need to help leaders, educators, and organizations to become more eco-literate, not only in order to understand environmental issues, but also to deconstruct the ideology of rationalism and growth that remains so endemic. I find myself working with leaders who are "dislocated" and disorientated, having lost their sense of place and often self. The first task is to help them "locate themselves" before I can move on to deeper work on how to create eco-leadership in their organizations. We go to art galleries, we ask them to observe the world around them, to sit in railway stations and parks and simply observe others and nature and then to observe their internal worlds, their thoughts and emotions. We work with "disruptive interventions," organizing a "Free Association Matrix" (Western, 2008b, pp. 188–190), asking them to sit silently in chairs arranged incoherently, and to free-associate, to let go of striving for answers and to become aware of their bodies, their unconscious minds, and their collective sense of who they are and what's happening in the here and now. Doing so creates a space for new thoughts, for reflection, for creativity. We then can move to how they might rethink their organizations, how they can liberate leadership throughout the organization, become more ethical, and challenge the status quo. Once a space is created and normal activity is disrupted, the results can be profound.

Across the globe organizations are stepping tentatively forward to make eco-leadership happen. There is no template so we learn from each other as we go, and we can learn from those already leading from the edges. I stayed with the Amish for a short period and observed their method to discern whether technology is useful to their quality of life and "faithful living." They have found a way of putting their faith community first, discerning how to use technology in the service of it, rather than be dominated by it. We need to do the same. I have stayed in other marginal communities, the countercultural community of a hermitage, where monks live without possessions, living a sustainable life that has been followed for over 1,500 years. I learned much from monastic formation and how monks are not trained in monk skills but are formed by the monastic life. So it is with eco-leadership, it cannot be learned through skills training, rather it is a way of being and we must create contexts that form us, and form future eco-leaders throughout the organization (see Western, 2008b, pp. 198–208).

I work with leaders running complex hospital and health systems who are inspired by the ideas of eco-leadership and realize that the concepts speak to their dilemmas. With colleagues I run an experiential event called "The Leadership Game" where we ask from 40 to 100 managers/leaders to work in teams under the four different discourses, and we reflect on the experience and analyze the results together before getting them to work across teams in an eco-leadership way, learning how easily they can resist collaboration, learning how exciting it is when they self-organize, work together with leadership but without hierarchy, and manage themselves to produce very creative results.

Harnessing the talent of all is vital. Apple Computer, Inc., began their commercial activity producing amazing computers but working on business models out of sync with their inventions. Now with the iPhone, the business model has changed. A key income stream now comes from selling "apps" (applications), by which they have "outsourced" creativity and innovation to everyone. Constant updating means more people want an iPhone to access this flow of inventiveness. This is eco-leadership in a commercial sense, democratizing creative leadership to anyone capable of invention, not just to creative employees. Eco-leadership is generative, it creates new capability and new creativity and it pays attention to "all in the assembly."

Eco-leadership is the application of an ecological worldview to organizations and workplaces, and to social and political movements. It describes a way of organizing based on organic and sustainable principles, many of them learned from nature. Yet it doesn't ignore technology and human potential. Technology is increasingly a part of our inner and outer landscapes, it can provide great benefits and many answers to environmental and social challenges, but only if each of us, individually and collectively, accept our responsibilities to become leaders. Eco-leadership is about recognizing the multitude of talent and goodwill in society, and harnessing the creativity and adaptability in our social and natural ecosystems.

Challenging the status quo and becoming eco-literate is the first step: learning how biodiversity is vital in social systems as well as nature, learning how to harmonize and integrate technology, humans, and nature in our ecosystems so that they are sustainable and socially just places. The eco-leadership discourse comes out from a new *zeitgeist*, and now is the time for organizational leaders—public, private, and not-for-profit—to stop observing from the sidelines because in ecosystems there are no sidelines, we are all in this together.

NOTES

1. For a full account of these discourses, see Western (2005, 2008b).
2. For detailed discussion of the leadership literature, see Western (2005).

REFERENCES

Armstrong, K. (2000). *The Battle for God*. London: Harper Collins.

Axtell Ray, C. (1986). Corporate Culture: The last Frontier of Control. *Journal of Management Studies, 23*(3), 286–295.

Bass, B. (1990). From Transactional to Transformational Leadership: Learning to Share the Vision. *Organizational Dynamics, 18*(3), 19–31.

———. (1998). *The Ethics of Transformational Leadership*. In J. Ciulla (Ed.), *Ethics: The Heart of Leadership* (pp. 169–192). Westport, CT: Praeger.

Bass, B., & Riggio, R. (2006). *Transformational Leadership*. Mahwah, NJ: Lawrence Erlbaum Associates.

Binney, G., Wilke, G., & Williams C. (2004). *Living Leadership: A Practical Guide for Ordinary Heroes*. London: Pearson Books.

Burns, J. (1978). *Leadership*. New York: Harper and Row.

Butler, J. (1990). *Gender Trouble: Feminism and the Subversion of Identity*. New York: Routledge.

Capra, F. (1996). *The Web of Life*. New York: Doubleday.

Casey, C. (1995). *Work, Self, and Society: After Industrialism*. London & New York: Routledge.

Coopey, J. (1995). The Learning Organization: Power, Politics and Ideology. *Management Learning, 26*(2), 193–213.

Florida, R. (2003). *The Rise of the Creative Class: And How It's Transforming Work, Leisure, Community and Everyday Life*. New York: Basic Books.

Foucault, M. (1972). *The Archaeology of Knowledge*. New York: Pantheon Books.

Friedman, M. (1962). *Capitalism and Freedom*. Chicago: University Of Chicago Press.

Greenleaf, R. (1977). *Servant Leadership*. Mahwah, NJ: Paulist Press.

Habermas, J. (1984). *The Theory of Communicative Action*. Boston: Beacon Press.

Klein, N. (2000). *No Logo*. New York: Picador.

Kunda, G. (1992). *Engineering Culture: Control Commitment in a High Tech Corporation*. Philadelphia: Temple University Press.

Lasch, C. (1979). *The Culture of Narcissism: American Life in an Age of Diminishing Expectations*. New York: Norton.

Latour, B. (2004). *Politics of Nature: How to Bring the Sciences into Democracy*. Cambridge, MA: Harvard University Press.

Law, J. (1991). *A Sociology of Monsters: Essays on Power, Technology and Domination*. London & New York: Routledge.

Law, J. (1993). *Organizing Modernity: Social Ordering and Social Theory*. Oxford: Wiley-Blackwell.

Meddis, S. (1999). Digital Activism in Seattle. *USA Today*. Retrieved from http://www.usatoday.com/tech/columnist/ccsam011.htm

Mintzberg, M. (2004). *Managers Not MBAs: A Hard Look at the Soft Practice of Managing and Management Development*. San Francisco: Berrett-Koehler Publishers.

Parker, M. (2002). *Against Management: Organization in the Age of Managerialism*. Cambridge, UK: Polity Press.

Peters, T., & Waterman, H. (1982). *In Search of Excellence: Lessons from America's Best Run Companies*. New York: Harper and Row.

Putnam, R. (2000). *Bowling Alone: The Collapse and Revival of American Community*. New York: Simon and Schuster.

Rieff, P. (1966). *The Triumph of the Therapeutic: Uses of Faith after Freud*. New York: Harper and Row.

Rogers, C. (1951). *Client-Centered Therapy: Its Current Practice, Implications and Theory*. London: Constable.

Rose, N. (1990). *Governing the Soul*. London: Routledge.

Snyder G. (1990). *The Practice of the Wild*. San Francisco: North Point Press.

Taylor, F. (1911/1997). *The Principles of Scientific Management*. New York: Dover Publications.

Weber, M. (1930). *The Protestant Ethic and the Spirit of Capitalism*. London: Allen and Unwin.

Western, S. (2005). *A Critical Analysis of Leadership: Overcoming Fundamentalist Tendencies*. Doctoral Dissertation, Lancaster University Management School.

Western S. (2008a). Democratising Strategy. In D. Campbell & D. Huffington (Eds.), *Organizations Connected: A Handbook of Systemic Consultation* (pp. 173–196). London: Karnac Publications.

Western, S. (2008b). *Leadership: A Critical Text*. Los Angeles & London: Sage Publications.

Wheatley, M. (2006). *Leadership and the New Science*. San Francisco: Berrett-Koehler Publishers.

Yeats, W. (1919). *The Second Coming*. Retrieved from http://www.poets.org/viewmedia. php/prmMID/15527

Zizek, S. (2008). *Violence: Six Sideways Reflections*. London: Profile.

3 Challenges and Strategies of Leading for Sustainability

Benjamin W. Redekop

INTRODUCTION

My aim in this chapter is to highlight some of the fundamental human challenges faced by those intent on leading for sustainability and to propose strategies for meeting those challenges. I draw upon research on future orientation, environmental management, and from the growing field of environmental psychology. The latter is a field of particular interest, and one goal of this chapter is to introduce some of the research findings from this field to students and practitioners of leadership who may be unfamiliar with it. The chapter briefly outlines some of the intellectual and motivational challenges that come with trying to get people to cooperate in solving social dilemmas like climate change and other environmental problems and offers some suggestions for how to facilitate intrinsic motivation to act for the common good. The chapter concludes with an examination of our affinity for nature and natural scenes and how leaders can help to foster love of nature among their constituents as an important first step towards achieving sustainability.

THE CHALLENGE OF THE FUTURE

The move towards sustainability will entail a host of changes to how we do things and how we think about the world, and perhaps one of the biggest challenges to attitudinal and behavioral change is the fact that the negative environmental effects of many present behaviors will not be fully felt for decades. This presents a problem, since "we are biased to process information that is local, dramatic, and simple" (Osbaldiston & Sheldon, 2002, p. 45). It took a vivid catastrophe like the recent Great Recession for Americans to begin saving for the future, as they did in the wake of previous economic catastrophes like the Great Depression (Zuckerman, 2009). Whatever we are feeling at any one moment in time tends to condition our expectations of the future, including our future happiness (Gilbert, 2006). In the case of climate change, polls show that a majority of

Americans are convinced that it is a problem requiring action, but that they also believe it will have a distant effect (temporally and geographically) and is less important than nearly all—and in some cases all—other issues (Leiserowitz, 2007; Pew Research Center, 2009). Under "normal" conditions, which in the past tended to be more localized, populations typically (but not always—see Diamond, 2005) have been able to adjust to environmental threats as they have emerged. However, as human populations have expanded and technological innovations have multiplied our impact on the planet, we are increasingly able to wreak harm in a more far-flung manner, both temporally and spatially. Anthropogenic climate change is clearly the most severe and pressing example of this problem, although acid rain and ozone depletion are also relevant cases among others.

Avoiding global environmental catastrophe and achieving sustainability is thus an enormous challenge not least because doing so entails resolving a conflict between immediate individual perceptions and wants and long-term collective good. Acting as self-interested individuals, we tend to exploit common resources, especially if the benefits are clear and immediate and the costs are diffuse and located far in the future. Garrett Hardin (1968) called this the "tragedy of the commons," while it has become common for social scientists to refer to it as a "social dilemma" or "temporal trap" (Joireman, 2005; Osbaldiston & Sheldon, 2002; Oskamp, 2002). As Hardin suggested, there is no problem so long as populations are limited and resources are plentiful. But at some point, unlimited population growth and resource depletion can lead to the general collapse of a finite system, which hurts everyone. We become ensnared in a trap that we have set for ourselves earlier in time. In order to avoid this tragic outcome, individuals need to align their behavior with the long-term best interests of the community and, indeed, biosphere. Doing so is enormously difficult to achieve, and represents a genuine leadership[1] challenge (for discussion of the pitfalls as well as promise of collaborative attempts to solve social dilemmas, see Chapter 4 of this volume).

In historical terms, modernity brought with it an unprecedented future orientation. In contrast to the cyclical patterns that characterize most traditional, preliterate, and nonentrepreneurial cultures, a widely shared linear time orientation arose in the west during the early modern period. The idea that history was progressive and that conditions were improving for "man" at large became pervasive during the period of the Enlightenment. For the first time in history it became thinkable that new knowledge was better than old knowledge and that moderns were advancing beyond the achievements of the ancients. The Industrial Revolution, built as it was on technological advancement and the rationalization of production processes, helped to secure the notion that time is linear, progressive, and governable, and that the future can be predicted and controlled in ways that go beyond the traditional methods of astrology, divination, and reliance on prophets and soothsayers. During subsequent centuries "progress" became a guiding theme of western civilization.[2]

Yet as Reading (2004) suggests, "There is [now] a growing apprehension about the future. As people begin to realize that nature often exacts a price for the gains that science and technology bring, progress is no longer seen as an unalloyed blessing. Threats of environmental or nuclear disaster make the future seem less hospitable than it once did" (p. 126). The buildup of ecological waste (including atmospheric CO2) is one of the products of time that weighs on the present and belies the modern conception of the future as a limitless repository of all our hopes and dreams—but not our waste.

OVERCOMING HUMAN SHORTSIGHTEDNESS

Research in the growing field of environmental psychology provides leaders with helpful clues about how to overcome our natural shortsightedness. Joireman, Strathman, and Balliet (2006) have proposed an integrative model of a personality variable called Consideration of Future Consequences (CFC). According to this research, individuals high in CFC tend to be more conscientious, academically successful, able to delay gratification and avoid unhealthy habits, and less impulsive and hedonistic. They also tend to be more interested and involved in pro-environmental behaviors (Joireman, 2005; Joireman et al., 2006). People low in CFC tend to focus on the immediate consequences of behaviors, engage in riskier behaviors, and are higher in present hedonism, fatalism, depression, and drug use, among other things. Those high in CFC are apparently better able to connect present behaviors with future consequences than those lower in CFC and they act accordingly. One implication for leadership is the need to identify and empower individuals high in CFC. Leaders will also need to help individuals low in CFC to recognize and act on those connections in a meaningful and enduring fashion. Research shows that in order to do so, leaders will need to be able to make clear to people low in CFC how cooperating with proposed solutions to environmental problems will benefit them in *both* the short and long term (Joireman, 2005, pp. 298–299). It is worth noting here that "[w]omen are typically higher than men in environmental concern and ecocentrism" (Oskamp, 2002, p. 314), so their fuller participation in public affairs is also desirable from an ecological point of view.

Leaders must furthermore be able to induce positive emotional states, if constituents are to engage in future-oriented behaviors, since people tend to emphasize short-term outcomes when they are in a negative emotional state. Hope is a positive emotion that allows us to delay present satisfactions for future rewards, and as such must be nurtured if people are to be convinced to act in a future-oriented manner. When people become less hopeful about the future, they typically become more short-sighted, cynical, and self-centered (Joireman et al., 2006; Cottle & Klineberg, 1974; Reading, 2004). As Reading (2004) notes, "Hope gives us a vision that things can be better . . . an expectation that some desired goal can be attained. It has been the driving force behind all of humanity's great achievements through the ages . . . Future-oriented behavior is the behavioral signal of hope" (pp. 3–5). Hopeful behaviors are augmented by clearly articulated, achievable goals that are congruent with an individual's value system (Snyder, Rand, & Ritschel, 2006). From this perspective, then, "one of the main tasks of leadership is to articulate a credible vision of the future that embodies the hopes and aspirations of their followers . . . Successful leaders raise a group's morale and bolster its members' hopes of achieving their desired goals" (Reading, 2004, p. 143).

In a similar vein, even though there is some utility in raising awareness of future threats, a strong correlation has been found to exist between Future Anxiety (FA) and negative expectations of solutions to global problems, threats, and dangers, with concomitant (negative) behaviors (Kals & Maes, 2002; Osbaldiston & Sheldon, 2002; Zaleski, 2005; Moser, 2007). Empirical studies have shown that fear appeals tend to motivate constructive responses only under certain conditions, including: a sense of personal risk (I am vulnerable); a sense of self-efficacy (I can do something about it); a sense of response efficacy (what I do will make a difference); the specific actions to be taken are known; there is no sense of manipulation; and there is social support for taking the prescribed actions (Moser, 2007, pp. 69–71).

Leaders must therefore engage in a delicate balancing act, identifying threats while communicating optimism about the chances of countering them. Complicating the issue, however, are two related findings. One is that "[c]ooperation in social dilemmas declines as the size of the resource becomes more uncertain" (Joireman, 2005, p. 298). We cooperate less in solving resource problems if we are unsure just how limited the resource is—maybe the problem is not so pressing after all and will be solved at some future date! Secondly, "[w]e are more frequently cooperative as the endpoint of the interaction seems ever-farther away" (Parks & Posey, 2005, p. 238). Cooperation, in other words, is paradoxically heightened if we are all convinced that it is a long-term issue that will not be solved tomorrow (by someone else's sacrifice). Taken together, these findings suggest that too much optimism about the extent of available resources and the probability of immediate success can result in backsliding and exacerbation of the problem. If too much FA is counterproductive, so is too little.

Further compounding the problem, the environmental goal to be reached is what psychologists call an "avoidance goal" rather than a more positive "approach goal" (Snyder et al., 2006). Environmental collapse is something to be avoided, even if spiritual and social benefits may accompany lifestyles that are less destructive and more in harmony with the natural world. The problem with avoidance goals is that they often do not have a clear end point. Consequently, "Such goal pursuits do not result in positive emotions nor in the general sense of well-being that are the sequelae of approach goals" (Snyder et al., 2006, p. 109). Leaders will need to reframe the avoidance goal of environmental collapse into a more positive approach goal or, better yet, a series of goals that can be celebrated as they are met. Environmental degradation has already gone so far in many parts of the world that "regeneration" of nature is an increasingly attractive approach goal that can be identified. Perhaps instead of talking so much about "ecological crisis," we need to start talking more about "ecological regeneration."

A loss of hope, as often happens among the poor and indigent, is a likely cause of short-term behaviors (Cottle & Klineberg, 1974; Edwards, 2002), and this fact raises the issue of economic inequality: is it possible to expect future-oriented behavior from people hardly able to survive? Cottle and Klineberg (1974) argue that fatalism among the poor is most likely a result of bad or hopeless living conditions, not "any psychological inability to imagine a different future as a personal possibility" (p. 183). If the health of the planet requires that all human beings engage in environmentally sensitive behaviors, then is it not a requirement of sustainability that the poor be raised up to a level of prosperity that allows them to be more future-oriented? It is well known that wealth and prosperity are correlated with CFC (Cottle & Klineberg, 1974; Friedman, 1990; Joireman et al., 2006). Whether CFC causes wealth and success or wealth and success cause CFC is an open question. But clearly it is much easier to be future-oriented and concerned about the natural environment for its own sake when one is not simply struggling to survive (Knopf, 1987, p. 786). The bottom line is that the wealthy—many of us in North America, for example—are in a better position to be future-oriented than poor nations, and thus we have a responsibility to lead the way on sustainability. To claim that we cannot act to curb greenhouse gas emissions until developing nations do the same, especially given the fact that we are one of the main parties responsible for the existing problem, is a clear abdication of leadership and, indeed, responsibility.

THE MOTIVATIONAL CHALLENGE

Beyond the specific challenges presented by human shortsightedness, leaders must confront a host of motivational challenges when it comes to leading for environmental sustainability. One way to get a handle on the motivational issues at stake in solving social dilemmas is to understand the variability in what researchers call "social value orientation." Similar to future orientation, there seem to be inherent differences in the way people approach social dilemmas (Osbaldiston & Sheldon, 2002). According to this research, around 60 percent of people tend to conform to the category of "individualists": their main concern is to maximize their own payoff regardless of its effect on others. "What's in it for me?" is the most important question to be answered. Such individuals will go along with solutions to social dilemmas if they perceive that it brings a benefit to themselves. (I would add that, at some level, *everyone* thinks this way.) People in the second category, around 20 percent of the population, can be characterized as "cooperators." They are concerned with maximizing the payoff for everyone, and will tend to go along with most solutions to social dilemmas regardless of the immediate impact on themselves. The third and most recalcitrant type is the "competitor": these individuals are concerned to maximize the payoff for themselves *in comparison* to others. Also comprising about 20 percent of the population, they may never cooperate because to do so does not enhance the differential between the payoff to themselves and to others whereas *defecting* from the system does. Punitive sanctions may be the only way to get this group to cooperate, and indeed, experimental "tit-for-tat" simulations have produced greater cooperation for both individualists *and* competitors (Osbaldiston & Sheldon, 2002, pp. 42–44).

But although the most obvious motivational tool for changing any set of behaviors is the use of punitive sanctions, are they always effective? Research has shown that punitive sanctions *can* work if a population directly feels the negative effects of the behaviors in question and consequently feels it is in their own best interest to curb them. In such situations, people are more likely to choose and empower leaders to impose limits on everyone (Osbaldiston & Sheldon, 2002, p. 44). The most obvious example is murder and other violent crimes: how many local leaders have been elected on a platform of "getting tough on crime"?

However, there are limits to a regime of punitive sanctions when it comes to tackling environmental problems, including the already-mentioned fact that negative environmental effects are not always immediately apparent to those who cause them. As long as water is not lapping around our ankles, many of us will be hesitant to empower leaders to force us to act in ways that curb climate change if such changes involve some sort of sacrifice. Secondly, a difficult question to answer in many cases is: what are the "best" sanctions? In other words, which sanctions will be effective and have the intended effect? We are very good at finding loopholes and exploiting weaknesses in laws we do not find compelling, while even "good" laws can often have unintended consequences. Closing off one set of behaviors may simply result in a new and more destructive set taking their place. The bottom line is that punitive sanctions undermine intrinsic motivation and enjoyment of the behaviors in question: "People must 'feel the need' or 'hear the call' to make major changes in their lifestyles" (Osbaldiston & Sheldon, 2002, p. 47).

"Self-Determination Theory" (SDT) provides evidence that internal motivation is the best way to promote long-term cooperative behaviors with a "cascading" effect where such behaviors are willingly spread to others (see the literature review in Osbaldiston & Sheldon, 2002). Results from this research suggest that "autonomy supportive requests" are more likely to foster intrinsic motivation and a cascading effect. Such requests include: acknowledging the target's perspective; allowing the target choice as to how to comply with the request; and providing a meaningful rationale for the request when choice provision is not possible. If requests are made in this manner, it is more likely that targets of such requests will not only engage in the behaviors in question, but will take ownership of them and pass them on to others (Osbaldiston & Sheldon, 2002, pp. 47–53).

However, it is here that "leadership" may conflict with "environmentalism." For example, many environmentalists are opposed to nuclear power as an alternative to carbon-intensive forms of power generation. Nuclear waste is just another form of pollution to be avoided and nuclear accidents are potentially very dangerous. Yet, it may be necessary for those wanting to exercise leadership on global warming, for example, to let their constituents decide if they are willing to accept the risks of nuclear power in order to avoid the severe disruptions that will likely be the result of unchecked climate change. If not, then they are going to need to be very good at explaining why nuclear power is unacceptable, and they are going to need to demonstrate clear and practical alternative pathways towards independence from fossil fuels.

A further complication lies in the fact that providing information and exhorting people to act in a sustainable manner are not in themselves terribly effective tactics for changing behavior (Stern & Oskamp, 1987; Osbaldiston & Sheldon, 2002; Jackson, 2005). Rather than exhorting people to change their behavior, *modeling* of appropriate behaviors has proven more effective when combined with other factors like the internalization of pro-environmental social norms, feedback loops that clarify the personal consequences of environmental resource problems and how individual behaviors are related to those larger problems, and local control over natural resources (Stern & Oskamp, 1987). Such actions help to raise awareness and overcome what Gifford (1976, 2007) calls "environmental numbness": our general inattention to our external environment as we go about our daily routines like work, play, socializing, and preparing and consuming food.

Thus although informational appeals, on their own, are not particularly effective in promoting sustainable behaviors, a link has been demonstrated between "ecological awareness" and pro-environmental behaviors (Kals & Maes, 2002). Such awareness is promoted by developing an emotional affinity for nature. When combined with a sense of self-efficacy ("I can make a difference"), it is correlated with higher levels of environmental responsibility, which is "one of the most decisive predictors of sustainable behavior" (Kals & Maes, 2002, p. 104). Environmental responsibility is heightened if people construe environmental problems as issues of fairness and social justice: "The more people construe . . . socio-ecological conflict as a justice dilemma, the more they are willing to contribute to the reduction of [the] dilemma and to the reestablishment of justice" (p. 104). This is an important finding that should be of value to leaders of all kinds: the more that environmental problems are framed as problems of fairness and justice to other human beings (and perhaps animals), the more people will feel inclined to take responsibility for them.

AFFINITY FOR NATURE

One of the more interesting and well-documented findings from the field of environmental psychology is the fact that exposure to nature scenes has a calming, restorative effect on people who are stressed. A host of studies has documented the stress-relieving functions of nature. The positive emotional states elicited by exposure to natural scenes "may be a mechanism underlying the finding that hospital patients recovering from surgery had more favorable recovery courses, including shorter hospital stays, lower intake of potent narcotic pain drugs, and more favorable evaluations by nurses, if their windows overlooked trees rather than a brick building wall" (Ulrich et al., 1991, p. 204; see also Knopf, 1987; Parsons, 1991; Kaplan, 1995). Stress reduction and recovery from illness would seem to be one of the most immediate and salient benefits of preserving nature, yet we rarely hear about it from leaders intent on promoting pro-environmental causes. Most individuals want to know "what's in it for me?" when it comes to adopting sustainable behaviors (Stern & Oskamp, 1987, pp. 1054–1067; Osbaldiston & Sheldon, 2002, pp. 42–43). This being the case, those intent on showing leadership on environmental issues are well advised to emphasize the immediate physiological and emotional benefits of natural environments.

Leaders will also want to make every effort to get their constituents into natural environments where they can experience firsthand the restorative effects of nature, since the development of an emotional "affinity for nature," as we have seen, has been found to be one of the primary motivating factors for sustainable behaviors. Love of nature seems to be primarily instigated by experiences in nature, particularly with significant others (Kals & Maes, 2002). Indeed, "The outdoor experience is clearly a group experience . . . fewer than 2% of visitors to the wilderness are alone . . . Sociological research forces us to consider action in the outdoors as being highly responsive to, even oriented to, social stimulation" (Knopf, 1987, pp. 793–794).

Researchers furthermore argue that the voluntary outdoor group "is an important source of self-affirmation used to reinforce confidence in the rightness of one's values, perspectives, and lifestyle" (Knopf, 1987, p. 803). Organizing an outdoor group—of whatever kind—would seem to be a fundamental act of leadership for environmental sustainability, promoting both affinity for nature and a strengthened sense of moral purpose for those that participate in such groups. Making the kinds of changes that are needed to achieve environmental sustainability is going to take an enormous commitment and sense of moral purpose, at the local level, if it is ever going to happen. Hence the local outdoors group may well become one of the most important building blocks in the process.

It may also be useful for those in leadership positions to know that there is solid evidence showing that human beings prefer nature scenes over urban scenes, and they prefer urban scenes with vegetation over urban scenes without vegetation. And there appears to be an innate preference for savanna-type environments, with large open grassy areas punctuated by well-defined areas of trees, water, and vegetation (Kaplan & Kaplan, 1972; Balling & Falk, 1982; Knopf, 1987, pp. 804–805; Pitt & Zube, 1987, p. 1023). But although there is a broad visual preference for natural environments, people pursue outdoor activity for a variety of reasons, including escape, social reinforcement, competence building, and aesthetic or spiritual enjoyment (Knopf, 1987, p. 801).

Experiences in nature thus satisfy different needs, and individuals impose different meanings on nature according to their own frames of reference. People "construct images of what each setting has to offer, and the image creates more information about the external environment than [it] actually carries" (Knopf, 1987, p. 806). As such, research indicates that it matters how we talk about nature: words with a more positive, "natural" connotation (e.g., "wilderness" or "national park") will make the areas in question more highly valued than identical areas that are described in more "nonnatural," negative terms ("commercial timber stand" or "leased grazing area"). The application of labels implying human influence consistently *lowers* the perceived value of the resource in question (Pitt & Zube, 1987, p. 1024; Knopf, 1987, p. 806). The implication for environmental leadership is clear: it matters what terms you use when talking about the natural environment, with a preference for terms that emphasize wildness and/or a "special" status. National pride also no doubt plays a role in the preference for terms like "national parks," especially given the historic role that "natural wonders" and scenic landscapes have played in the formation of American national identity (Pitt & Zube, 1987, p. 1012). But the effect is doubtless similar in all nations: natural landmarks and refuges are consistent points of pride around the world.

CONCLUSION

This chapter has touched upon some of the challenges leaders face when they seek to help constituents act in a future-oriented, environmentally sensitive manner, and it proposes some strategies and tactics that are supported by social-scientific research. As such it only represents a tiny fraction of possible leadership behaviors and strategies—much more research and reflection is needed in this area. Readers who are intrigued by the findings presented here are encouraged to explore the fascinating work being done in the field of environmental psychology and related fields—my references are only the tip of the iceberg and my suggestions are provisional at best. They are also urged to read Chapter 4 of this volume, titled "Leadership and the Dynamics of Collaboration: Averting the Tragedy of the Commons," which delves deeper into collaborative approaches to solving social dilemmas like climate change and other environmental problems.

Readers may find many of my suggestions to be commonsensical; if so, all the better. My hope is that readers will, if nothing else, become more intentional and confident in their pro-environmental leadership behaviors after reading this chapter. And I would suggest that none of the suggested strategies and tactics are in themselves harmful or counterproductive if they are pursued thoughtfully and with sensitivity to the situation at hand. Whether leading or following, we must find ways to move forward that are noncoercive and congruent with our nature and aspirations. Doing so will be neither easy nor simple, but then again doing things the easy and simple way has led us to our current environmental impasse and hence is no longer a viable option.

NOTES

1. Here I define *leadership* as an influence process or relation between an individual or group of individuals and a larger group, aimed at clarifying and achieving group goals. See the Introduction of this volume for further discussion of what is meant by "leadership for environmental sustainability."
2. Many historical and anthropological sources could be cited here, but these developments are so well known that I will limit myself to mentioning a few synthetic works on time orientation: Cottle & Klineberg (1974); Nowotny (1994); Bell (1997); Reading (2004). Suffice it to say that these are broad generalizations to which there are numerous exceptions and that can be qualified in various ways.

REFERENCES

Balling, J., & Falk, J. (1982). Development of Visual Preference for Natural Environments. *Environment and Behavior, 14*(1), 5–28.

Bell, W. (1997). *Foundations of Future Studies: Human Science for a New Era.* New Brunswick: Transaction Publishers.

Cottle, T., & Klineberg, S. (1974). *The Present of Things Future.* New York: Free Press.

Diamond, J. (2005). *Collapse: How Societies Choose to Fail or Succeed.* New York: Viking.

Edwards, A. J. (2002). *A Psychology of Time Orientation: Time Awareness across Life Stages and in Dementia.* Westport, CT: Praeger.

Friedman, W. (1990). *About Time: Inventing the Fourth Dimension.* Cambridge, MA: MIT Press.

Gifford, R. (1976). Environmental Numbness in the Classroom. *Journal of Experimental Education, 44*(3), 4–7.

Gifford, R. (2007). Environmental Psychology and Sustainable Development: Expansion, Maturation, and Challenges. *Journal of Social Issues, 63*(1), 199–212.

Gilbert, D. (2006). *Stumbling on Happiness.* New York: A. A. Knopf.

Hardin, G. (1968). The Tragedy of the Commons. *Science, 162*(3859), 1243–1248.

Jackson, T. (2005). *Toward a "Social Psychology" of Consumption. End of Award Research Report, Sustainable Technologies Programme, Economic & Social*

Research Council. RES-332-27-0001. Retrieved from http://www.sustainabletechnologies.ac.uk/final%20pdf/End%20of%20Award%20 Research%20 Reports/Final%20Report %2014.pdf

Joireman, J. (2005). Environmental Problems as Social Dilemmas: The Temporal Dimension. In A. Strathman & J. Joireman (Eds.), *Understanding Behavior in the Context of Time: Theory, Research, and Application* (pp. 289–304). Mahwah, NJ: Lawrence Erlbaum Associates.

Joireman, J., Strathman, A., & Balliet, D. (2006). Considering Future Consequences: An Integrative Model. In J. Sanna & E. Chang (Eds.), *Judgements over Time: The Interplay of Thoughts, Feelings, and Behaviors* (pp. 82–99). Oxford: Oxford University Press.

Kals, E., & Maes, J. (2002). Sustainable Development and Emotions. In P. Schmuck & W. Schultz (Eds.), *Psychology of Sustainable Development* (pp. 97–122). Boston: Kluwer Academic Publishers.

Kaplan, S. (1995). The Restorative Benefits of Nature: Toward an Integrative Framework. *Journal of Environmental Psychology, 15*, 169–182.

Kaplan, S., & Kaplan, R. (1972). Rated Preference and Complexity for Natural and Urban Visual Material. *Perception & Psychophysics, 12*(4), 354–356.

Knopf, R. (1987). Human Behavior, Cognition, and Affect in the Natural Environment. In D. Stokols & I. Altman (Eds.), *Handbook of Environmental Psychology* (pp. 783–811). New York: John Wiley and Sons.

Leiserowitz, A. (2007). Communicating the Risks of Global Warming: American Risk Perceptions, Affective Images, and Interpretive Communities. In S. Moser & L. Dilling (Eds.), *Creating a Climate for Change: Communicating Climate Change and Facilitating Social Change* (pp. 44–63). Cambridge: Cambridge University Press.

Moser, S. (2007). More Bad News: The Risk of Neglecting Emotional Responses to Climate Change Information. In S. Moser & L. Dilling (Eds.), *Creating a Climate for Change: Communicating Climate Change and Facilitating Social Change* (pp. 64–80). Cambridge: Cambridge University Press.

Nowotny, H. (1994). *Time: The Modern and Postmodern Experience*. Cambridge: Polity Press.

Osbaldiston, R., & Sheldon, K. (2002). Social Dilemmas and Sustainability: Promoting Peoples' Motivation to "Cooperate with the Future." In P. Schmuck & W. Schultz (Eds.), *Psychology of Sustainable Development* (pp. 37–57). Boston: Kluwer Academic Publishers.

Oskamp, S. (2002). Summarizing Sustainability Issues and Research Approaches. In P. Schmuck & W. Schultz (Eds.), *Psychology of Sustainable Development* (pp. 301–324). Boston: Kluwer Academic Publishers.

Parks, C., & Posey, D. (2005). Temporal Factors in Social Dilemma Choice Behavior: Integrating Interdependence and Evolutionary Perspectives. In A. Strathman & J. Joireman (Eds.), *Understanding Behavior in the Context of Time: Theory, Research, and Application* (pp. 225–241). Mahwah, NJ: Lawrence Erlbaum Associates.

Parsons, R. (1991). The Potential Influences of Environmental Perception on Human Health. *Journal of Environmental Psychology, 11*, 1–23.

Pew Research Center. (2009). Economy, Jobs Trump All Other Policy Priorities in 2009. Retrieved from http://people-press.org/report/485/ economy-top-policy-priority

Pitt, D., & Zube, E. (1987). Management of Natural Environments. In D. Stokols & I. Altman (Eds.), *Handbook of Environmental Psychology* (pp. 1009–1039). New York: John Wiley and Sons.

Reading, A. (2004). *Hope and Despair: How Perceptions of the Future Shape Human Behavior*. Baltimore: The Johns Hopkins University Press.

Snyder, C., Rand, K., & Ritschel, L. (2006). Hope over Time. In J. Sanna & E. Chang (Eds.), *Judgements over Time: The Interplay of Thoughts, Feelings, and Behaviors* (pp. 100–119). Oxford: Oxford University Press.

Stern, P., & Oskamp, S. (1987). Managing Scarce Environmental Resources. In D. Stokols & I. Altman (Eds.), *Handbook of Environmental Psychology* (pp. 1043–1080). New York: John Wiley and Sons.

Ulrich, R., Simons, R., Losito, B., Fiorito, E., Miles, M., & Zelson, M. (1991). Stress Recovery and Exposure to Natural and Urban Environments. *Journal of Environmental Psychology, 11*, 201–230.

Zaleski, Z. (2005). Future Orientation and Anxiety. In A. Strathman & J. Joireman (Eds.), *Understanding Behavior in the Context of Time: Theory, Research, and Application* (pp. 125–141). Mahwah, NJ: Lawrence Erlbaum Associates.

Zuckerman, M. (2009). Consumer Spending Turns to Saving as Recession Aftershocks Shake Confidence. *US News and World Report*, April 27, 2009. Retrieved from http://www.usnews.com/articles/opinion/ mzuckerman/ 2009/04/27/consumer-spending-turns-to-saving-as-recession-aftershocks-shake-confidence.html

4 Leadership and the Dynamics of Collaboration

Averting the Tragedy of the Commons

Robert L. Williams

INTRODUCTION

It was a short, simple article in *Science* on December 13, 1968, that focused on the environmental impacts of unrestrained population growth and the social dynamics of decision-making that pitted benefits to others against benefits to self. While Garrett Hardin's basic thesis on population control in "Tragedy of the Commons" has not withstood the test of time, it did introduce a term that has endured (Hardin, 1968, 1998). From 10 citations in other academic works in 1969, the article would be cited over 150 times by 1979 before it began to decline in the eyes of other natural scientists and was cited by them less than 10 times in 1990. That same year, social scientists cited the original article over 50 times and by 1996 the number of annual social science citations had risen to over 90 per year (Burger & Gochfeld, 1998, p. 7).

In many ways, the trajectory of Hardin's article was the impetus for the research that undergirds this chapter. The transition in citations of Hardin's original work from the natural sciences to the social sciences bespeaks a subtle but telling shift in the approach to understanding the dynamics of environmental collaboration and cooperation. (For the purposes of this chapter, I define *collaboration* as an ongoing process involving two or more organizations or groups that retain individual autonomy and identity while sharing resources, governance, and risks and rewards during the pursuit of a common goal or goals.)

In the 1960s, many in the fledgling environmental movement assumed that science and data would be a sufficient motivator to change behavior and guide people to make better decisions about use of environmental resources. In many ways, awareness and even understanding of environmental issues and individual environmental choices have increased as the science and data has increased. But at the same time, the abundance of new information has not necessarily simplified or clarified choices or even increased collaboration (Jager, Janssen, & Hulbert, 2002; Levin, 2006; Scheffer, Westley, & Brock, 2003; Vincent, 2007).

Instead, early approaches to collaboration among environmental organizations and other social action groups were fueled more by passion and common beliefs than by systematic organizational development and intentional leadership (Cartwright & Zander, 1968; Level, 1967; Lippitt & Seashore, 1962; Snow, 1992). One common belief was that collaboration was an inherent good and represented the most effective and productive relationship among individuals and groups, a belief that has persisted among nonprofits (and is evident in some of the other chapters in this volume). While I do not wish to question the value of collaboration, my research has led me to see it as a complex phenomenon that requires more than just good intentions to succeed. Much of this chapter is built upon in-depth interviews with environmental leaders done in the last two years, but I have worked with social advocates, nonprofit leaders, and environmental groups for more than 20 years. Their cautionary tales of collaboration helped me begin to identify important attributes influencing successes and failures of collaboration and ways in which environmental leaders can promote realistic and long-lasting collaboration.

> *I always thought there was something naturally appealing about collaboration. I had visions of lots of different people "co-laboring" or laboring together for a common purpose. It just seemed natural that humans are social creatures and so they would want to work together. After a couple very bad experiences with collaboration, I realized that my approach to collaboration was like my approach to my first marriage: it was love at first sight, filled with romance and dreams, and natural. Then it all fell apart because I had not worked at the relationship or even my naiveté about marriage.* (Director, state agency[1])

Because most people have believed in the inherent value of collaboration, it remains, for the most part, an unstudied phenomenon. The few formal studies tend to focus on collaboration in one sector or on one issue, not the interplay of many sectors and the complexity of issues necessary to ensure environmental sustainability (Curtis, 2001; Nelson, Thomas, & Cynthia, 2000; Rosenthal, 1998; Thompson, Socolar, Brown, & Haggerty, 2002; Wagner, 1995). If there has been little research on the dynamics of collaboration, there has been even less on the role that environmental leadership plays in cultivating or facilitating collaboration (Beaulieu, D'Amour, Ferrada-Videla, San Martin-Rodriguez, 2005; de Gibaja, 2001; Dovey, 2002).

It has become increasingly clear to me—in part because of experiences with failed collaboration and the realization that passion and commitment are not sufficient to build and maintain collaborative efforts—that efforts at collaboration must be purposeful and exposed to the same critical analysis and ongoing assessment as any other form of organizational or group relationship. Bryan (2004) aptly states both the promises and pitfalls of collaboration:

> Collaboration, to be sure, is often time-consuming, messy, and unpredictable . . . Collaboration engages people, often adversaries, in ways

> that are quite unique, and therefore may be uncomfortable for those not fully aware of its underlying structure and purpose . . . [yet] a deeper understanding of these elements places collaboration in a much more favorable light. That is not to say that collaborative processes, like other problem solving processes, do not have their drawbacks. They do. But collaboration, I argue, offers an important promise other forms of public decision making seem to lack—that of creating a sense of 'shared ownership' of our larger and more complex problems and challenges. (p. 882)

While specific research on collaboration and environmental leadership is limited, a multidisciplinary scan of related research helps build a more general framework of the leadership experience in collaboration that can be applied to environmental issues and groups (see, for example, Gaertner et al., 1999; Komorita, Parks, & Hulbert, 1992; Koole, Jager, van den Berg, Vela, & Hofstee, 2001; Parks, Sanna, & Posey, 2003).

The questions I seek to answer in this chapter begin with the metaphor of the "tragedy of the commons": if seeking to maximize individual benefit from shared resources almost always leads to loss or degradation of that resource—and the facts are known—then what are the attributes that either promote or discourage collective action through cooperation and collaboration? (*Cooperation*, which also appears frequently in this chapter, more accurately describes an individual behavior or attitude and is well researched in psychology and sociology. It is, however, not the same as collaboration, but rather a significant factor in collaboration.) Second, how does the intersection of three critical players in collaboration—the individual, the organization (or group), and the process—influence the relative strengths and weaknesses of any collaboration? Third, what is the role of leadership in promoting, developing, and sustaining collaboration?

The answers to these questions, as we shall see, are intriguing and can help us better understand how to make collaborative partnerships "work." Some of the findings include:

1. Perceptions of the collaboration values of environmental leaders are not always as positive as the leaders view themselves.
2. Most environmental leaders have made significant contributions to building and sustaining collaborative efforts but those contributions are often in a few narrow areas and may differ by role and gender.
3. Individual behaviors and interpersonal dynamics seem to have a greater impact on the success of collaboration than do organizational influences or procedural influences.
4. Exploring the lessons learned from successful and unsuccessful collaboration and interpersonal cooperation offers specific suggestions upon which environmental leaders should focus.

Readers will also find, interspersed with the data, extensive quoted comments from interviewees that illustrate the results and findings of this study in practical, everyday terms. In what follows I first summarize the results of surveys on collaboration experiences from environmental leaders, then compare the perceptions of others about the collaboration values of environmental leaders with how the leaders view themselves, and finally discuss five areas of greatest influence on the success and failure of collaborative efforts (power and control, conflict, trust, tolerance of ambiguity, and risk and reward) and the role leaders play in the process.

THE STUDY

Complex issues—certainly sustainability and the quality of the global environment would qualify—require a form of leadership that views adaptive change as collective action, rather than technical solution control and individual effort. In other words, the scale of the issue or opportunity requires different forms of leadership (Heifetz & Linsky, 2002; Hermann, 1995; Rutte, 1990; Snow, 1992; van Knippenberg, Haslam, & Platow, 2007). For this study, I focused on a population of 185 individuals, all of whom had participated in the Institute for Georgia Environmental Leadership (IGEL), a yearlong program developed by the Fanning Institute at the University of Georgia at the request of a former governor who challenged: "We have to find other ways to resolve environmental issues than by suing each other." The program, which many say was "born out of conflict," focuses on established leaders from many different sectors or organizations including government, nonprofit, business and industry, elected officials (local, statewide, and national), science and education, advocacy groups, and many others. IGEL, currently in its eighth year, has 30 to 35 participants selected each year to ensure the broadest diversity imaginable. The program focuses less on skills building or technical solutions than on complexity, conflict, influence, collaboration, peer coaching, relational leadership, interpretations of science and public policy, and "leading from the back of the room."

Each of the former participants was contacted via e-mail and asked to provide examples of collaborations and to indicate whether or not they would be willing to complete a short survey and be interviewed about that collaboration. Forty-five individuals (or 24 percent) responded with examples and agreed to participate, and 24 were randomly selected for the first round of surveys and in- depth interviews completed in October, 2009.[2] The survey and interviews focused on three intersecting areas of influence on the success or failure of collaboration (see Figure 4.1):

1. *individual* or social psychological attributes—such as locus of control, dominance, social reciprocity, trust, values, leadership, and oth-

ers—of individuals directly involved in a collaboration process who influence, either negatively or positively, the quality and outcome of collaboration

2. *organizational* attributes—such as structure, power and control, internal relationships, mission, communications, and others—that influence, either negatively or positively, the quality and outcome of collaboration
3. *procedural* steps and activities used to form and maintain collaboration—such as governance, meeting design, evaluation, feedback, and others—that influence, either negatively or positively, the quality and outcome of collaboration

The interplay of these three sets of attributes appeared at very early stages in the interview process, which were more open-ended. Drawn from the words of those we interviewed, the three areas guided more in-depth interviewing later in the study.

> *It was not one thing that made the collaboration a success but rather the way the individuals involved directly interacted with their*

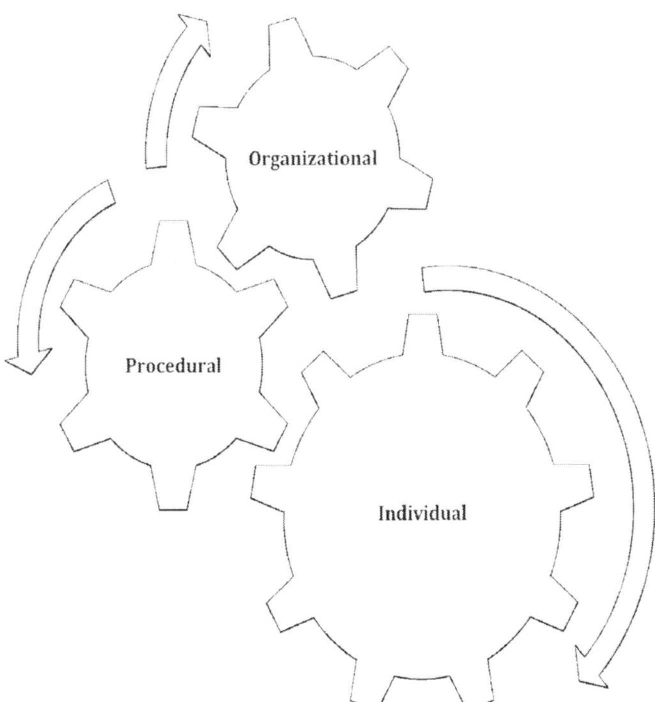

Figure 4.1 Interacting influences on collaboration.

organizations and how those organizations reacted to key issues and resolving differences. (Environmental activist)

We had differences to overcome but I think they were doable. Unfortunately, the leadership of [a collaborative] . . . never involved the leadership of the [organizations involved] in the process. We were like three orbiting planets: those of us trying to work together, our bosses, and the leadership of [a collaborative]. (City manager)

[The collaborative] was never meant to last. It was for one purpose. And that would take a year or so. [Two of the organizations involved] took the lead but did not dominate. We were lucky to have [individuals involved] who seemed to know specific steps to take and when we ran into obstacles it seemed like the people and organizations involved said their piece and then let those running [the collaborative] do their thing. It was neat. Kind of like watching the inner workings of a clock. (Local environmental educator)

AREAS OF INFLUENCE AND LENGTH OF COLLABORATION

Twenty-four environmental leaders who agreed to in-depth interviews were first asked to complete a survey that included:

- A brief description of collaboration(s) in which they had been involved (there were 37 different collaborations described by the 24 respondents).
- Give the length of each collaboration in months.
- Was the collaboration successful? Yes, No, or Partially.
- Rate the influence of individual attributes, organizational attributes, and process attributes on each of the different collaborations on a 5-point scale in ascending value from "strongly negative" to "strongly positive."

Figure 4.2 shows the mean scores on the rankings of influence from the survey for each of the three areas of influence, cross-tabbed with the length of collaboration:

In general, respondents rated longer collaborations as successful more often than shorter collaborations.[3] The graph suggests several conclusions that were pursued in later interviews and that appear in more detail in the discussion of key predictors of success in collaboration later in the chapter:

1. *Individual attributes were viewed as a more negative influence in the shortest collaborations and positive influences in the longer*

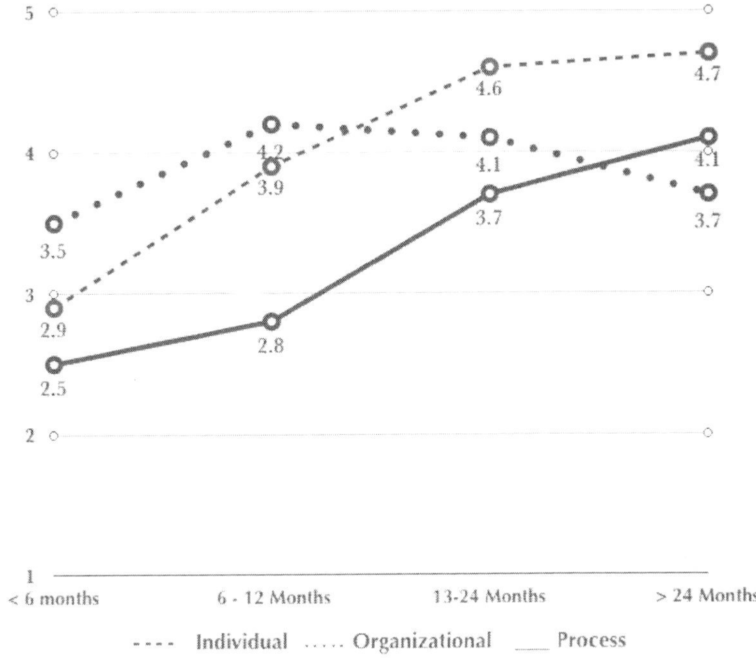

Figure 4.2 Types of influence on collaboration related to longevity.

collaborations. Based upon the mean scores and later interviews, the leaders interviewed saw a definite connection between problems forming and sustaining collaboration, and the personalities, styles, and behaviors of key individuals participating. From the interviews, the most often mentioned (in descending order) attributes that could have either positive or negative impacts were (a) how the individual dealt with conflict; (b) how the individual handled power and control—both their own and that of other participants; and (c) how the person communicated or related to others.

2. *Organizational attributes were moderately positive in all lengths of collaboration, having the least positive influence in the longest collaborations*. The interviews provide a couple of possible explanations for the distribution of mean scores on organizational attributes and their influence on collaboration. First and foremost, the interviews suggest that given the right individuals with the right skills and attitudes, most collaborations can moderate the organizational influences on the collaborative. That does not mean that organizational attributes do not influence the relative successes and failures of collaborations but rather that the individuals involved could determine the degree and length of that influence. Second,

those interviewed thought that organizational influences were more apparent early on, primarily because of the fact that the organizations were preexisting to the collaboration and had resources, power, and influence. Over time, procedural and individual influence began to account for a greater share of influence on the collaboration.

3. *Procedural attributes seemed to correlate most closely with longevity (and thereby success) of collaborations but were often least influential of the three sets.* When discussing the influence of procedural attributes in the interviews, the environmental leaders almost always talked about facilitated meetings or role of consultants. It was only later that they talked more about the "hidden" or informal procedures and processes and how they impacted the collaboration. For example, several of those interviewed pointed to the lack of timelines, or if there were timelines, to managing those timelines. As one of those interviewed said: "It was almost as if we never understood our steps or process until we looked backwards. And then it was often too late to fix something."

INDIVIDUAL LEADERSHIP CONTRIBUTIONS

The second part of the survey completed by 24 environmental leaders asked the leader to self-identify individual contributions that she or he had made to a specific collaboration(s). Each respondent could pick any number of contributions and then distribute up to 10 points across all contributions picked to show the degree of the contribution: 1 point = very minor contribution, 2 points = minor contribution, 3 points = major contribution, and 4 points = very major contribution. The descriptions of individual contributions were:

- technical knowledge that contributes to accomplishing the task
- facilitation skills that shape and implement the collaboration process
- direction setting and control for completing tasks
- securing resources that support the collaboration goals and process
- creativity and generating ideas, innovation and new approaches that support the collaboration goals and process
- developing relationships to support the collaboration goals and process
- making decisions, encouraging decisions, and creating "decision rules"
- communicating with members of collaboration and others
- challenging others and staying true to goals and values
- developing others, mentoring, training, and coaching

The chart in Figure 4.3 reflects the variations in self-reported individual contribution to collaboration efforts. Out of the 24 leaders who responded, there were 16 males and 8 females. (The total population of the IGEL program is roughly 65 percent male and 35 percent female.) The numbers listed are the total points assigned by all the environmental leaders participating and reflect a relative weight for the impact of that area of individual contribution. The total number of points assigned by the 8 females was doubled for purposes of comparison.

In terms of individual contributions to collaboration, interesting results include:

1. *Both genders reported relatively greater contributions in securing resources and communicating.* Later in interviews, the leaders often referred to the importance of resources and the amount of time it took to secure them. Interestingly, very few of the unsuccessful collaborations failed for want of resources alone. Similarly, those interviewed frequently pointed to the importance of communications in a collaboration: "Look, you don't own them or control them, you can only influence them. And that takes lots and lots of communication. Sometimes not very sophisticated or complex communication, just a quick, 'What are you thinking? What do you need? What are the problems?' and so on," said one interviewee.

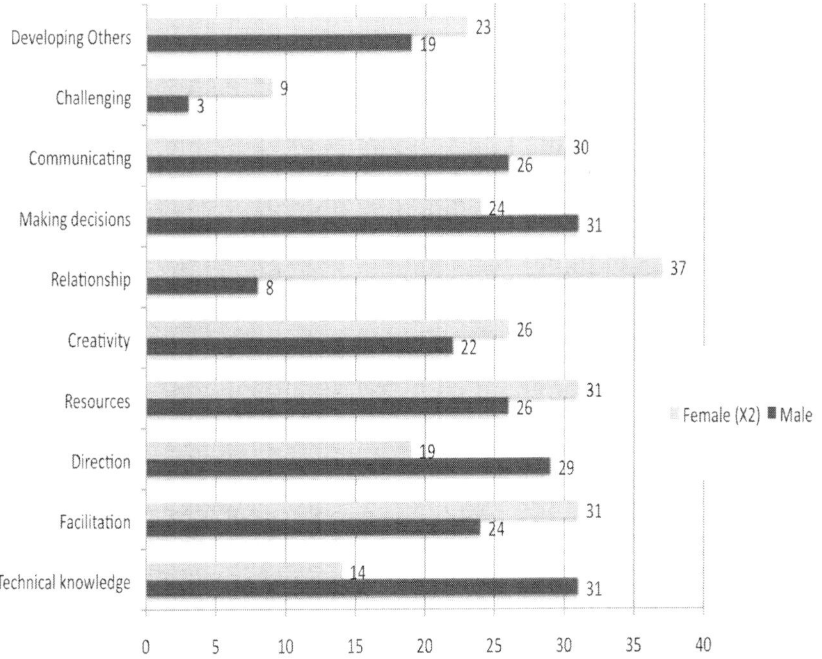

Figure 4.3 Individual contributions to collaboration by gender.

2. *Females reported significantly greater contributions in facilitation and developing relationships and significantly lesser contributions in technical knowledge, direction setting, and challenging others when compared to males. Males reported significantly greater contributions in technical knowledge, direction, and making decisions and significantly lesser contributions in developing relationships and developing others.* The interviews provided little insight into the degree to which these gender-differentiated contributions are a result of "nature or nurture." In the interviews, several of the women pointed to "roles" or "expectations" that often guided their contributions. When asked pointedly if the gender differentiation was the result of sexism, most of those interviewed replied either "probably" or "definitely." Several participants volunteered that most of the "isms" were present in one form or another in the collaborations just as they were present in society at large, and suggested that how the collaboration handled those "isms" often determined the relative success or failure of the collaborative.

VALUES AND COLLABORATIVE LEADERSHIP

Beginning in the 1950s, Robert F. Bales at Harvard University began his research on the dynamics of groups, increasingly turning his attention to what values about appropriate leadership are held by leaders and members of groups (Bales, 1951, 1999). His process became known in the field of group dynamics and leadership as "social interaction analysis" and quickly became one of the standards for studying the relationships and performance of groups and organizations. Originally, his studies relied upon trained observers with coded scoring sheets called "systematic multiple observation of groups" (SYMLOG), but by the 1970s, the research relied upon more standardized questionnaires, allowing the research to expand exponentially on both the group and individual level. Of the 185 environmental leaders surveyed for this study, 64 of them completed the Bales SYMLOG assessment on leadership values. There are 19 women and 14 minorities (African-American, Hispanic, and Asian-Pacific) among the 64 environmental leaders who completed the assessment.

The questionnaire asks respondents to rate the frequency that a leader displays 26 values related to leadership and followership. They are also asked how often those 26 values should be displayed for them to be more effective. Each of the leaders was rated by up to 10 "others"—peers or direct reports and one "supervisor"—on the 26 values using a "rarely," "sometimes," and "often" scale. The 592 "others" were asked to rate the leader twice: once on the values they actually displayed and then a second set of ratings on what an "ideal environmental leader" would display. For the purposes of this chapter, I am focusing on the feedback on 6 of the 26 value items that seem most related to collaboration:

1. active teamwork toward common goals, organizational unity
2. tough-minded, self-oriented assertiveness
3. equality, democratic participation in decision-making
4. responsible idealism, collaborative work
5. self-protection, self-interest first, self-sufficiency
6. trust in the goodness of others

In their self-assessments, the 64 leaders perceived themselves, in general, as often displaying values 1, 3, 4, and 6 and only infrequently displaying values 2 and 5. To be more effective, the leaders thought they should be slightly less frequently trusting in the goodness of others and slightly more frequently valuing "active teamwork toward common goals, organizational unity" and "responsible idealism, collaborative work."

The collective scores of the 592 "other" raters of the leaders indicate that others view the leaders as displaying values 3 and 4 (equality, responsible idealism, and collaboration) significantly less frequently, and value 5 (self-protection, self-interest) more frequently than the leaders viewed themselves. The "others" agreed with the leaders that, to be more effective, they, as a group, should be less "trusting in the goodness of others" (value 6) and more frequently displaying "equality, democratic participation in decision-making" (value 3). The "others" disagreed on the need to display more "responsible idealism, collaborative work" (value 4) in order to be more effective as a leader. Of the 64 leaders, the self-ratings of 36 of them on the 6 values statements related to collaboration are very close to the ratings given by those who work with them. Only 12 of the leaders gave themselves significantly different ratings from their "others" on at least 4 of the 6 value statements while only 5 leaders had significantly different ratings from their "others" on 3 of the values items. The remaining leaders had significant variations from their "others" on only one or two ratings. These variations mirror the Bales SYMLOG research findings in terms of the internal validity of the items and tend to reflect variations in leader performance and accuracy of self-perceptions rather than problems in instrumentation (Bales, 1999).

The SYMLOG results offer some insight into interpersonal dynamics of collaboration and the role of leadership, especially when combined with interviews with many of these leaders about their SYMLOG results and the tension between collaboration as an inherent "good" and the difficult and often unpleasant aspects of building effective collaborations.

> *I think I valued collaboration and working together above all other leadership or organizational strategies. For me, collaboration was not only important; it was also the "best" way to address environmental problems. And that required that you, you know, trust other people. When I first looked at my SYMLOG results in which people I work with thought I was too trusting of others and that I should show less value for "responsible idealism, collaborative work," I initially*

dismissed the results as . . . a reflection of values more appropriate in for-profit organizations. It was only in talking with those who rated me that I started to understand that my assumptions about collaboration were not shared by everyone and that by assuming all the benefits of collaboration, I didn't do the hard work necessary. (Executive director, environmental nonprofit)

I viewed myself as valuing others, trusting them as a leader. Those who work with me saw me [on the SYMLOG] as being less trusting, even not trust[ing], other people. I can't say that it was a shock to see that feedback. It was a shock that they knew that about me because I thought I had hidden it pretty well. I used to trust people more but then there were several problems with people I trusted, especially in terms of integrity and performance, and I basically stopped trusting as much. They saw that in me even when I thought I was able to hide it. Working with others, cooperating or collaborating on something, I had a switch: trust or don't trust, trust or don't trust [making flipping motion like the on-and-off function of a light switch] *that I used. If I trusted you, I was more likely to work together, but if I did not trust you, I did not collaborate. And without saying why. What I was missing was a middle ground: building trust. Any complex relationship . . . takes work and, for me, constructing trust often required honesty and feedback that I previously chose not to use.* (Senior executive, utility company)

Collaboration was, for me, about, friendship, shared goals, and shared philosophy. So I could collaborate with my friends but not [with] my enemies. The SYMLOG feedback said I overly valued self-interest and protecting myself and did not value idealism and collaboration. Needless to say, that's not how I saw myself and it was a stinging criticism [that] I tended to ignore or reject. A month or so later, I was in the midst of lobbying efforts at the legislature and I realized that I created a little "gang" of friends and we spent more time creating monsters out of anyone that did not agree with us then we did on developing good public policy. So I decided to practice a little more collaboration and you should have seen the skepticism and avoidance when I approached some of my "enemies" to discuss alternative policies that might meet both of our needs. (Lobbyist with association)

TRI-FACTOR INFLUENCES ON COLLABORATION

Interviews with the 24 environmental leaders began with a short (20–30 minute) telephone interview followed with several longer interviews, some by telephone and some in person. In the initial interview, each leader was asked to briefly describe the scope, size, duration, and purpose of the collaboration(s); identify the impact or influence of individuals both negative and positive; identify the impact or influence of organizations both negative and positive; and identify the impact or influence of the procedures followed in the collaboration.

I designed follow-up questions based upon both the individual interview and the emerging themes from the literature search, the written survey, SYMLOG, and interviews of the whole group. After all the interviews had been transcribed, I used "Atlas.ti," software that enables researchers to pursue subtle forms of qualitative analysis (Hwang, 2008; McKether, Gluesing, & Riopelle, 2009).[4] Using qualitative software simplifies and shortens many analytical steps but it does not fully replace the "inquiring mind" of a researcher. I thus explored five interviews in depth, using an older form of hand coding and "constant comparison" of terms to see how closely the software and I would agree. I did identify some additional areas for further electronic analysis, but, in general, the software had done a good job of analysis.

From the data and literature, I constructed a "tri-factor matrix" of the five areas of influence on collaboration (see Table 4.1) most often mentioned in the interviews and that seemed, to the environmental leaders interviewed, to have the greatest impact on the relative success or failure of collaboration efforts. They are also attributes that appear, in one way or another, in all three areas of influence.

For example, the first attribute is power and control. As discussed later, the way individuals involved in collaboration exercise, respond to,

Table 4.1 Tri-Factor Matrix of Influences on Collaboration

	Personal	*Organizational*	*Procedural*
Power and Control	Locus of control	Centralized or decentralized	Centralized or decentralized
Conflict	Range of styles	External or internal conflict Conflict over scarce resources	Managing differences Conflict resolution
Trust	Implicit or explicit trust	Trust in organizational representative Trust culture	Measures of trust "Open" communications
Tolerance of Ambiguity	Multiple perspective taking	Degrees of certainty in daily operations	Role of science and information Predetermined standards or principles
Risk and Reward	Individual perspective on shared social dilemmas	Organizational perspective on shared social dilemmas	Broad spectrum of tracking and accounting tools like "triple bottom lines" or multigenerational equity

Source: the author.

and view power and control affects how they behave as part of a collaborative effort. At the same time, how much control an organization involved in collaboration wants to exercise affects both the individuals from that organization directly involved in the collaborative *and* how the organization will act as a corporate body in relationship to the collaborative effort. Finally, many aspects of the procedures followed in forming a collaborative can support or encourage the centralization of power and control, or support the distribution of power and control, or encourage some blend. That could mean that an individual more comfortable being in charge or in control, or one of the organizations participating in the collaborative that has a very strong board used to being in charge, could be discomforted by procedures that encourage distributive power and control. In the five sections that follow, I discuss more fully each of the five attributes in all three areas of influence.

POWER AND CONTROL

Power and control have long been associated with both theories of leadership and with the effectiveness and quality of groups (Ames & Flynn, 2007; Bolden, Gosling, Marturano, & Dennison, 2003; Rooke & Torbert, 2005; Ruth, 2006). Therefore, it is not surprising that the environmental leaders interviewed discussed power and control and its influence on efforts to collaborate more frequently than any other attribute of individuals, organizations, or the procedure involved in collaboration. The well-developed research field of locus of control identifies variation among individuals in the degree to which they view the locus of control as being internal or external. With internal locus of control, the individual believes that he or she has significant control over what they do and the consequences. Conversely, with external locus of control, the individual believes that others have significant control over what she or he does and the consequences (Langan-Fox, Sankey, & Canty, 2009; Twenge, Liqing, & Im, 2004).

> *Collaboration and cooperation are viewed as positive social behaviors and many people are so focused on collaborating that they do not communicate what they need in order to remain in the collaboration. When I first became involved in collaborative efforts to address a common problem, I was unaware of how hard I—and others—tried to make the collaboration work. I guess in a way, I viewed others as being in control of what was going to happen and I was just along for the ride. I would fail to set conditions or expectations for the collaboration that were important to my organization and would affect our participation. I found myself withdrawing from collaborations that did not meet my needs.* (Executive director, nonprofit organization)

Bottom line, when there is a lot to be done or the stakes are high, I like to be in control. I know I can make things happen and I know that I am dependable and responsible. When working collaboratively, too many people think that means you have to sit back and wait for the group to make a decision. (Environmental lobbyist)

I have seen it happen too many times: a couple people want to be in charge of the process of bringing people together to collaborate because one of those individuals will not give up the chance at power. What's even more amazing is how that person says that they want to be in charge to be responsible, to get things done, to serve the group. I think they just like power. (Engineering consultant)

Rarely have I experienced pure "win-win" situations. Typically, even in the most successful collaborations, someone benefits a little more or a little less. I think everyone participating knows that and it divides the competitors from the cooperators. And it appears to be instinctual or just part of some people's personalities to want to win or to cooperate regardless of the impact on the group. (Manufacturing executive)

Boards of nonprofits—and I guess businesses—talk about collaboration and even direct their staff to collaborate but they want to continue to act like they are the board of the collaboration, not just the board of one organization in the collaboration. The staff often have their hands tied when collaborating. (Environmental lawyer)

The environmental leaders interviewed could point to several specific aspects of power and control that influenced the collaboration effort:

- The early stages of building a collaborative tend to suppress even appropriate forms of power and control. Everyone wants to be equal. Too little power and control can be as harmful as too much power and control.
- Even if you simply draw straws, collaborative efforts need a leader, even if that is someone to facilitate meetings and communications.
- "Decision rules" go a long way toward establishing an appropriate use of power and control (for example, setting a time frame—two weeks, three meeting, and the like—for attempting to make a consensus decision and then automatically moving to simple majority vote).
- Organizations involved in collaborations have their own internal power and control procedures and they may, without much thought, assume that the same procedures will be used by the collaborative or assume that an internal decision of the organization is binding on all the organizations in the collaborative. "At one meeting of [the collaborative], the representative from [one organization participating] said

that his board had decided that the collaborative should have a board to make sure there was a balance of power. Now that was a strange moment," said one of the leaders interviewed.

- For many organizations power and control includes different degrees of autonomy, usually because of the amount of resources and the relationship to the external environment. Highly autonomous organizations appear less collaborative. "Our organization has very limited resources and we are very dependent upon public perception and politics," said one of the leaders interviewed. "The most successful collaborations I have experienced are typically among organizations with similar constraints. All it takes is one organization that has lots of resources and independence and building a sustainable collaboration is very, very difficult."
- "The smartest thing I have ever done in encouraging new efforts at collaboration [was] to seek help from a competent external facilitator experienced in the resources and barriers of collaboration," said one of those interviewed. "The dumbest thing I have ever done is not to realize that the sooner the collaborators can begin to 'self-facilitate' their process, the more successful they will be in the long run."

CONFLICT

According to several of the environmental leaders interviewed, one of the primary reasons to form a collaborative was to reduce conflict, yet frequently it only increased conflict.

> *Imagine a nonprofit environmental group, a conservation group, a wildlife group, two utilities, and four local governments "collaborating" on a very large land acquisition. At about our fourth meeting, with a dozen attorneys, bankers, wildlife biologists, neighborhood groups, and others in attendance, I was worn down by the incessant conflict in strategies, scientific studies, financing options, tax codes, deed formats, and on and on. My counterpart in the collaboration from one of the local governments was seated across from me and she must have seen the look on my face. She leaned over and whispered, "Just think what it would be like if we were not collaborating."* (Local elected official)

> *Two of us in [the collaborative] had disagreed with each other for more than 10 years. Recently, we spent more time being disagreeable than just disagreeing. When I arrived at the first meeting of what would become [the collaborative] . . . there he sat and he was obviously just as unhappy to see me as I was to see him. We had a great facilitator and the vice president from a statewide environmental group and they were both great at getting to the root of conflicts and managing conflicts. They did not try to get us to resolve our differences—that would have taken years at*

> *best—but rather [to] focus on the purpose of the collaboration and what, if anything, we could agree upon. Turns out there was lots we agreed on as part of the collaborative but, three years later, we still have fundamental disagreements on other things.* (State director of nonprofit)

In general, the presence of conflict was never mentioned as the primary reason for the failure of efforts to collaborate. Similarly, and for many of the same reasons, the absence of conflict was not a primary reason for successful collaboration. Instead, a significant number of those interviewed thought that conflict was an important ingredient to problem solving, creativity, and identifying the need for additional information. "It is not 'co-love-aration,'" said one of the interviewees, "it's working together and work often involves conflict." Those interviewed could point to several specific aspects of conflict that influenced the collaboration effort:

- There is a need to find out how much conflict members of the collaborative can stand. For most of them, it was not the presence of conflict that negatively affected collaboration efforts but rather "the never-ending conflicts over issues that cannot be resolved," said one. For many, there was a fine line between "resolving" conflicts and just repeatedly talking about them.
- Most of the individuals involved in collaborations have a fairly narrow range of ways to deal with conflict and most have preferred styles they use even more. Multiparty collaboration, especially when it involves individuals and organizations from very different settings and cultures, requires leaders with an ability to choose wisely from among many different ways of managing or resolving conflict.
- Conflict often involves or triggers emotions and that may be the root difficulty that most people have with conflict.
- Most nonprofit and public-sector environmental organizations spend inordinate amounts of time developing resources. The formation of a new collaborative can often be viewed as a new competitor for those limited resources and managing that conflict may be the key to the success of the collaboration.
- By definition, individuals and organizations collaborating retain their autonomy and individual identity. That can make it too easy for them to withdraw in times of conflict and not expend the time and effort to work out differences.

TRUST

Extensive research on trust and betrayal in the workplace, and its impact on relationships and effectiveness in general and within environmental organizations in particular, supports what interviewees had to say on the topic: trust often figures as a key to building collaboration and the absence or loss of trust may be the single most common reason for the failure of an effort to collaborate (De Cremer & Stouten, 2003; McDonell, 1997; Newton, 2001; Parks, 1994; Reina & Reina, 1999).

> *Of all the possible stumbling blocks to collaboration I have faced, the absence of trust or possibly the inability to trust others, is the one I have the most trouble overcoming. Attempts at collaboration are often a way to bring groups together and I have found that the most common reason they are not "together" is that they just don't trust one another. Sometimes that lack of trust is based upon past experiences but sometimes the lack of trust is the result of stereotypes like, "You just can't trust the power companies" or you fill in the blank. . . . I am pretty sure that a lot of distrust or lack of trust is not based on any facts at all.* (Organizational consultant)

> *I thought that trust was mostly about shared values or philosophy. I am finding in several different collaborative efforts that a lot of it is more procedural: did you do what you said you would do, did you share the information you had, did you tell the truth, did you tell me what you wanted and why? I won't say it's simple stuff because it's not, but it is pretty basic and certainly a reasonable expectation.* (Environmental lawyer)

> *Conflict and disagreements are inevitable, especially in the early days of an active collaboration. What was missing in our failed attempts to collaborate was enough conflict to explore all sides of an issue and a willingness to be transparent about what you and your organization needed from the collaboration. I don't think we trusted each other.* (Commercial forester)

> *People make too much fuss about trust. I think they start off trusting folks without checking it out and then one of their assumptions doesn't happen and they are all bent out of shape and vow never to trust the person again. I find it refreshing when, as a first step in forming a collaboration, we just go around the table and say what we expect or want out of the relationship. It gives me a chance to do right by others and not try to guess what they are expecting of me. And I can trust someone a lot more if they tell me directly what they want and expect. It's a two-way street.* (Community environmental activist)

The leadership lessons regarding trust, learned by those interviewed, may have been some of the most painful to relate: "You just don't want to face the fact people have stopped trusting you," said one. The SYMLOG discussion earlier in this chapter underscored the point that many environmental leaders trust too much and others trust too little. It seems a difficult leadership competency to get just right. According to those interviewed, small variations in trust and distrust often had a major impact on the success or failure of a collaborative effort:

- Trust is very fluid, especially in times of conflict, difficult and unpopular decisions, and when resources are scarce. The movement—or fall—from trust to distrust is quite fast but the movement from distrust to trust can be very protracted with lots of intermediate or transitional steps.
- What the leader did *not* say or did *not* do is often much more influential on trust and collaboration than what the leader said or did. Those interviewed said they hesitated to say something out loud because they had been told that leaders are better off not speaking their minds or feelings. Ultimately, that silence resulted in a loss of trust that was more long-lived than the anger or conflict over a spoken thought or feeling would have been.
- Incremental or "transactional" trust building is important in the early part of any collaborative effort. It involves very clear, small, and specific steps that, when taken, build trust. For example, a regular e-mail with budget updates, or volunteering for and completing a task beneficial to the collaborative are all forms of incremental trust building.
- When there has been a break in trust or a betrayal, it is important to stop and deal with it. Members of the collaborative may think it is just between a few parties or it is not as important as fund-raising, but it *is* as important, and trust and distrust tend to spread in a culture.

TOLERANCE OF AMBIGUITY

The title of this section could just as appropriately be: degrees of certainty. For years, social psychologists have used variations on social dilemmas in decision simulations to provide a social laboratory to explore individual and group psychology and behavior. The most widely known—the "Prisoner's Dilemma"—creates a situation in which different decisions result in either personal benefit, personal loss, or some shared version of both benefit and loss (Exline, Geyer, Lovel, & Single, 2004; Garling, 1999; Suleiman & Rapoport, 1988; Utz, 2004; Van Vugt, 2002). At its most basic, the scenario can help measure cooperation and competition, among other attitudes and behaviors. More recently, again fueled by the continuing conundrum of the "tragedy of the commons," the scenarios have been modified to reflect situations in which "individually rational behavior can prevent the securing of socially rational outcomes" (Bianco & Bates, 1990, p. 133).

Climate change provides a real-life example of a collective-risk social dilemma in which the group has to work together (and perhaps give up things) to hit a necessary goal, but if they fail to reach that goal everyone suffers individually (Bianco & Bates, 1990; Dreber & Nowak, 2008; Lloyd, 2007; Milinski, Sommerfeld, Krambeck, Reed, & Marotzke, 2008). Both the extant literature and my interviews with environmental leaders come to similar conclusions: individuals are more likely to act collectively or collaboratively in cases of shared risk if they accept the premise and scope of the risk, and if leadership plays a key role managing the ambiguity the group faces. Thus current debates on global warming tend to correlate different responses—or no response—with different degrees of certainty in the science or data. Increasingly, with very complex environmental issues, certainty is elusive, even with the best science.

> *I really hate to start off discussions about a joint effort by focusing on the threat or risk of not doing anything, but that seems to be the only thing that people pay attention to.* (State environmental regulator)

> *Our efforts over the past five years to create [the collaboration] have shown me that some people can roll with uncertainty and some people can't. I think in our first meeting five years ago, a couple people wanted to discuss specifics such as timelines, specific steps, specific outcomes, when the rest of us were still trying to get our hands around the big concepts or plans . . . After working with some of these folks for years, I think I now understand that they get nervous, or anxious or something [and consequently] . . . they focus on the details . . . I think that if we had a few more of those needing decisions on the details we could have never launched [the collaborative].* (University faculty member)

> *I don't think we have to agree on* all *the facts to figure out our common interests in [the collaborative] and be successful; we just need to agree on most of them.* (Federal agency executive)

> *Too many collaborative efforts are really just a way that a few overly concerned or zealous folks want the rest of us to share in their anxiety. Just show me the facts and if they affect us all, I am the first to pitch in.* (Business owner)

The role that information, or the lack thereof, plays in determining the success or failure of collaborative efforts seemed to frustrate many of the environmental leaders we interviewed: "It's like wrestling with smoke," said one. They described some of the key influences of ambiguity and uncertainty thus:

- For most of them, their first inclination in ambiguous or uncertain situations was to "be a leader and take responsibility," according to one, and try to fix the information gap. They mostly agreed that not only was that the wrong step because they seldom had the additional information needed, but it also fueled the group's anxiety that lack of information was a major problem.

- Several of the leaders interviewed had specific examples of time and resources spent in search of information that, when collected, did little to advance the discussions or decision-making. As one put it: "I felt like a retriever dog, they would throw the stick—need for more information—and I would go fetch it, bring it back, only to watch it being thrown further out."
- Increasingly, the complexity and scale of environmental issues, especially the ones that have not been addressed, mean that no one person or organization can have all the facts they need. Those interviewed said it will require trust to proceed collaboratively.
- Some individuals are uncertain and need certainty, and that can slow down or impede collaboration building. Equally problematic, according to those interviewed, are the individuals that have too much certainty and hold on to "absolute truths" when they should develop competencies for seeing things from different perspectives.

RISK AND REWARD

The fifth area influencing the success or failure of collaborations reflects the balance between what individuals and organizations put into collaborations and what they get out of them. When discussing leadership and collaboration building, those interviewed viewed risk and reward very differently, but tended to fall within three frameworks: those with the most business backgrounds tended to use business language of profit and loss, cost and benefit, and other familiar terms; those with the most nonprofit and advocacy background tended to use public goods and common resources language; and those with government and public policy backgrounds tended to use tax and public services language. (As one laughingly put it: "No wonder we can't collaborate, we don't even speak the same language.")

> *For many folks, collaboration is simply a group of signatures on a grant application hoping to convince the foundation that folks are working together. For some that would be "no risk–maximum reward," but my experience with true collaborations is that everyone puts something in before anyone takes anything out . . . I don't care if it is sweat equity or in-kind contributions or providing coffee and doughnuts, collaborations don't work if people don't have some "skin in the game."* (Environmental foundation program officer)

> *It doesn't have to be equal shares or equal contributions but it should be equitable: put up in relationship to your size or resources or something. I have seen too many collaborations fail because one organization that*

really wants the collaboration to work puts in almost everything in the beginning and then, when it is time to share the costs, the others drop out . . . and it doesn't take much of a request to cause them to drop. I heard about "freeloaders" somewhere; they're people who benefit from services, or a change, or something new but do not pay their way. (Economic developer)

There are other "costs," like "opportunity costs" that says the time you put into building a collaboration cannot be used for another purpose; like "status" costs that says you might lose friends or influence by associating with those in a collaboration that you don't agree with, and others. (Elected official)

I don't think collaborations need business plans or elaborate accounting. They are supposed to be something different than an organization, which has all that. That's part of the problem, few collaborative efforts are satisfied being collaborations, instead they want to become permanent, have a budget, office space, and someone gets to be CEO. Successful collaborations I know about harness the resources and energy of member organizations to get done what no single one of the organizations can do. And there should not be rewards to the collaboration. Should it make money, get a grant, or attract new resources, those should be split among the members of the collaboration. (Federal agency manager)

The leaders interviewed tended to agree that it was not the question of how much risk or how much reward that influenced the success or failure of collaborations, but rather how the risks and rewards were communicated, agreed upon, and managed:

- Silence is not consensus. When it comes to agreeing upon a cost or risk to assume, environmental leaders will be more successful if they have members of the collaboration publicly state their agreement or disagreement with assuming joint risks.
- The impact of risks is not evenly spread among members of the collaboration. "Remember President Truman had a sign that said 'The buck stops here,'" said one those interviewed, "but I don't think that is always the case. Enron employees suffered more than the CEO and that often happens when collaborating: those making the decision may not bear the greatest risk."
- Conflicts related to resources discussed in the section on conflict bears repeating here. Member organizations may see the collaboration as "another mouth to feed" and a concern with ever-shrinking public-sector and nonprofit funds.
- Calculating and tracking risks and rewards or costs and benefits requires more than the standard accounting systems. Businesses

using a "triple bottom line" to track resource sustainability and other environmental considerations and "intergenerational equity" to track long-term impacts provide models for collaborations.

- "A collaboration is its own reward," said one of those interviewed. Others agreed that participants in a collaboration benefit in ways unrelated to the original purpose of the collaboration. Working together on one project develops transferrable skills for working together on other projects, and investments in building relationships in a specific collaboration result in relationships helpful in other undertakings.

CONCLUSION

While sprinkled with cynicism and disappointment, the stories of collaboration efforts of established environmental leaders remain generally positive and hopeful. A significant number of the findings discussed in this chapter seem to reflect what happens when leaders assume too much and place too much hope in one form of relationship that will fix all problems and resolve all issues. Rather than leave readers of this chapter with the mistaken impression that the findings argue against collaboration, I will simply state my continuing belief in the need for a collective effort to address global challenges to a sustainable future. That said, I am reminded of one community activist who, when accused of "playing politics," responded: "'Playing' hell, I am working at it as hard as possible." Broadly speaking, the collaboration experiences of environmental leaders suggest that if you choose to collaborate, you should not assume you can "play at it." Rather, you will need to work at it like the future depends upon it.

NOTES

1. Here and in what follows, I quote directly from interview material that is in my possession (some quotes have been italicized). In order to protect confidentiality, names have been substituted with the professional identity of the speaker.
2. For many of those initially contacted, we also had a 360-degree assessment (called SYMLOG) on their values related to leadership and followership, which will be discussed later in the chapter.
3. The actual length of each collaboration was later compared to "planned length" as best as those interviewed could remember. It would be difficult to accurately correlate which of the shorter collaborations were intended to be shorter or simply ended before their time. However, more than eight of the shorter collaborations (a year or less) were expected to be short-lived according to the interviews, and six of them definitely ended before their time.
4. During the interview process, I noted what appeared to be interesting or common themes and concepts and used those as initial search terms within the "Atlas.ti" hermeneutic unit that included all the transcripts. "Atlas.ti" provided coding and memoing options by which I could write descriptions of

common themes or identify additional related terms such as synonyms. The software could also construct a "network analysis" to show relationship of terms or themes in the interviews.

REFERENCES

Ames, D., & Flynn, F. (2007). What Breaks a Leader: The Curvilinear Relation between Assertiveness and Leadership. *Journal of Personality and Social Psychology, 92*(2), 307–324.

Bales, R. (1951). *Interaction Process Analysis: A Method for the Study of Small Groups*. Cambridge, MA: Addison-Wesley Press.

Bales, R. (1999). *Social Interaction Systems: Theory and Measurement*. New Brunswick, NJ: Transaction Publishers.

Beaulieu, M., D'Amour, D., Ferrada-Videla, M., & San Martin-Rodriguez, L. (2005). The Determinants of Successful Collaboration: A Review of Theoretical and Empirical studies. *Journal of Interprofessional Care, 19*(1), 132–147.

Bianco, W., & Bates, R. (1990). Cooperation by Design: Leadership, Structure, and Collective Dilemmas. *American Political Science Review, 84*(1), 133–147.

Bolden, R., Gosling, J., Marturano, A., & Dennison, P. (2003). *A Review of Leadership Theory and Competency Frameworks*. Exeter, UK: Centre for Leadership Studies.

Bryan, T. (2004). Tragedy Averted: The Promise of Collaboration. *Society & Natural Resources, 17*(10), 881–896.

Burger, J., & Gochfeld, M. (1998). The Tragedy of the Commons 30 Years Later. *Environment, 40*(10), 4–13, 26–27.

Cartwright, D., & Zander, A. (1968). *Group Dynamics: Research and Theory*. New York: Harper and Row.

Curtis, R. (2001). Successful Collaboration between Hospitals and Physicians: Process or Structure? *Hospital Topics, 79*(2), 7–13.

De Cremer, D., & Stouten, J. (2003). When Do People Find Cooperation Most Justified? The Effect of Trust and Self–Other Merging in Social Dilemmas. *Social Justice Research, 16*(1), 41–52.

de Gibaja, M. (2001). An Exploratory Study of Administrative Practice in Collaboratives. *Administration in Social Work, 25*(2), 39–59.

Dovey, K. (2002). Leadership Development in a South African Health Service. *International Journal of Public Sector Management, 15*(6/7), 520–533.

Dreber, A., & Nowak, M. (2008). *Gambling for Global Goods*. Paper presented at the Proceedings of the National Academy of Sciences of the United States of America.

Exline, J., Geyer, A., Lobel, M., & Single, P. (2004). Glowing Praise and the Envious Gaze: Social Dilemmas Surrounding the Public Recognition of Achievement. *Basic and Applied Social Psychology, 26*(2/3), 119–130.

Gaertner, S., Rust, M., Mottola, G., Dovidio, J., Nier, J., Banker, B., et al. (1999). Reducing Intergroup Bias: Elements of Intergroup Cooperation. *Journal of Personality and Social Psychology, 76*(3), 388–402.

Garling, T. (1999). Value Priorities, Social Value Orientations and Cooperation in Social Dilemmas. *British Journal of Social Psychology, 38*(4), 397–408.

Hardin, G. (1968). The Tragedy of the Commons. *Science, 162*(3859), 1243–1248.

Hardin, G. (1998). Extensions of "The Tragedy of the Commons." *Science, 280*(5364), 68–69.

Heifetz, R., & Linsky, M. (2002). *Leadership on the Line: Staying Alive through the Dangers of Leading*. Boston: Harvard Business School Press.

Hermann, M. (1995). Leaders, Leadership, and Flexibility: Influences on Heads of Government as Negotiators and Mediators. *Annals of the American Academy of Political and Social Science, 542*, 148–167.

Hwang, S. (2008). Utilizing Qualitative Data Analysis Software: A Review of Atlas.ti. *Social Science Computer Review, 26*(4), 519–527.

Jager, W., Janssen, M., & Vlex, C. (2002). How Uncertainty Stimulates Over-harvesting in a Resource Dilemma: Three Process Explanations. *Journal of Environmental Psychology, 22*, 247–263.

Komorita, S., Parks, C., & Hulbert, L. (1992). Reciprocity and the Induction of Cooperation in Social Dilcmmas. *Journal of Personality and Social Psychology*, 62(4), 607–617.

Koole, S., Jager, W., van den Berg, A., Vlek, C., & Hofstee, W. (2001). On the Social Nature of Personality: Effects of Extraversion, Agreeableness, and Feedback about Collective Resource Use on Cooperation in a Resource Dilemma. *Personality and Social Psychology Bulletin, 27*(3), 289–301.

Langan-Fox, J., Sankey, M., & Canty, J. (2009). Incongruence between Implicit and Self-Attributed Achievement Motives and Psychological Well-Being: The Moderating Role of Self-Directedness, Self-Disclosure and Locus of Control. *Personality and Individual Differences, 47*(2), 99–104.

Level, D. (1967). *Leadership and Group Dynamics: A Decade of Selected Research Reports: 1948–1958*. Lawrence: Communication Research Center, University of Kansas.

Levin, S. (2006). Learning to Live in a Global Commons: Socioeconomic Challenges for a Sustainable Environment. *Ecological Research, 21*(3), 328–333.

Lippitt, G., & Seashore, E. (1962). *The Leader and Group Effectiveness*. New York: Association Press.

Lloyd, B. (2007). The Commons Revisited: The Tragedy Continues. *Energy Policy, 35*(11), 5806–5818.

McDonell, G. (1997). Scientific and Everyday Knowledge: Trust and the Politics of Environmental Initiatives. *Social Studies of Science, 27*(6), 819–863.

McKether, W., Gluesing, J., & Riopelle, K. (2009). From Interviews to Social Network Analysis: An Approach for Revealing Social Networks Embedded in Narrative Data. *Field Methods, 21*(2), 154–180.

Milinski, M., Sommerfeld, R., Krambeck, H., Reed, F., & Marotzke, J. (2008). The Collective-Risk Social Dilemma and the Prevention of Simulated Dangerous Climate Change. *Proceedings of the National Academy of Sciences of the United States of America, 105*(7), 2291–2294.

Nelson, P., Thomas, B., & Cynthia, H. (2000). Inter-Organizational Collaboration and the Dynamics of Institutional Fields. *Journal of Management Studies, 37*(1), 23–43.

Newton, K. (2001). Trust, Social Capital, Civil Society, and Democracy. *International Political Science Review/Revue internationale de science politique*, 22(2), 201–214.

Parks, C. (1994). The Predictive Ability of Social Values in Resource Dilemmas and Public Goods Games. *Personality and Social Psychology Bulletin, 20*(4), 431–438.

Parks, C., Sanna, L., & Posey, D. (2003). Retrospection in Social Dilemmas: How Thinking about the Past Affects Future Cooperation. *Journal of Personality and Social Psychology, 84*(5), 988–996.

Reina, D., & Reina, M. (1999). *Trust and Betrayal in the Workplace: Building Effective Relationships in Your Organization* (1st ed.). San Francisco: Berrett-Koehler.

Rooke, D., & Torbert, W. (2005). Seven Transformations of Leadership. *Harvard Business Review, 83*(4), 66.
Rosenthal, B. (1998). Collaboration for the Nutrition Field: Synthesis of Selected Literature. *Journal of Nutrition Education, 30*(5), 246–267.
Ruth, S. (2006). *Leadership and Liberation: A Psychological Approach.* London & New York: Routledge.
Rutte, C. (1990). Solving Organizational Social Dilemmas. *Social Behaviour: An International Journal of Applied Social Psychology, 5*(September–October), 285–294.
Scheffer, M., Westley, F., & Brock, W. (2003). Slow Response of Societies to New Problems: Causes and Costs. *Ecosystems, 6*(5), 493–502.
Snow, D. (1992). *Inside the Environmental Movement: Meeting the Leadership Challenge.* Washington, DC: Island Press.
Suleiman, R., & Rapoport, A. (1988). Environmental and Social Uncertainty in Single-Trial Resource Dilemmas. *Acta Psychologica, 68*(September), 99–112.
Thompson, D., Socolar, R., Brown, L., & Haggerty, J. (2002). Interagency Collaboration in Seven North Carolina Counties. *Journal of Public Health Management and Practice, 8*(5), 55–64.
Twenge, J., Liqing, Z., & Im, C. (2004). It's Beyond My Control: A Cross-Temporal Meta-Analysis of Increasing Externality in Locus of Control, 1960–2002. *Personality and Social Psychology Review, 8*(3), 308–319.
Utz, S. (2004). Self-Construal and Cooperation: Is the Interdependent Self More Cooperative than the Independent Self? *Self and Identity, 3*(3), 177–190.
van Knippenberg, D., Haslam, S., & Platow, M. (2007). Unity through Diversity: Value-in-Diversity Beliefs, Work Group Diversity, and Group Identification. *Group Dynamics: Theory, Research, and Practice, 11*(3), 207–222.
Van Vugt, M. (2002). Central, Individual, or Collective Control? Social Dilemma Strategies for Natural Resource Management. *American Behavioral Scientist, 45*(5), 783–800.
Vincent, J. (2007). Spatial Dynamics, Social Norms, and the Opportunity of the Commons. *Ecological Research, 22*(1), 3–7.
Wagner, J. (1995). Studies of Individualism-Collectivism: Effects on Cooperation in Groups. *Academy of Management Journal, 38*(1), 152–172.

5 Leadership for Sustainability in Business

It's all about the Stories We Tell

Martin Melaver

INTRODUCTION

I'm a businessperson. Since 1992, I've run a real estate company focused on sustainable principles and practices. Typical of small companies, I wear numerous hats: crunch numbers and write for our Web site, paint office walls, and negotiate deals. But mostly, I tell stories, such as this one:

> *Our family business began with a grocery store my grandmother Annie started in Savannah, Georgia, in 1940. After my father Norton finished college, he joined the business, growing it into a 14-store supermarket chain. In 1985, our family sold the business but held on to the real estate. At that point, we discovered two things: (a) we had always been in real estate—building stores, warehouses, and an office for our operations—only we had never recognized this fact; (b) we didn't like real estate, with its tendency to homogenize place and its widespread despoliation of nature. So we decided we either had to exit real estate or envision a different, more restorative approach to the business. The result has been a 20-plus year journey toward sustainability, a journey that continues to this day. My colleagues and I are focused on being both thought and product leaders in sustainable real estate. Our purpose is to leverage our business to be agents of change: to restore our lands and our communities. We look to share our mission and knowledge with anyone willing to listen.*

It's an okay story, I guess, addressing a question often asked about our evolution (*how did you get started with all this green stuff?*). But the story distorts as much as it clarifies. It's told from the vantage point of hindsight and relative omniscience. My colleagues and I know where we are at the present moment. We are simply looking back across the passage of years and selecting and ordering key details that confirm our sense of this present moment. Missed are the false starts and blind alleys and stupid mistakes we made (and are still making).

Moreover, while this story celebrates possibility (*we made this journey, so can you*), it cannot escape being nostalgic. How helpful is such a backward-looking story in shaping the world we are hurtling into? Are stories generally of much help addressing issues of global deterioration? If so, what stories are needed?

These questions are not intended to be academic. My purpose is to elaborate upon some essential tools that can redress global conditions (economic, social, and environmental) that are out of whack. A key resource is storytelling—not just any storytelling but a specific type of narrative. But let's pause and raise a basic, skeptical question: *why dither about storytelling when there's a planet to save?*

THE RELEVANCE OF STORYTELLING

> *We need to find a "story of meaning" in exchange for the feeling of emptiness that so many people harbor today . . . But finding a meaningful myth, a "story of what it is all about," that would fit a modern society, is not easy . . . How can the evolution of such stories be promoted? How can a story like that be authentic enough to win the hearts of modern people?*
>
> (Karl-Henrik Robert[1])

Let's face it: how many decision-makers in government or business ever read books like this? Why should they? Such leaders, like the rest of us, lead time-starved lives. Who's got time to read this stuff?

For another thing: yawn. If we are going to be honest here—and staring at ecosystemic meltdown globally demands such honesty—essays on business leadership and sustainability seem better suited to academia. As a businessperson or government leader trying to effect more sustainable practices, wouldn't one be more productive effecting change in the field rather than engaging in discursions about sustainability?

Here's a third problem: There is no shortage of big, compelling ideas regarding sustainable principles and practices. If we stopped this burgeoning industry of discussions about sustainability *right at this very instant* it would still take us decades to implement just a few of these worthwhile ideas:

- focusing on ethics and consumption, learning to do more with less (Schumacher, 1989)
- shaping a new capitalism, based upon establishing trusts to oversee our commons (Barnes, 2006)
- creating a baseline environmental literacy (Orr, 2002; Louv, 2008)

- stabilizing greenhouse gases through greater efficiencies and breakthrough technologies (Romm, 2008; Monbiot, 2009; Brown, 2008)
- reinvigorating democratic advocacy by means of a more localized and more politicized environmental movement (Speth, 2007)
- inhibiting the pernicious control of government by business through campaign reform and by overturning the jurist view of a corporation as a "person" (Reich, 2007; Wolin, 2008)

At the risk of sounding philistine, many of the necessary, big ideas are already "out there." Perhaps we should focus our energy on implementing them.

Finally, there's the point made by Pietra Rivoli in her book *The Travels of a T-Shirt in the Global Economy*: "In general, stories are out of style today in business and economic research" (2005, p. xiii). Rivoli's study is brilliant. But on this point, I think she's wrong. Storytelling may be out of style in business but its presence is pervasive. Her miscue here points to the need for understanding how leadership, business practices, and sustainability need to be interwoven.

Business is permeated by storytelling. We business folk have simply become adept at calling our storytelling by other names. Marketing, obviously, is replete with stories. The simplest ads contain a narrative line: use a certain product and wonderful results happen. PR articles narrate. Web sites provide background stories on companies. And marketing is only the tip of the iceberg.

Management of personnel and operations is embedded with narratives. We create work plans for staff; devise incentives built around if-then stories of behavior and results. Stories promote cultural norms and make a business more cohesive (Prusak, 2004, pp. 23–25). Stories are critical to change management, enabling a company to cut through present reality, envision alternatives, share knowledge, create a shared future, and inspire action (Denning, 2004, 2007).

Businesses of virtually any size constantly evaluate their financial performance with a narrative inference behind it: *business was off this past quarter because of such and such.* Our numbers are shorthand, capturing the complex engagement of numerous actors and actions. Most businesses engage in longer-term storytelling. We call it "gap analysis" or "multiyear strategies" or "scenario planning." But essentially we are telling a basic story in time: here's the situation at the current moment, there's where we want to be in the future, and in front of us are our plans to bridge the "now" and that future date.

Business leaders are storytellers extraordinaire. The real problem is this: we are not telling the right stories. We lack a sense of how *what* we do specifically ties into the larger context around us. And we focus on short-term measures of performance to the detriment of a much longer and more comprehensive view of what is sustainable. In short, we are lacking two master narratives: one that takes a holistic view of business and a second that locates this holism within a long-term vision of possibility. Let's consider these two master narratives in greater detail.

ENVISIONING A MASTER NARRATIVE OF HOLISTIC THINKING

I once guest-taught a high school class on environmental studies. And I got into trouble posing a seemingly easy question I couldn't answer: why should we care about poverty in, say, Africa or deforestation in Malaysia? How do we connect what is occurring in some remote part of the world with what's happening in our backyard?

Let's pose the question differently. In *Green to Gold,* authors Esty and Winston (2006) identify the top 10 environmental issues businesses should focus on: climate change, energy, water, biodiversity and land use, chemicals and toxins, air pollution, waste management, ozone layer depletion, oceans and fisheries, and deforestation. The list is good. But it lacks a key ingredient: the linkages among them. We know, intuitively, that these issues are interrelated, just as we know that issues of social justice—poverty—are related to issues of environmental justice—cutting down forests for basic energy needs (Sachs, 2008; Brown, 2008). But how are these issues interrelated?

We need an aluminum can story for the planet. The lifecycle story of the aluminum can begins with the strip-mining of bauxite ore in Australia, a process that scars the landscape and leaves a caustic red mud behind. The ore is then smelted, separating the alumina from the mined rock. The alumina is shipped to northern Europe where it is processed into bars and then sent to England. There, the bars are rolled into sheets, cut, and manufactured into cans. The cans are then transported to soda manufacturing sites in the U.S., where the cans are filled, sealed, and shipped to distribution warehouses and, from there, to retailers. Shoppers make their purchase, drive home, open, drink, and then chuck the can—ten months after the mining process had started halfway across the world. A complex story of waste elegantly told.

A few statistics dress up the story. The U.S. could rebuild its commercial fleet of aircraft with the amount of aluminum discarded each year. The EPA estimates that a return to refillables could conserve 100,000 barrels of oil daily, and the Natural Resources Defense Council calculates that the energy conserved through recycling is five times more valuable than the cost of disposal. Eighty percent of U.S. products are used once and discarded. Exporting waste in the U.S. grew from a $200 million business in 1997 to over $1 billion by 2002 (Rogers, 2005). We need a similar master narrative that integrates the major environmental and social justice issues being faced today.[2]

CONSTRUCTING A MASTER NARRATIVE OF HOLISTIC THINKING

Enter Joe and Jane Columbia. Joe, after years working at a local manufacturer, has just been fired. His bosses call it "redundancy." Economists would describe it as an effect of globalization, with Joe's company moving offshore where labor and environmental regulations are lax, enabling the business to remain competitive. For Joe and Jane, it seemed the last nail in the coffin of an American dream gone awry.

Joe and Jane Columbia are a typical American couple, although more fortunate than many. They live in Westville, a suburban development 40 miles from Historiaville where Joe works in a modular home–building plant. Jane teaches social studies in a nearby school. The couple makes $105,000 a year, well above the median income for their area. Still, they are barely breaking even.[3] *It seemed strange. The economy had been going gangbusters for three decades, and yet they were unable to save more than a few hundred dollars a year. At least they weren't one of the 46 million Americans without health insurance. Jane knew they'd be in real trouble without it.*

The couple moved to Westville 10 years ago when Joe's company relocated to the Sunbelt from Ohio. Joe and Jane chose to live in Westville for two reasons: a spacious house on a half-acre lot was cheaper than anything in Historiaville, and the schools in Westville were reportedly better. They didn't, however, factor many of the hidden costs of their decision.

There was the commute to and from work, which consumed two hours of Joe's day. Joe didn't think about the effect of this lost time on the national economy or that it was a major factor in the loss of community volunteerism. But he knew he had less time with his family.

It seemed a shame, all this time in the car. Their house was nice, but they rarely had time to enjoy it. The kids—Seth and Annie—couldn't walk or ride bikes to school or any after-school activities, as Joe and Jane had done when they were kids. Westville was a vast tract of low-density housing removed from other facets of community life. In fact, the couple was about half as social as their grandparents, with little time and fewer opportunities to socialize (Putnam, 2001). The lack of physical mobility and restricted socialization was affecting the family's mental and physical well-being.

Their kids averaged about four hours of TV a day, which accounted for their capacity to recognize so many corporate brands (around 1,000). Joe was concerned that the kids had little appreciation for the outdoors and even less capacity to identify local flora and fauna. Jane was concerned about her kids' lack of exercise and weight gain. Their choice of habitat was costing the family a lot more than they had bargained for when they signed the mortgage.

Westville was part of a nationwide phenomenon that, in a generation, has resulted in 1 million acres annually given over to sprawl, the loss of 50 percent of the nation's wetlands, the loss of 45 acres of farmland every hour, the loss of topsoil 20 to 40 times faster than the replacement rate, the development of one shopping center every 7 hours, and the increase in average house size from 1,000 to 2,300 square feet.[4] *The loss of farmland has complemented the consolidation and industrialization of agriculture, multifold use of nitrogen-fixing chemicals in food, a nutrient-diminishing monocultural diet, a trend away from locally grown produce, and a growing dependency on transportation for putting food on the table. The roads and infrastructure developed to support low-density sprawl have not only created ever-greater traffic and longer commute times, but have also led to impairment of air quality, contributing to the growing trend of childhood asthma. They've also contributed significantly to carbon emissions—as have the building practices associated with inefficient energy design and construction. This same growth has impaired water quality and quantity. Water quantities, mostly influenced by inefficient agricultural irrigation, have also suffered because of rampant residential consumption. Water quality has been affected as development has caused nonpoint source pollution into our rivers and streams, negatively impacting the purity of our surface waters and the viability of aquatic life, which in turn affects the long-term livelihood of local fisherman.*

And so it goes. The couple's seemingly innocuous choice of a cheap home is caught up in a complex web involving consumption habits, land planning, food production, and investment in and decisions about infrastructure, transportation, and energy. The resulting entanglement of business interests across multiple industries has created a perfect storm of environmental devastation involving climate change, energy, water, biodiversity and land use, chemicals and toxins, air pollution, waste management, ozone layer depletion, oceans and fisheries, and deforestation.

As we look back at the evolution of American culture, we can see unfolding a story in time characterized by: (a) laying waste to the environment while providing short-term livelihood and growth; (b) laying waste to a domestic economy by outsourcing jobs to locales where labor and environmental regulations are more lenient; (c) creating environmental *and* economic havoc for a global citizenry when the full environmental consequences of bad business practices abroad finally come to roost. Surely, another scenario is called for.

ENVISIONING A MASTER NARRATIVE OF POSSIBILITY

The story of Joe and Jane is complex. It's easy to get lost in the details of their life, to lose sight of a big-picture, feedback system. As a political system matures over time, securing rights for its citizenry, an economic system also evolves, one that externalizes many of the true costs of business onto society. Eventually, there is pushback from various groups seeking to hold businesses accountable, which leads businesses either to fight (resisting accountability through lobbying, litigation, and weakening regulation) or flight (going abroad where labor and environmental regulations are lax). In this system, the major sectors of society—business, government, nonprofit, and academia—square off against one another.

It's a zero-sum game among social sectors, with society itself the loser. And the big question facing us today is this: do capitalism and democracy have the adaptive capacity, are they robust enough, to change how they have traditionally functioned, so as to shape a sustainable world order? If so, what would this look like? What kind of story could be told about how we get there from here? Called for is a narrative that connects one's inner and outer spheres, that connects past generations to present and future ones, that assembles the parts of one's life and gives it coherence and meaning (Suzuki & McConnell, 1997, p. 10). Some of the most visionary thinkers today share two corollary thoughts when it comes to a master narrative of possibility. First, the old master narrative of humankind prevailing over nature has run its course (Brand, 1999, p. 48). Secondly, we need a compelling new master narrative that includes peoples who have been written out of the traditional frame, illustrates how our land and community are in harmony, and provides a sense of redemption (Hawken, 2007, p. 25).

Max De Pree, former CEO of Herman Miller, noted that our leaders are akin to tribal elders or storytellers who "insistently work at the process of . . . renewal. They must preserve and revitalize the values of the tribe" (De Pree, 1987, p. 91). That's the charge for sustainable leadership in an uncertain age. The question is: what does that master narrative look like?

This master narrative of possibility needs to be holistic. It needs to link the various elements of the natural order: air, water, land, energy, climate, biodiversity, etc. Let's call that *narrative condition #1: natural synthesis.* A second critical element entails synthesis within society. The current system is one in which the various sectors of society are working at cross-purposes from one another (for more, see Melaver, 2009, pp. 166–172). A corrective to this complex feedback system is to have our political and economic systems—and the various tribes that comprise them—working in concert for the overall interests of future generations and for the overall interests of our planet. What is required is integrative work among all sectors of a society. Call this *master narrative condition #2: social synthesis.*

A master narrative of possibility calls for a few other things. It should be reasonably brief. It should focus on decision-makers who will shape our notions of stewardship of land and community. It needs to provide a home for the key critical ideas floating out there today. It has to be both credible and offer hope. It should reflect the grave realities facing us today—global warming, increasingly chronic water shortages and desertification, loss of biodiversity, growing disparity between the wealthy and the poor—while also providing a reasonable road map that leads us in another direction. It needs to inspire, without seeming to be full of hot air. It should be long on vision, while also being tactical enough for each of us to see the role we can play. It needs to have epic breadth, while having specific relevance to day-to-day life in our communities. It needs to provide a sobering account of consumption run amok without causing listeners to resist the message. Most of all, it needs to be authentic.

CONSTRUCTING A MASTER NARRATIVE OF POSSIBILITY

Hillsboro seemed a rather ordinary town: about 100,000 residents with a four-year community college, a vocational training institute, a smattering of aging manufacturing companies and numerous local businesses providing most employment. Hillsboro had for many years seen its population aging, its (brighter) kids going off to college and not returning. About 10 years ago, you might have called it "sleepy," a nice place to retire, a great place to be if you didn't mind the streets rolling up around 5 p.m., a place more focused on its 19th-century origins than its 21st-century possibilities.

Not now. Hillsboro had become the poster child for a new type of community. Delegations from far-flung locales studied the city's practices. It was featured in urban-planning magazines and health journals and green-living periodicals. What had turned Hillsboro around was a question often asked. How had they pulled this miracle off?

Despite appearances, the municipality's evolution hadn't been orderly. There were false starts and numerous blind alleys pursued; chaotic, interminable meetings from which it seemed no common purpose would evolve. And yet, from the perspective of hindsight, the steps Hillsboro had taken seemed methodical, commonsensical.

The town first convened a cross-functional team from across professional disciplines—government and urban-planning folks, health care professionals and businesspeople, teachers and administrators, faith-based leaders and heads of key nonprofit organizations. A "dream team" of outside experts in fields as diverse as energy, biology, economic development, permaculture, etc., rounded out the team.[5]

This core steering group began by articulating overarching principles that would govern their work. Fortunately, much of what townsfolk were looking for was readily available from work done elsewhere. They were drawn to the system conditions established by Natural Step founder Karl-Henrik Robert, which holds that in a sustainable society, nature is not subject to systematically increasing:

1. *concentration of substances extracted from the Earth's surfaces*
2. *concentration of substances produced by society*
3. *degradation by physical means*
4. *conditions that systematically undermine the capacity of people to meet their needs (Robert, 1997;Nattrass & Altomare, 1999, 2002)*

Alongside these core concepts, the Hillsboro citizens added principles from The Earth Charter, Hanover Principles, and the UN Global Compact. Kerala, India, Curtiba, Brazil, and Gaviotas, Columbia, served as influential role models in sharpening their thinking (Edwards, 2005; Hawken, Lovins, & Lovins, 1999; Weisman, 1998).

The steering group then conducted a thorough stocktaking, looking at the numerous assets provided by both natural and human environments. Leaders examined the city's supply chain, from the sources for its materials to the sinks where wastes were disposed. They looked at the entire range of infrastructure at their disposal. Resources that seemed to be duplicative—school libraries and municipal libraries, recreational facilities—were duly noted, as were resources that had odd half-lives, such as hotel parking lots used only in the evenings and office parking lots used only during the day. They looked at waste products generated by one user—scraps of food, excess steam—and considered how these might be utilized elsewhere. They undertook an economic "leakage test," assessing how dollars exited the system for other locales (Shuman, 2007).

The steering group then engaged in future scenario building. This went beyond envisioning what they wanted Hillsboro to be a generation hence. Instead, their jumping-off point was the pioneering work of Royal Dutch/Shell from the 1970s, which charted its strategic direction in the face of certain "what-ifs" likely to occur in the coming decades. Arie de Geus, one of the architects of Shell's planning program, liked to refer to scenarios as alternative stories with the powerful characteristics of a folktale (de Geus, 1997).

Hillsboro's scenario for the future assumed the following outlines: it made little sense for its Economic Development Authority to lure big corporations. Such a "race to the bottom" never paid for itself. Instead, the focus would be on attracting and retaining local businesses having a natural affinity for the place. Finding synergies among these various local businesses would also be critical. Imagined was a closed-loop economy of sources and sinks: a local hotel outsourcing its laundry to a nearby facility. The excess heat from the laundry to be captured and reused for a neighboring restaurant, which sourced its ingredients from the local farmers' market, which came from urban gardens throughout the city. The vision became a reality and the synergies among local businesses picked up momentum at a geometric rate. Before long, over 1,000 local businesses would sign on to Toward Net Zero pledge, a commitment to achieving a carbon-neutrality.

In keeping with this local entrepreneurship and zero-footprint orientation, the town decided it would own its utilities, tapping in to local biofuel scraps, tidal wave movement, wind, and solar to provide a more highly efficient distributive energy system. This green utility company, along with a mandated green building program, fostered a strong local green-collar job base around: weatherization, passive solar and PV, geothermal, green modular construction, and related activities.

Hillsboro had undertaken an intensive urban-planning program, with higher, mixed-income, mixed-use densities within the urban core linked by linear parks. The green space was financed by a 1 percent transfer tax on real estate transactions and by a sophisticated system of Transfer Development Rights that enabled the municipality to equilibrate land values between high-density areas and zero-density green spaces. An electric public transportation network, fueled by solar cells over public parking facilities connected the pieces of this urban fabric.

Hillsboro became the leading light for a net-zero approach to living: net-zero emissions, net-zero brain drain, net-zero waste, net-zero financial leakage. The only thing about Hillsboro that wasn't net zero was its overall sense of contentment and well-being—which was pretty much sky-high.

I suppose the story of Hillsboro sounds fanciful—even though everything in this story has been borrowed from actual case studies around the globe. It's just too fanciful, says a skeptical voice, to synthesize all of these various practices into one place. And even if that happened, the doubtful voice continues, it would still be a little example, an outlier—hardly the place to launch transformational behavior. And then finally, from our skeptical voice, the cruelest cut of all: it is, after all, just a story.

CONCLUSION: HILLSBORO IS EVERYWHERE

Really? In this last section, I want to adopt a less formal, more personal manner with you, my reader. I hope that's okay. For, you see, that skeptical voice is a part of a persona I think I know well—an old "me."

So, Hillsboro is an outlier community? Perhaps. But not too long ago I finished writing a business book built around our journey at Melaver, Inc., becoming a more sustainable enterprise. It is a book that literally begins with the word *no*. And the last word in the book is *yes*. In between is the story of taking an oppositional stance toward things you believe are no longer viable and converting that stance into a positive vision. The poet Wallace Stevens has a couplet that captures this dynamic:

> After the final no there comes a yes
> And on that yes the future world depends.
> (Stevens, 2009)

When I first began running Melaver, Inc., I was only dimly aware of the things amiss with business's engagement—or lack of engagement—with the other aspects of our lives on this Earth. However, I was aware of Ben and Jerry's. And Tom's of Maine. And Patagonia. And eventually Interface and Zingerman's and White Dog Cafe, and a bunch of other businesses clear about what the overarching purpose of a business should be. Those stories took root. They shaped the development of our own company. So, to those skeptical detractors questioning the power of outlier stories, I can only offer up my own story of Melaver, Inc., being influenced by outliers that preceded us.

So is Hillsboro just a small-scale place, unlikely to be replicated elsewhere? Admittedly, even today, I feel a bit odd speaking before an audience about the things my colleagues and I are doing. We are, after all, just a small company taking baby steps toward functioning sustainably. But even small enterprises and out-of-the limelight places have last-chance landscapes that are entitled to our passion to conserve. Every place on this planet has habitats worth fighting for. The political scientist Sheldon Wolin, who has written critically of our loss of democracy in the United States, has this to say about shaping reform at the local level: "Democratic consciousness, while it may emerge anywhere at any time, is most likely to be nurtured in local, small-scale settings, where both the negative consequences of political powerlessness and positive possibilities of political involvement seem most evident" (Wolin, 2008, pp. 290–291).

Instead of being dismissive about using the small, fictional town of Hillsboro as a setting for a more sustainable revolution, we should embrace it for the potential embodied within. As Anita Roddick, founder of The Body Shop once noted: "Anyone who thinks he is too small to make a difference has never been in bed with a mosquito" (quoted in Hirshberg, 2008, p. 194).

So, this vignette about Hillsboro is just a story? Hmmmm. I came to this business of running Melaver, Inc., from a literature background, feeling that this background was a liability. I studied stories, for chrissake, whereas my business counterparts had all studied spreadsheets and accounting and financing. It took me a long time to realize that I was distancing myself from the very thing that was most familiar, most meaningful, and most effective in expressing many of the things I lacked a business language for.

So what do stories have to do with running a business, with leadership, with sustainability? Everything. Author and businessman David Korten has, for me, captured the critical importance of storytelling for a 21st-century ethic. It's a lengthy quote, but I think worth savoring:

> The human species is entering a period of dramatic and potentially devastating change as the result of forces of our own creation that are now largely beyond our control. It is within our means, however, to shape a positive outcome. The outcome will depend in large measure on the prevailing stories that shape our understanding of the traumatic time at hand—its causes and its possibilities. Perhaps the most difficult and yet essential aspect of this work is to change our stories. If we succeed, future generations may look back on this as a time of profound transition and speak of it as the time of the Great Turning. If we fail, our time may instead be known simply as the tragic time of the Great Unraveling. (Korten, 2006, pp. 20–21)

Stories shaping a Great Turning. In the elegance of a turn of phrase, the lowly story, a thing associated with getting our kids to sleep, or a rhetorical device associated with prevarication, or a pedestrian form of entertainment, seems to hold the ongoing viability of our planet in the palm of its hand.

NOTES

1. Taken from a speech delivered in 2001, see Robert (2006, p. 240).
2. *The Story of Stuff*, a short 20-minute video produced by the Tides Foundation and Free Range Studios (http://www.storyofstuff.com/) is an excellent step in the right direction. It focuses on the links among extraction, production, sales, and disposal, and foregrounds how a culture of consumption plays a key role in the story.
3. Here's the basic calculation: their home mortgage eats up about 30 percent of their after-tax income, while the cost of operating and maintaining their two cars consumes another 25 percent. Tuition for their two kids Seth (15) and Annie (13), health insurance, food, clothing, plus debt service on about $9,000 of credit-card debt eat up the balance.
4. For more, see Beatley and Manning (1997); Suzuki and McConnell (1997); and James and Lahti (2004).
5. Interface, Inc., provides an example of such a dream team (see Anderson, 1998).

REFERENCES

Anderson, R. (1998). *Mid-Course Correction: Toward a Sustainable Enterprise; The Interface Model*. White River Junction, VT: Chelsea Green.

Barnes, P. (2006). *Capitalism 3.0: A Guide to Reclaiming the Commons*. San Francisco: Berrett-Koehler Publishers.

Beatley, T., & Manning, K. (1997). *The Ecology of Place: Planning for Environment, Economy, and Community*. Washington, DC: Island Press.

Brand, S. (1999). *The Clock of the Long Now: Time and Responsibility; The Ideas behind the World's Slowest Computer*. New York: Basic Books.

Brown, L. (2008). *Plan B 3.0: Mobilizing to Save Civilization*. New York: W. W. Norton and Company.

de Geus, A. (1997). *The Living Company: Habits for Survival in a Turbulent Business Environment*. Boston: Harvard Business School Press.

De Pree, M. (1987). *Leadership is an Art*. New York: Doubleday.

Denning, S. (2004). *Squirrel Inc.: A Fable of Leadership through Storytelling*. San Francisco: John Wiley and Sons.

Denning, S. (2007). *The Secret Language of Leadership: How Leaders Inspire Action through Narrative*. San Francisco: Jossey-Bass.

Edwards, A. (2005). *The Sustainability Revolution: Portrait of a Paradigm Shift*. Gabriola Island: New Society Publishers.

Esty, D., & Winston, A. (2006). *Green to Gold: How Smart Companies Use Environmental Strategy to Innovate, Create Value, and Build Competitive Advantage*. New Haven, CT: Yale University Press.

Hawken, P. (2007). *Blessed Unrest: How the Largest Movement in the World Came into Being and Why No One Saw It Coming*. New York: Viking.

Hawken, P., Lovins, A., & Lovins, H. (1999). *Natural Capitalism: Creating the Next Industrial Revolution*. Boston: Little, Brown, and Company.

Hirshberg, G. (2008). *Stirring It Up: How to Make Money and Save the World*. New York: Hyperion.

James, S., & Lahti, T. (2004). *The Natural Step for Communities; How Cities and Towns Can Change to Sustainable Practices*. Gabriola Island: New Society Press.

Korten, D. (2006). *The Great Turning: From Empire to Earth Community*. San Francisco: Berrett-Koehler Publishers and Kumarian Press.

Louv, R. (2008). *Last Child in the Woods: Saving our Children from Nature-Deficit Disorder*. Chapel Hill, NC: Algonquin Books.

Melaver, M. (2009). *Living above the Store: Building a Business that Creates Value, Inspires Change, and Restores Land and Community*. White River Junction, VT: Chelsea Green.

Monbiot, G. (2009). *Heat: How to Stop the Planet from Burning*. Cambridge, MA: South End Press.

Nattrass, B., & and Altomare, M. (1999). *The Natural Step for Business: Wealth, Ecology, and the Evolutionary Corporation*. Gabriola Island: New Society Publishers.

Nattrass, B., & and Altomare, M. (2002). *Dancing With the Tiger: Learning Sustainability Step by Natural Step*. Gabriola Island: New Society Publishers.

Orr, D. (2002). *The Nature of Design: Ecology, Culture, and Human Intention*. New York: Oxford University Press.

Prusak, L. (2004). Storytelling in Organizations. In J. Brown, S. Denning, K. Groh, & L. Prusak (Eds.), *Storytelling in Organizations: Why Storytelling Is Transforming 21st Century Organizations and Management* (pp. 15–52). Burlington: Elsevier Butterworth-Heinemann.

Putnam, R. (2001). *Bowling Alone: The Collapse and Revival of American Community*. New York: Simon and Schuster.

Reich, R. (2007). *Supercapitalism: The Transformation of Business, Democracy, and Everyday Life*. New York: Alfred A. Knopf.

Rivoli, P. (2005). *The Travels of a T-Shirt in the Global Economy*. Hoboken, NJ: John Wiley and Sons.

Robert, K. H. (1997). *Natural Step: A Framework*. Critical Press.

Robert, K. H. (2006). Problems are Not Enough in Themselves to Create a Momentum for Change. In A. Tal (Ed.), *Speaking of Earth: Environmental Speeches that Moved the World* (pp. 232–246). New Brunswick, NJ: Rutgers University Press.

Rogers, H. (2005). *Gone Tomorrow: The Hidden Life of Garbage*. New York: The New Press.

Romm, J. (2008). *Hell and High Water: The Global Warming Solution*. New York: Harper Perennial.

Sachs, J. (2008). *Common Wealth: Economics for a Crowded Planet*. New York: Penguin Press.

Schumacher, E. (1989). *Small is Beautiful: Economics as if People Mattered*. New York: Harper Perennial.

Shuman, M. (2007). *The Small-Mart Revolution: How Local Businesses Are Beating the Global Competition*. San Francisco: Berrett-Koehler Publishers.

Speth, J. (2007). *The Bridge at the Edge of the World: Capitalism, the Environment, and Crossing from Crisis to Sustainability*. New Haven, CT: Yale University Press.

Stevens, W. (2009). *The Well-Dressed Man with a Beard*. Retrieved from http://www.americanpoems.com/poets/Wallace-Stevens/1029

Suzuki, D., & McConnell, A. (1997). *The Sacred Balance: Rediscovering our Place in Nature*. Vancouver: Greystone Books.

Weisman, A. (1998). *Gaviotas: A Village to Reinvent the World*. White River Junction, VT: Chelsea Green.

Wolin, S. (2008). *Democracy, Inc.: Managed Democracy and the Specter of Inverted Totalitarianism*. Princeton, NJ: Princeton University Press.

6 Green Heroes Reexamined

An Evaluation of Environmental Role Models

Beth Birmingham and Stan L. LeQuire

INTRODUCTION: BROADENING OUR SPECTRUM OF GREEN HEROES

Who are the heroes of the green movement? Who are the iconic leaders for environmentalism? Would the average American citizen know the name of Wangari Maathai without the assistance of Google? Perhaps not. How about Former Vice President Al Gore, Jr.? Leonardo DiCaprio? The Prince of Wales? More likely. In this chapter we review the celebrity activist model and citizen leader model of environmental activism, and we encourage a reexamination of our green heroes. Who are the unsung heroes, particularly from the developing world, that can provide us with a broader spectrum of role models? Environmental issues are so complex and so pressing perhaps it is time to expand the models we follow.

We are not proposing an either-or position here, but a challenge for educators, parents, and individuals alike to broaden their pool of environmental leadership models to include both celebrities, as spokespersons for environmentalism, and citizen environmentalists, as those who often launch local environmental movements. What are the leadership characteristics of the men and women at the grassroots whose commitment to an environmental challenge raises the awareness and reaction of those around them, at times at great personal sacrifice? While appreciating both models of engagement, we will highlight the differences in the celebrity activist model, or as we refer to them in the following, those that are "celebrities first." Then, we will compare this model with the citizen leadership model. These citizen leaders are "environmentalists first," average and often unknown citizens who have made significant sacrifices and contributions in their endeavor to protect the environment.

These grassroots sources of environmental work are the model we want to focus on in this chapter, the citizen leader as environmental hero. Whether it is Wangari Maathai planting trees to stop land erosion in Kenya, or José Matilde Bonilla protecting the land for his community in Honduras, or Chico Mendes's confronting deforestation efforts in the Amazon, these environmental causes often start with people at the grassroots getting involved to enact change. While they do not have the media spotlight to shine on their cause as celebrity activists have, theirs is the catalyst that accomplishes great change on the local level. Furthermore, we believe citizen leaders are more likely to motivate a new generation of environmental leaders, due to the cultural skepticism of contemporary youth who will be the environmental leaders of the future. Youth appear wary or even scornful of leadership, especially when the credentials of leadership are bestowed by powerful interest groups or the mass media. The challenge is finding and telling the stories of citizen leaders to whom the average person can relate.

THE CELEBRITY ACTIVIST MODEL

We are familiar with the leadership of Gore, DiCaprio, the Prince of Wales and other celebrity activists in the environmental movement because they are "celebrities first." They did not come to fame by way of their commitment to the environmental causes they now champion, but rose to fame by way of acting talents, political roles, or royal ancestry. Here is a brief overview of a few of these "eco celebs."[1]

Former Vice President Al Gore spans both our celebrity activist and citizen leader models in many ways, but for the purpose of this chapter, we will describe Gore as a celebrity activist because he became widely known as an environmental leader by way of his political positions in American government, most notably as vice president of the United States from 1992 to 2000. However, his résumé as an environmental champion precedes his involvement in the executive government of the United States. His interest in environmental issues began to grow after his son was involved in a serious automobile accident in 1989. "Gore later explained that this trauma had prompted him to reevaluate serious life issues, and he started to consider the effect an environmentally unstable world would have on the future of his four children" (Becher & Richey, 2008, p. 336). His first major contribution to environmentalism was the acclaimed volume, *Earth in the Balance*. This book explained complex environmental situations in understandable language. However, Gore is most known for his Oscar-winning documentary, *An Inconvenient Truth*. This film has opened an international conversation on climate change and has accomplished much in raising awareness of this global issue. To build on the film's momentum, Gore collaborated with others to found Live Earth, an organization seeking "to leverage the power of entertainment through integrated events, media, and the live experience to ignite a global movement aimed at solving the most critical environmental issues of our time" (Live Earth, 2008). While Live Earth continues as an activist organization, its main accomplishment was a series of concerts during a 24-hour period on July 7, 2007. The Live Earth organization boldly claims the concerts to be "the 'Most Watched Online Entertainment Event Ever.' The concerts were hosted on seven continents, broadcast in 132 countries, and inspired 2 billion people worldwide to engage with the issues and solutions surrounding the global climate crisis" (Live Earth, 2008). Certainly, only someone with power and celebrity can produce such an event and gather the requisite superstar musicians such as Snoop Dogg, Madonna, the Dave Matthews Band, and Red Hot Chili Peppers, among others.

Leonardo DiCaprio is an actor who claims instant recognition around the world. Also well known, albeit on a lesser scale, is DiCaprio's involvement in environmental activism. From a young age, the actor has been a committed environmentalist. Moreover, he has been able to parlay his celebrity and his personal wealth to provide visibility and financial support for the causes he champions. DiCaprio has thus far focused his greatest commitments and energies on green building and global warming. In 1998, he founded the Leonardo DiCaprio Foundation, which has received several environmental awards (Becher & Richey, 2008, pp. 236–237). In addition, DiCaprio has produced several films profiling environmental issues, including *The 11th Hour*, which toured college campuses from 2008 to 2009 to raise awareness of climate change.

While the Prince of Wales has yet to appear in a movie, he nonetheless owns significant celebrity status due to his royal lineage. However, the prince has just signed a book and movie deal, which may add movie credentials to his royal celebrity (Ward, 2009). Prince Charles is a longtime supporter of such environmental causes as biodiversity and sustainability. All proceeds from the prince's forthcoming movie, titled *Harmony*, will go to his charitable foundation for the support of environmental causes. The prince has also won several environmental awards, including the Global Environmental Citizen Prize, given by Harvard Medical School's Center for Health and the Global Environment (British Broadcasting Corporation, 2007).

It is not possible to deny the huge contributions that celebrity leaders make to environmental causes. What follows is a summary of a few of these benefits and contributions.

Name Recognition

The use of celebrity spokespeople is not a new concept. A number of international development organizations, including the United Nations, have sought the aid of public figures to shed light on international social and environmental problems for decades. Celebrities bring credibility and emotional attachment to attract new activists and potential donors to organizations that might not have otherwise reached this population. For the new converts, the credibility and favorable emotions already established with celebrities are transferred to whatever cause celebrities champion. At some future point, the mission of that cause will take root in the hearts and minds of those new converts beyond the celebrities' involvement. The potential downside of this benefit is that the association between celebrities and their environmental cause is only beneficial as long as their character and behavior maintain high standards. If celebrities are exposed for inconsistent actions or extravagant behaviors, their tarnished image may transfer to the causes they've championed and their decreased credibility may bring into question the credibility of the environmental organizations they support or even to environmentalism in general.

Influence

For better or worse, celebrities have the ability to influence behaviors of fans and followers. This is a well-established fact in the consumer behavior realm, with a heavy use of celebrity spokespersons, and has transferred to the philanthropic realm as well. Many a charity concert has been held in the hopes of drawing attention to, and garnering financial support for, some plight occurring in the world. Elton John's ability to tap the wallets of wealthy friends has made record-breaking amounts of money for his work for HIV/AIDS. Al Gore's work in organizing the Live Earth concerts, as mentioned earlier, has been a great success. The increased sales in hybrid automobiles, energy-efficient home appliances, and organic products are evidence of changed consumer behavior thanks, in large part, to these efforts. Our concern with the celebrity activist model, however, is the risk that their concern becomes the "cause of the day," to be replaced by another cause on another day, and that their involvement may be driven more by public relations ploys than long-term environmental commitment. As Charles Foster notes, such charismatic leaders have "the capacity to induce others to his or her views. Yet, in modern times, charismatic leaders are more frequently the product of mass persuasion techniques. They tend to arise in times of crisis and fade away when conditions moderate" (quoted in Berry & Gordon, 1993, p. 20).

An Established Platform

Thanks to an insatiable market for celebrity "news," celebrity activists have an established media platform at their disposal to spotlight whatever cause they choose. Usually, this tactic is a mix of altruism and public relations savvy; however, their celebrity does engage a number of popular media vehicles with far greater reach than academic journals or obscure environmental publications on the shelves of the already converted. The danger of this established platform is that the same public platform that is a blessing to celebrity activists for getting their environmental message out is the same platform that can come crashing down on them when there is any rumor of questionable behavior. Unlike the general public, celebrities must be on guard for the watchful paparazzi.

THE CITIZEN LEADER MODEL

In his book *Environmental Leadership in Developing Countries*, Paul Steinberg (2001) highlights the propensity for researchers and storytellers to bypass the grassroots source of environmental work in favor of easier access to the data of multinational environmental groups. He states:

> The inordinate amount of attention given Northern scientists and donors [and celebrity activists] obscures the essential role played by domestic environmentalists in developing countries and draws our attention away from an entirely different category of resources in need of further study. (p. 201)

We propose that attention to domestic environmental "citizen leaders" enriches and deepens our understanding of environmental leadership. Richard Couto (1995) defines citizen leaders as those who:

> facilitate organized action to improve conditions of people in low-income communities and to address other basic needs of society at the local level. Their goal is to raise the floor beneath all members of society, rather than to enable a few to touch its vaulted ceiling. (p. 12)

They are "environmentalists first"—committed to significant sacrifices in the name of what is right for the environment. These men and women may never find a global audience on the scale of celebrity activists, but to their local communities and countries, they are heroes nonetheless. We will discuss some known examples of citizen leaders, but first we will anchor our discussion on one unknown leader who provides an inspiring example of environmental leadership.

A CITIZEN LEADER AS GREEN HERO

José Matilde Bonilla was just such a citizen leader. Born in 1962, Bonilla grew up, married, and started a family in the indigenous Lenca communities of central Honduras. Eventually, Bonilla settled in the village of Palmital, which is just down the mountainside from the Cerro Azul Meambar National Park. In this spectacularly beautiful region of cloud forests and mountain peaks, Bonilla came to understand that unless the forests and watersheds of the mountain peaks were protected, the villages of the lower slopes would not have clean, healthy water. He became a park ranger with a nongovernmental organization, Proyecto Aldea Global, which co-manages the national park with the Honduran government.

Bonilla's ranger duties were sometimes paid and sometimes volunteer. In addition to these duties, he farmed corn and beans to support his eight children and his wife, Telma.

In this region of Honduras, working as a park ranger does not mean wearing a crisp uniform and answering questions from appreciative tourists. It often means confronting poachers, illegal loggers, and local drug

Figure 6.1 The only known photograph of José Matilde Bonilla.

barons. It is a dangerous job. By arrangement, the rangers carry no weapons but report illegal activity within the park to the Honduran police for action. Bonilla understood the dangers and confronted them fearlessly. He is known to have said, "If people are going to kill me for what I am doing, then let them kill me. I am not afraid of death" (J. M. Rodrigues, personal communication, November 20, 2006).

Beyond his work as a ranger, Bonilla served in a wide variety of spiritual, environmental, and community leadership positions in Palmital. He was an active preacher in his village church. As an environmental educator, Bonilla taught villagers the vital role of the national park and its benefit to their livelihood. Bonilla also served as president of various committees and community organizations. He led a committee working to bring electricity to Palmital and presided over the village parent organization, which advocates on behalf of better schools and teachers. Despite the economic duress of this region, Palmital is an organized village with structures and leaders in place to improve the lives of the citizens. Chet Thomas, the executive director of Proyecto Aldea Global, noted that Bonilla approached his various leadership roles with a high degree of seriousness and commitment. Park ranger and friend José Max Rodrigues says Bonilla "was a dedicated volunteer. If someone would ask for his help as a volunteer he would set aside the necessary time to get the job done" (J. M. Rodrigues, personal communication, November 20, 2006). Bonilla encouraged the citizenry to active and dedicated leadership roles within a region where poverty is endemic and where leadership roles are often unpaid and unrecognized.

In July of 2003 Bonilla paid the ultimate price for his environmental leadership. Despite his "peaceful, soft-spoken" demeanor, Bonilla had a reputation of confronting poachers and loggers. In late June Bonilla discovered men tending a large plot of marijuana on clear-cut land within the national park. He fearlessly confronted these men for operating in their own interests rather than the best interests of the wider community. On July 2, as he ate dinner with his family, "hooded gunmen stormed the home and murdered him in front of his terrified wife, Telma, and their eight children" (LeQuire, 2008, p. 16).

Perhaps the greatest testimony to Bonilla's leadership came at his funeral. His village of 400 doubled in size as "800 people attended from his community and from surrounding communities" (J. M. Rodrigues, personal communication, November 20, 2006). This high attendance in such a remote, sparsely populated area speaks of the loss felt by the local Lenca communities. The day after the funeral, his murderers returned to his simple grave plot and desecrated the simple marker that was placed over it. Honduran authorities have not prosecuted Bonilla's murderers. While the village awaits justice, the volunteer park rangers continue to protect the watershed and park despite being under threat of retaliation and violence.

His leadership impact in the village is ongoing. While alive, he would encourage the Lenca villagers to pick up litter and garbage in the village. This practice continues out of respect for Bonilla's memory and without the assistance of municipal garbage collection. At the conclusion of the author's interview with Rodrigues (2006), he solemnly said, "A leader like José Matilde Bonilla will never again be born in that village."

OTHER CITIZEN LEADERS

Environmental history is filled with the biographies of others, like José Matilde Bonilla, who have been local, citizen leaders. We will examine a few of them. Some are relatively unknown; others began as unknown but have reached an iconic status.

In 1988, a cattle rancher's son murdered Francisco Alves Mendes Filho, better known to the world as Chico Mendes. Revkin (2005) states that Mendes "gave [global issues] a human face." He knew the value of partnership with powerful international environmental organizations, yet he "would chuckle sometimes about these head-in-the-clouds types" (p. 23). Born in 1944 to poor peasant rubber farmers on a Brazilian plantation, Mendes grew up without education and began work as a rubber tapper at 9 years of age. Wealthy landowners strictly forbade their workers from gaining an education, which would have helped them to make sense of their oppression. Not until he was 20 had he learned to read and write.

In the 1970s, rubber tappers organized into a union and elected Mendes as their president. Mendes gained international attention from his fearless confrontations and strikes against the clearing of more rain forest. Environmental organizations brought him to the United States to lobby for an end to Inter-American Development Bank funds for a road into the forest. He succeeded. Respect and honor for Mendes accumulated. He won several awards, including the United Nations Global 500 Environmental Prize.

> Perhaps the most significant element of the legacy of Mendes is the enhanced power and voice of the organizations associated with him and the rubber tappers' cause—the National Council of Rubber Tappers, and the Amazon Work Group—from whose membership emerged a new generation of environmental leaders and activists. (Palmer, 2000, p. 305)

Affirming his lasting role as a citizen leader, Revkin (2005) states, "With all of Mendes's successes, the central lesson of his life may well be that the vigilance and resolve of the individual must be passed to the community, and then down from one generation protecting an environmental legacy to the next" (p. 25).

Ken Saro-Wiwa is another citizen leader who demonstrates the high cost of environmental activism. The Ogoni people of Nigeria are a small ethnic group inhabiting the oil-rich delta of the Niger River. Already, the reader will sense the potential for conflict because oil and power share a long and intimate history. Indeed, the Ogoni suffered the oppression of their indigenous culture and environmental devastation of their traditional lands at the hands of more powerful ethnic groups who wanted to control the oil wealth. One of the Ogoni native sons, Ken Saro-Wiwa, helped to organize his people to stand for their rights and for their land.

Saro-Wiwa was uniquely suited for this task. As a former government official, he had served within the very power structures that he sought to challenge. In addition, as a writer and a television producer, he possessed the communication skills needed for grassroots activism. In 1990, he helped form the Movement for the Survival of the Ogoni People (MOSOP). Traveling and speaking tirelessly throughout Ogoniland, Saro-Wiwa's communications skills served to unify many disparate groups under the MOSOP umbrella. His success also brought him into conflict with the Nigerian government who wanted a quiet, docile people whose land could pump more wealth into their coffers. Through the early 1990s, the government's anger grew apace with the Ogoni struggle for autonomy and environmental justice. Furthermore, the Ogoni struggle captured the attention of the global community.

In 1994, the Nigerian government decided to crack down on the movement and "arrested Saro-Wiwa and nine top MOSOP leaders on trumped-up charges of complicity in the murders of four Ogoni chiefs" (Bob & Nepstad, 2007, p. 1386). The MOSOP organization began to fall apart under harsh repression; some leaders fled into exile abroad. The government dealt its heaviest blow to the Ogoni cause when in 1995 they executed Saro-Wiwa along with eight other Ogoni leaders after a "blatantly unfair" military trial (Bob & Nepstad, 2007, p. 1386). Bob and Nepstad (2007) call Saro-Wiwa a "prophetic leader . . . [who] attracted substantial media attention and generated great moral outrage both at home and abroad" (p. 1387). A successor to Saro-Wiwa was never found; his "key role in bridging personal, generational, subethnic, and political rivalries among the Ogoni elites made his replacement difficult" (p. 1388). Despite the failure of the movement, the environmental community can learn from Saro-Wiwa's leadership, particularly in the power of indigenous people to speak for themselves and to provide their own leadership. Perhaps the environmental community can also learn from some of its mistakes in responding to Saro-Wiwa's death. According to Bob and Nepstad (2007), Saro-Wiwa's son recalls that, after his father's execution, international NGOs competed to raise money to keep Saro-Wiwa's memory alive. Surely, the NGOs had noble goals, but as Bob and Nepstad (2007) state, "Saro-Wiwa's death created a shallow basis on which overseas advocates opportunistically sought to build support" (p. 1389).

There are many more inspiring stories of green heroes that could be told. (See Table 6.1 in Appendix 6.1). The lives and stories of these citizen leaders highlight seven leadership characteristics of our environmental heroes:

(1) Organic

There is an organic quality to citizen leaders, drawing from Preskill and Brookfield (2009) who paraphrase Antonio Gramsci's concept of "leadership from below":

> where the leader is part of a collective that through dialogue crafts a vision to challenge dominant ideologies, structures and practices. In organic leadership, the leader is concerned less with being the progenitor of a branded vision that is announced and imposed from above and more with helping members of the community realize what talents, knowledge and skills they can contribute to a vision they themselves have generated. (p. ix)

(2) Reluctant

Unknown environmental activists do not have a public platform through which to deliver their stories, and in most cases would shun the role of leader or public figure. As Couto (1995) suggests:

> Citizen leaders usually do not choose leadership. They do not even seek it. They leave their private lives reluctantly for these public roles.

> Often they intend to take some public action, to achieve their purpose quickly, and then to return to private matters . . . Somewhere in that chain they acquire the truly distinguishing characteristic of leadership, the gift of trust bestowed by others with whom they work . . . Citizen leadership is leadership with far fewer perks and far less glamour than that which marks those in the threadbare political and national leadership we lament. At the same time, citizen leadership comes with the same or greater personal costs as other forms of leadership. (pp. 13–14)

(3) Addresses the Felt Needs of the Community

In the epilogue of his book, *Transforming Leadership*, James MacGregor Burns (2003) articulates a leadership strategy for global poverty alleviation. In such a strategy, it is the transforming leader's ability to first listen to the local community that is central. Such leaders know best the wants and needs of the community and can gather those voices for thoughtful listening, and can mobilize action around those needs, which are often matters of survival for the community.

(4) Courageous

Inevitably, citizen environmental leaders face adversity. The gluttony of industry in land and natural resource consumption, coupled with governments lured by revenue and possible employment opportunities for local citizens, confronts these citizen leaders with powerful adversaries. They must possess the courage to challenge powerful entities with an interest in ignoring or even destroying the natural environment. Others may view their environmental activism as an impediment to development and a threat to economic security and future of the community. Nevertheless, citizen environmental leaders persevere for the sake of environmental protection and longer-term social objectives.

(5) Committed for the Long Term

The courage just discussed is often needed as citizen environmental leaders may not see the benefit of their work for many years. Local victories, if any, are often the first in a series of ongoing threats by industry and land developers, and only when localized action moves to policy change and protection at regional and national level does the burden end. Despite this, these leaders stay committed to their cause, knowing it is right and necessary. Their sacrifice is in the form of time with family and possible estrangement from family and friends not totally committed to the sacrifice that environmental activism requires of citizen leaders. Ultimately, as in the case of Bonilla and others, they all too often give their lives for their cause.

(6) Role Models

Citizen leaders are "environmentalists first." They operate "from a strong ethical base and a fully formed code of personal belief and conduct" (Berry & Gordon, 1993, p. 273). Their aspirations are not toward leadership itself, but their respective environmental cause. Thus, it is in their modeling and active engagement that they lead, not any positional status. Burns (2003) says such leaders have strong motivations to action relevant to serving followers' unrealized wants. As such, they display the characteristics of servant leadership (Greenleaf, 2002).

(7) Inspiring

Environmentalists have long struggled to inform and engage the public. Cold, scientific fact does little to inspire action across broad themes (Osbaldiston & Sheldon, 2002). While science remains crucial, perhaps it is time for a commitment to find and tell the stories of grassroots environmental heroes like those highlighted in this chapter. For every issue celebrity activists point us to with their powerful public platform, somewhere a citizen leader owns the same issue and works on it in obscurity. The stories of José Matilde Bonilla, Chico Mendes, Ken Saro-Wiwa, and others have the power to inspire; they draw us into the lives, and deaths, of people who did not write a check to save the rain forest, but who paid with their lives. "When you tell a story you invoke a power that is greater than the sum of the facts you report. It has emotional content and delivers a contextual framework and a wisdom that reaches past logical rational analysis" (Simmons, 2006, p. 80). Perhaps now more than ever, the environmental movement needs leadership that arises from citizens in communities far beyond our own in the Northern Hemisphere, and stories that foreground the relevant social justice issues. Researchers have suggested that linking environmental issues to issues of social justice heightens our sense of environmental responsibility. When environmental issues are perceived to involve social injustice and unfairness, our moral emotions are engaged and we are more likely to take responsibility for solving environmental problems (Kals & Maes, 2002, pp. 105–106). A human element is introduced that moves people to action.

As we stated at the beginning of this chapter, we would encourage all of us—educators, parents, and citizens—to broaden our pool of environmental leadership models to include *both* celebrity and citizen environmentalists. If one accepts this suggestion, the question then becomes: how do we find these citizen leaders? How do we uncover or discover their stories? How do we develop a fuller attention for all kinds of possible leaders? Some suggested steps to uncovering stories of alternative environmental role models follow:

Mind Your Culture and Context

If the environmental movement is beholden to a cultural context where powerful, glamorous leaders are preferred, then leaders from minority contexts or whose glamour is determined by other standards may remain outside our awareness. If environmentalists have grown accustomed to letting celebrities speak for the movement, then other spokespersons may remain voiceless. As Herwitz (2008) states, "Ours is a society where depth is continually converted into surface, emotion into consumer choice" (pp. 31–32). How will the powerful narratives of Bonilla and many others motivate and inspire new environmental leadership if our cultural bias ignores the contributions of those beyond our immediate context? The premise of this chapter is that other, compelling leadership models do indeed exist. Nonetheless, every effort must be made to acknowledge that context and culture may predispose us to prefer glamorous heroes and leaders.

Develop a Healthy Suspicion of Environmental Legalism

One of the environmental movement's downfalls is its dependence upon a list of dos and don'ts for its core message: thou shalt recycle, thou shalt buy green, etc. While such activities are important, they can preclude thoughtful, adaptive reflection and action. A second downfall might be the tendency of environmentalists to scorn eco-scofflaws. Even though green rules are based in truth and have good intentions, to sustain environmentalism, the movement must rise above motivation through legalism and its enforcement. Environmental stewardship is more than obedience to a list of commandments. Perhaps the lives and work of a new cadre of heroes, such as José Matilde Bonilla, can inspire and motivate us in a more idealistic fashion. Their commitments show us that deep stewardship can be more costly than it is glamorous. Simmons (2006) advocates the use of story as a superior motivator: "Rules aren't as useful as case histories (stories). Harvard Business School has known that for a long time" (p. 196).

Name and Avoid Environmental Elitism

Environmentalism has long been accused of an elitism that puts the movement beyond the sympathies of most people. For example, an environmental issue for elites might be the preservation of pristine water quality for water-skiing and bathing. In fact, clean water is a matter of elemental survival for most of the world's people. While some environmentalists focus on "charismatic megafauna" and plan their next safari to an exotic location, most people in the world will probably never travel more than a few miles from their homes. Simmons (2006) believes that we are in a moment characterized by a "worldwide search for authenticity and those things that are truly important—a search for meaning" (p. 112). While all these environmental themes and messages are valid, there exist messages of far greater consequence and depth, yet they are often overshadowed by the elitist and entertainment values of our culture.

CONCLUSION

Without denigrating the accomplishments and contributions of celebrity environmentalists, we affirm that radically different models of environmental leadership—and heroism—do exist. This chapter has sketched out the lives of a few such heroes. Discovering such citizen environmentalists would be a monumental but rewarding task that could renew environmentalism and its advocates. However, our cultural preferences for the celebrity activist model and our lack of access to the stories of citizen environmental leaders leave us with limited choices and jeopardize the sustainability of the environmental movement itself. Our contention is that the next generation of environmental leaders is not smitten by stardom and longs for alternative heroes. Therefore, let us commit ourselves to the task of finding and telling the compelling stories of new green heroes.

Table 6.1 Leaders Who Have Sacrificed Their Lives for Environmental Causes

Murdered	*Name*	*Country*	*Involvements*	*Source*
1980s–1990s	Ten priests, including one from the U.S., one from Italy	Philippines	Illegal logging	(4)
1991	Father Nerelitio Satur	Philippines	Illegal logging	(4)
2001	Godofredo Garcia Baca	Peru	Protests against mining	(3)
2001	Miguel Freitas da Silva	Brazil	President, Rural Workers Association	(2)
2001	Galdino Jesus dos Santos	Brazil	Indigenous rights	(2)
2001	Ademir "Dema" Federicci	Brazil	Land reform	(1)
2001	Digna Ochoa	Mexico	Lawyer representing two environmental activists	(2)
2002	Bartolomeu Morais da Silva	Brazil	Land reform	(1)
2003	José Matilde Bonilla	Honduras	Deforestation	(5)
2005	Dorothy Stang	Brazil	Deforestation and land issues	(4)

Sources: (1) Revkin (2005); (2) Bishop (2007); (3) Switzer (2003); (4) Franke (2005); (5) LeQuire (2008).

NOTES

1. The term *eco celeb* is borrowed from *The Environmental Magazine* (Connolly, 2008). In 2008, the magazine named the following as their top 10 eco celebs of the year. In order, they are: Ed Begley, Jr., Leonardo DiCaprio, Jackie Chan, Harrison Ford, Ted Danson, Dominic Monaghan, Daryl Hannah, Robert Redford, Carole King, Maggie Gyllenhaal.

REFERENCES

Becher, A., & Richey, J. (2008). *American Environmental Leaders: From Colonial Times to the Present* (Vol. 1). Millerton, NY: Grey House Publishing.

Berry, J., & Gordon, J. (1993). *Environmental Leadership: Developing Effective Skills and Styles.* Washington, DC: Island Press.

Bishop, J. (2007). Resisting the Death of Ideas: The Afterlife of Chico Mendes. *Social Alternatives, 26*(1), 43–47.

Bob, C., & Nepstad, S. (2007). Kill a Leader, Murder a Movement? Leadership and Assassination in Social Movements. *American Behavioral Scientist,* 50(10), 1370–1394.

British Broadcasting Corporation. (2007). Prince Wins Environmental Award. Retrieved from http://news.bbc.co.uk/2/hi/uk_news/6308609.stm

Burns, J. (2003). *Transforming Leadership: A New Pursuit of Happiness.* New York: Atlantic Monthly Press.

Connolly, B. (2008). E's Top Ten Eco Celebs. *The Environmental Magazine, 19*(November–December), 35.

Couto, R. (1995). Defining a Citizen Leader. In J. T. Wren (Ed.), *The Leader's Companion: Insights on Leadership through the Ages* (pp. 11–17). New York: Free Press.

Franke, J. (2005). Faith and Martyrdom in the Forest [electronic version]. *The Witness.* Retrieved from http://www.thewitness.org/article.php?id=785

Gore, A. (1992). *Earth in the Balance: Ecology and the Human Spirit.* Boston: Houghton Mifflin.

Greenleaf, R. (2002). *Servant Leadership: A Journey into the Nature of Legitimate Power and Greatness.* New York: Paulist Press.

Herwitz, D. (2008). *The Star as Icon: Celebrity in the Age of Mass Consumption.* New York: Columbia University Press.

Kals, E., & Maes, J. (2002). Sustainable Development and Emotions. In P. Schmuck & W. P. Schultz (Eds.), *Psychology of Sustainable Development* (pp. 97–122). Boston: Kluwer Academic Publishers.

LeQuire, S. (2008). Finding Untold Stories. *Journal of Theology for Southern Africa, 131,* 16–29.

Live Earth. (2008). Friends of Live Earth: Frequently Asked Questions (FAQs). Retrieved from http://liveearth.org/2008/10/fole-faq/

Osbaldiston, R., & Sheldon, K. (2002). Social Dilemmas and Sustainability: Promoting Peoples' "Motivation to Cooperate with the Future." In P. Schmuck & W. P. Schultz (Eds.), *Psychology of Sustainable Development* (pp. 37–57). Boston: Kluwer Academic Publishers.

Palmer, J. (2000). *Fifty Key Thinkers on the Environment.* London: Routledge.

Preskill, S., & Brookfield, S. (2009). *Learning as a Way of Leading: Lessons from the Struggle for Social Justice.* San Francisco: Jossey-Bass.

Revkin, A. (2005, March/April). Remembering Chico Mendes: The Martyr of the Amazon Lives On. *The Environmental Magazine, 16,* 23–25.

Simmons, A. (2006). *The Story Factor: Secrets of Influence from the Art of Storytelling*. New York: Basic Books.
Steinberg, P. (2001). *Environmental Leadership in Developing Countries: Transnational Relations and Biodiversity Policy in Costa Rica and Bolivia*. Cambridge, MA: MIT Press.
Switzer, J. V. (2003). *Environmental Activism: A Reference Handbook*. Santa Barbara, CA: ABC-CLIO.
Ward, D. (2009). Prince Charles Signs Green Movie Deal. Retrieved from http://www.cnn.com/2009/SHOWBIZ/books/04/24/prince. green/index.html

7 Communicating Leadership for Environmental Sustainability

The Rhetorical Strategies of Rachel Carson and Al Gore

Denise Stodola

INTRODUCTION

Strong communication skills are some of the most important qualities a leader can possess (Flauto, 1999). Within the realm of environmental leadership, the role of communication skills is of special importance, as activists wish to provide leadership that will not only inform the general public about ecological dangers, but also attempt to move the public to take action that may involve changes in behavior and personal sacrifices. The leader must furthermore be able to signal to the audience that there is an imminent risk to their well-being without causing panic-induced paralysis or apathy (Moser, 2007). In order to avoid audience paralysis in the face of seemingly insurmountable ecological obstacles, communicators must convey the hope that action can be effective, hopefulness being an essential emotion that must be generated by the communicator's message (Reading, 2004).

Two of the most effective communicators in environmental activism have been Rachel Carson and Al Gore. Carson is commonly known as the "mother of the modern environmental movement." Her book *Silent Spring*, first published in 1962, was integral in informing the public about the dangers posed by DDT and other toxic chemicals (Carson, 2002). Gore for his part has been very successful in raising public awareness about global warming. His documentary *An Inconvenient Truth* won the Academy Award for best documentary in 2007, and Gore himself won the Nobel Peace Prize in 2007. Despite the fact that these two environmental leaders have very different leadership styles, I will argue that both effectively combine and balance the rhetorical appeals of *ethos*, *pathos*, and *logos* as outlined by Aristotle, and that they do so in surprisingly similar ways, albeit through different media. I will further suggest that Carson and Gore's blending of these three forms of rhetorical appeal are crucial ingredients in their effectiveness as environmental leaders, and that their rhetorical strategies are further enhanced by their evocation of the sublime and their status as sociocultural "underdogs."

INDIRECT VS. DIRECT LEADERSHIP

The differences in Carson's and Gore's leadership styles appear quite pronounced. Carson, who had three major authorial successes prior to *Silent Spring* (*Under the Sea Wind*, *The Sea around Us*, and *The Edge of the Sea*), spent a large part of her life very quietly, working for the U.S. Fish and Wildlife Service as a marine biologist. Carson was an extremely private person. Indeed, when her first book appeared in November 1941, although there was a paragraph about Carson inside the back cover flap, there was no photograph of her. *The Sea around Us* was published in July 1951, and three weeks later was in fifth place on the *New York Times*'s best-seller list. This occurred despite the fact that Carson refused all but one of the many requests for radio and television appearances her publisher received. Ultimately, she did one television interview as a favor to Oxford University Press (Lear, 1997). In stark contrast to the shy Carson, Al Gore has spent many years in the public eye, for much of that time as a high-profile politician, and, since the release of *An Inconvenient Truth* he has also became a pop culture icon synonymous with the issue of global warming, even appearing on television shows like *The Simpsons*, *Futurama*, and *The Daily Show* (see also Chapter 6 of this volume for discussion of Gore as "celebrity activist").

Such different leadership styles are better understood through an application of Howard Gardner's distinction between "direct" and "indirect" leadership, a distinction he outlines in *Leading Minds: An Anatomy of Leadership* (1995). For Gardner, the two types of leadership exist on a continuum; in fact, one individual can exhibit both types of leadership in differing degrees and can move back and forth along the continuum over time. An indirect leader influences others through his or her works, including tangible artifacts like books or paintings, while a direct leader influences his or her constituents through leadership positions in institutions and organizations (Gardner, 1995, p. 6). Within this latter category one finds politicians, military leaders, and CEOs, for example. Clearly, Rachel Carson occupies the "indirect" end of the spectrum, while Al Gore occupies the more "direct" end. This is not to say that each figure employs only one strategy—indeed, they both employ varying degrees of each—but Carson exercised leadership primarily through her works, while Gore has more directly sought to enact change in the political arena and in the popular media. But despite the fact that the two occupy opposite ends of the direct–indirect spectrum outlined by Gardner, both must still use effective forms of communication in order to reach potential followers, and both use rhetorical appeals in similar ways within the works for which each author is most widely recognized.

CARSON AND GORE: ETHOS, LOGOS, PATHOS

In Book I of his *Rhetoric* (350 BCE), Aristotle defines rhetoric as the "faculty of observing in any given case the available means of persuasion." There are three modes of artistic persuasion: the appeals of *logos*, *ethos*, and *pathos*. *Logos* refers to the mode of persuasion grounded in the logic and reason of an argument; *ethos* refers to the mode of persuasion grounded in the speaker's credibility; and *pathos* to the mode rooted in the speaker's ability to arouse certain emotions in his or her audience. Both Gore and Carson use *logos* in order to establish for the audience that a problem exists. For example, Carson used a variety of credible sources that would be classified as "academic." These range from articles in medical journals to reports from the U.S. Fish and Wildlife Service and information conveyed in congressional hearings.

Significantly, though, Carson did not use an academic citation method, which would place the source citations within the text itself; rather, she included a list of sources at the end of *Silent Spring*, providing a methodical delineation of page numbers followed by the sources appearing on those pages. Her "Author's Note" at the beginning of the book makes clear that she made this choice consciously: "I have not wished to burden the text with footnotes but I realize that many of my readers will wish to pursue some of the subjects discussed. I have therefore included a list of my principal sources of information, arranged by chapter and page, in an appendix which will be found at the back of the book" (Carson, 2002, p. xi).

Approaching her source material in such a way means that her book can be experienced without the interruption of parenthetical citations or copious footnotes. Such a format is a concession to the nonacademic audience member, who might be put off by the tone such a format would entail—one that creates a division between author and audience, a strident "author as expert" and "audience as student" dynamic, which could potentially counteract one of the main messages in the book: that human beings and all life on the planet are inextricably linked, and that the poisoning of the environment threatens us all equally. By maintaining more of an egalitarian tone in her presentation of facts, Carson effectively reinforces this interconnectedness and equality.

Such a rhetorical stance does not detract from the power of her argument, but, for the broader audience, may serve to enhance it, and this enhancement is complemented by the *ethos* that Carson establishes. By the time *Silent Spring* appeared, Carson had become rather well known as a science writer, so her credibility would have been built in part upon the audience's awareness of her previous work.

Within *Silent Spring* itself, Carson is conspicuously absent, instead keeping her discussion almost exclusively in the third person. When she does use first person, it is most often in the plural form, so that she becomes an almost invisible speaker; in other words, she masks her identity as one individual speaker, instead becoming part of a larger group that includes the audience member. The main exception here, though, is in the chapter entitled "And No Birds Sing," where she narrates a series of first-person stories—stories of real people. For example, the chapter opens with a letter a housewife has written to ornithologist Robert Cushman Murphy:

> Here in our village the elm trees have been sprayed for several years. When we moved here six years ago, there was a wealth of bird life; I put up a feeder and had a steady stream of cardinals, chickadees, downies and nuthatches all winter, and the cardinals and chickadees brought their young ones in the summer . . . It is hard to explain to the children that the birds have been killed off, when they have learned in school that a Federal law protects the birds from killing or capture. 'Will they ever come back?' they ask, and I do not have the answer. The elms are still dying, and so are the birds. Is anything being done? Can anything be done? Can I do anything? (Carson, 2002, p. 103)

The effect here is that the audience gets to hear other voices that resemble their own: stories from real people who are concerned about the environment and that illustrate how DDT has adversely affected the natural communities they inhabit. Essentially, by removing herself as a personality from the text, Carson allows other voices, like the voice of the housewife in the letter, to take her place. By constructing her *ethos* through the use of many individual, "authentic" voices, she further supports the effect created by her handling of *logos*: she is emphasizing that the systemic poisoning of the environment with DDT is risking one and all. In other words, what could become a book in which a scientific expert proselytizes to an audience, the stance of the expert serving to put the audience into a disempowered position, takes a much different form—one that ultimately empowers the audience to act. Doing so would seem to be essential when one deals with environmental dangers, as what affects one portion of the ecosystem ultimately affects the entire globe. Moreover, by putting the question "Can I do anything?" into her text, she is inviting the audience to put themselves into a position as agent—one who can actually take on the issue and make changes to avert additional negative consequences.

Al Gore's use of *logos* and *ethos* does much the same things, but in somewhat different forms. For one thing, *An Inconvenient Truth* has two major components: the book and the documentary film. In the book, Gore (2006) thanks a group of scientists for their advice and assistance on the "book, and the movie that is part of the overall project" (p. 323), thus providing some references for the data he uses within it. Moreover, within the context of an extremely visual book layout, Gore provides general citations whenever he inserts text boxes containing data culled from other sources. Source information is presented differently in the film, although the book and film deliver much of the same information. The film basically shows Gore giving an oral presentation to a live audience, a narrative that is interspersed with his musings and memories, as well as his concern about global warming and its potentially devastating effects, and within the film he mentions some of the institutional and individual sources for some of his information but he does not do so in an academic manner. At the end of the film, though, he does include a list of researchers who worked on the film, as well as a list of organizations that provided data for his project. The Web site address climatecrisis.net is also provided there. If one navigates to that site and then clicks on the link entitled "the science," she or he is led to a list of significant sources of data that do have citations and footnotes.

Thus, while Gore establishes *logos* in the same manner as Carson—for a general nonacademic audience who would likely be put off by the tone of an academic text—the data he uses are substantiated, but, true to the multimedia world that we now inhabit, the documentation for that data appears in a text conceptually linked to the primary text(s). In other words, the book, the film, and the Web site form a textual system, one that works not only as individual pieces within different contexts, but also as a matrix of interrelated texts.

Similarly, Gore's *ethos* as an author and speaker is distributed across texts. In fact, the book references both the film and the Web site; the film references the Web site; and the Web site references the film. Significantly, while the *logos* of this textual system appears primarily at the Web site, the *ethos* is distributed within the contexts of the film and the book in structurally similar ways. Indeed, the Web site focuses on Gore only very marginally. He is almost "absent" from this particular textual component, in much the same way that Carson was absent from *Silent Spring*. Conversely, both the book and the film include bits of information about Gore as an individual that are designed to make him appear more credible as a speaker.

Throughout the book are sections that deal with Gore's attitude to the subject and why he has become so passionate about the environment. The book's introduction is the first of such sections, always brief, and always on yellow paper. Gore lends credibility to his case not only by articulating how and why he came to the subject of global warming, but also the degree to which nature has played an important role in his life. At the same time, he discusses and presents candid snapshots of himself and of his family, as well as significant stories from their lives. In doing this, he draws his audience in more closely to him emotionally, getting us to see that we share the same kinds of concerns. This creates more equality between the speaker and the audience, endowing him with more credibility and allowing us to feel more emotionally comfortable in listening to his message. Whereas Carson achieved this effect by removing herself and substituting "authentic" voices expressing their own personal experience of environmental decline, Gore achieves a similar effect by foregrounding his own more private personal experience of, and concern for, the natural environment.

Of course, emotion, or *pathos*, plays an important role in any argument addressing environmental dangers: the audience must be made aware of the imminent dangers facing them. As such, some degree of fear can and should be present in any rhetorical strategy designed to address such subjects. Without the simultaneous empowerment of the audience and the instillation of hopefulness, however, the audience will not be motivated to act on the problem. (For more see the discussion in Chapter 3 of this volume.) It is in this creation of an admixture of *pathos* that Carson and Gore are most similar.

In Carson's case, perhaps the most focused attention on the emotional tendencies in *Silent Spring* has been centered on what has been called the "opening allegory," which, as Oravec (2000) points out, is a misnomer:

> Commentators often use the word allegory to describe the first chapter of *Silent Spring.* Allegory, however, requires the personification of abstract values or principles . . . In its final version, 'A Fable for Tomorrow' does not go so far—the town is not an abstraction (Green Meadows) but a composite of factual events happening in existing towns, as the text makes clear. (p. 56)

Indeed, Carson's use of factual events undercuts a possible criticism that can be leveled at the passage—namely, that the tone is overly "apocalyptic." Moreover, the section combines the factual events (*logos*) with joy and contentment, as well as with sadness and fear: joy and contentment in response to the beauty of the town before its deterioration, and sadness and fear once the deterioration begins. Confusion is inevitably another emotional response to the section: the reader wonders why such a thing would happen in a story, in much the same way as a real individual would wonder why such things would happen in the actual world she or he inhabits.

Significantly, though, the book does not maintain an uninterrupted evocation of confusion and fear. Carson uses sentence-level constructions, as well as diction, to instill a poetic quality into her prose. As Gartner (2000) suggests, the "beauty of her writing beguiles the reader into reading and assimilating material that is both intellectually difficult to understand and emotionally difficult to accept" (p. 105). In addition, Carson included illustrations at the beginning of each chapter. These are quite simple but realistic drawings, the simplicity of the style thus serving to avoid the visual overstimulation of the reader, which could lead to an additional layer of anxiety. Carson believed that the drawings had an important role to play in the text: "[W]e have never planned for illustrations, but today we [she and Paul Brooks, editor-in-chief at Houghton Mifflin] talked seriously of having them (sketches—not photographs)—partly to aid understanding, partly to break it up and make reading easier. I'm delighted" (Carson, 1995, p. 380). By breaking up her argument this way, Carson allows her audience to assimilate facts at a steady but unhurried pace, while also allowing the reader breaks from the emotional distress instilled by the unpleasant, fear-inducing, and imminent threat posed by the dangers she describes.

This steady pace and the emotional balance it creates are also reinforced by the overall structure of the book, as one can see in its opening and closing. "A Fable for Tomorrow" evokes the image of roads and roadsides, and does so in both the positive and negative descriptions of the town:

> Along the roads, laurel, viburnum and alder, great ferns and wildflowers delighted the traveler's eye through much of the year. Even in winter the roadsides were places of beauty, where countless birds came to feed on the berries and on the seed heads of the dried weeds rising above the snow . . . The roadsides, once so attractive, were now lined with browned and withered vegetation as though swept by fire. (Carson, 2002, pp. 1–3)

This motif appears at the end of the book as well, in the last chapter, entitled "The Other Road." Carson takes the road motif one step further by evoking the notion of "beauty" with "road," as she makes reference to Frost's poem: "[W]e now stand where two roads diverge . . . But unlike the roads in Robert Frost's familiar poem, they are not equally fair" (Carson, 2002, p. 277). Carson is referring, of course, to the poem "The Road Not Taken," which ultimately suggests that taking the "road less traveled by" can alter one's life, in a positive way, forever. Thus, not only does the road motif tie together the first and last chapters, but it also raises the issue of individual choice and agency that permeates the poem. Significantly, too, the beauty of poetry she invokes adds a positive emotional element while simultaneously empowering the audience to act. The order and unity of the text serve to create an additional calming effect, since the world Carson is describing is "disordered," to some extent.

Like Rachel Carson, Al Gore uses the *pathos* of visual images to support the *logos* of his argument. The film *An Inconvenient Truth*, one long visual image, includes moments when lighting is used to create a pensive but determined tone—the moments at the beginning and end of the film, which show Gore walking, alone, down a darkened hallway toward the audience waiting for his appearance. These segments are also presented in black and white rather than in color, adding to the serious, solitary atmosphere. Much like the use of "road" at the beginning and end of *Silent Spring*, this image evokes the sense of individual agency and purposefulness, while also creating an overall unity to the piece. Gore's book has a similar structure: at the beginning is a two-page spread that shows a photograph of Caney Fork River taken by Tipper Gore in 2006; the book ends with another two-page spread of the same river from a slightly different angle.

Although Gore does not use poetic language to create a sense of beauty and contentment in either the book or the film, his voice is modulated in the film in such a way as to have a calming effect. This is especially true in the interposed meditative scenes where he is providing a voice-over to the visual images. These are inserted to break up the oral presentation he is giving to his audience—which is also broken up with little moments of humor—such as his introduction of himself as the man who was once the "next president of the United States." By interspersing his oral presentation with humor and meditative sequences, Gore, like Carson, paces his material in such a way as to avoid overwhelming the audience with a barrage of bad news, which would only serve to send them into despair.

Gore thus creates a level of anxiety that is conducive to audience awareness of the problem and to their motivation to act in response while not being overwhelming. This is further enhanced by the inclusion at the end of the film of the Melissa Etheridge song entitled "I Need to Wake Up," which reiterates audience agency by stating "I need to wake up/ I need to change/ I need to shake up/ I need to speak out." The song is energetic and upbeat, further associating a positive emotion with the need to act. The effect is further reinforced by the comforting lyrics that state "I am not an island/ I am not alone," lines that make the task at hand less insurmountable while reminding the audience of the interconnectedness of all those who hear the song. Moreover, the use of the first-person "I" makes the lines more directly applicable to the audience, who are experiencing it in the first person: in other words, the individual audience member becomes the "I" of the lyrics.

THE EVOCATION OF THE SUBLIME

The similarity in the way in which Carson and Gore use a sophisticated strategy of *pathos* to make their messages both urgent and readily addressed by the agency of the audience members is also evident in the way in which both evoke the sublime. The notion of the sublime has two major elements embedded within its definition: fear and beauty. For the 18th-century philosopher Edmund Burke, the fear and trepidation one might feel in witnessing a thunderstorm was a major component of the sublime (Oravec, 2001, p. 758). Later, Ruskin stated, "Anything which elevates the mind is sublime, and elevation of mind is produced by contemplation of greatness of any kind; but chiefly, of course, by the greatness of the noblest things" (quoted in Oravec, 2001, p. 759).[1]

Carson's use of the sublime is chiefly evident in her allusion to a Keats poem in the chapter entitled "And no birds sing." This is a very famous line from his poem "La Belle Dame Sans Merci," the first and last stanza of which are as follows:

> O, what can ail thee, Knight at arms,
> Alone and palely loitering?
> The sedge is wither'd from the Lake,
> And no birds sing! . . .
> And this is why I sojourn here

> Alone and palely loitering;
> Though the sedge is wither'd from the Lake,
> And no birds sing. (Keats, 1983, pp. 658–659)

This poem, which uses the images of decay juxtaposed with the beauty of the female "faery" described elsewhere within it, underscores the ways in which the gothic was used by Romantic poets as a means to achieve the sublime. Clearly, the poem, like Carson's work, is a warning, but, infused as it is with beauty and poetic language, the warning is delivered to the audience in an aesthetically and emotionally pleasing way. Moreover, the images of the poem are also reminiscent of the dead and dying vegetation along the roadways in the second half of "A Fable for Tomorrow," a parallel that lends an additional element of the sublime to Carson's text, which takes on a nobility of tone that elevates the mind: the two pieces not only illustrate the sublime, but also become part of a larger network of texts that "speak to" each other over an expanse of time.

Gore also uses a sublime image—but his is a purely visual one, and it appears in both the book and the film. It is the first photograph taken of the Earth from space: *Earth Rise*. The image is awe-inspiring in two main ways: not only does the image show us the view of the Earth, but presented as it is in the darkness of space, the audience cannot help but feel a sense of fear. Gore reinforces our response to the visual elements through his use of language, telling the audience that the photo was taken during the *Apollo 8* mission, the first time that human beings had left the Earth's orbit. Significantly, however, the audience's emotional response is not an end in itself. Since the sublime also serves to elevate one's thoughts, the audience members are not just slightly fearful and awestruck, but also inspired, since they have encountered the sublime and the complex emotional responses it raises in the context of equally strong elements of *ethos* and *logos*: in this case, the confluence of *ethos*, *pathos*, and *logos* with the sublime can inspire the audience to protect the beauty that they see in the image before them.

CONCLUSION: UNDERDOGS EMPLOYING ETHOS, PATHOS, AND LOGOS

While Carson and Gore exerted authorial control over the texts they created, their arguments are also aided by elements over which they had no control at the time they composed the texts. Both works are aided by the fact that the authors are embedded within a larger narrative—the narratives comprised of events in their lives. In fact, both authors speak as individuals who have overcome substantial obstacles in order to even articulate their views: Carson was a female scientist at a time when women were rarely part of the scientific establishment, and she not only had a position in a scientific field, but she also became a widely read author. Similarly, Gore had lost the 2000 U.S. presidential election to George W. Bush and had to reinvent himself, to some extent. Also, during his campaign, he uttered some unfortunate verbal gaffes, which made him a subject of ridicule on late-night comedy shows.

As such, both authors speak from the position of "underdogs." Indeed, there is a large conceptual gap between their underdog statuses and what they ultimately accomplished as environmental leaders. The dynamic of this narrative functions in several main ways: it aligns the notion of "underdog" with the environmental leaders, the audience members, and the natural environment itself. More specifically, this dynamic functions as the means whereby each author speaks a particular message while also embodying for their audiences an image of just how the audience can be successful: after all, if Carson and Gore can overcome such obstacles individually in order to produce such important and influential works, certainly the audience members can work together to overcome the obstacles inherent in the environmental challenges they face. Moreover, the environment itself is an underdog—and the challenge it faces is one that can only be overcome with active, collective assistance from environmental leaders and their constituents.

This empowerment and motivation of the audience is at the heart of the authors' use of Aristotle's rhetorical appeals. They accomplish this by presenting their arguments logically, through the use of data, and by using diction, tone, and textual structure to develop their *ethos* as speakers who share life experiences and concerns with the audiences to whom they are speaking. Most importantly, both authors construct a complex matrix of affective impulses that serve to generate concern, hope, motivation, and inspiration in their audiences, all of which are necessary for us as audience members if we, like Carson and Gore, are to effectively address the serious and growing environmental challenges that we face.

NOTE

1. The notion of the sublime appears in many of the current discussions of environmental rhetoric, most notably in the work of scholar Christine Oravec, who warns that in current usage, the notion of "sublime" could have deleterious results: the repeated use of the sublime as a rhetorical trope diminishes its linguistic power, moving it toward cliché, conventionality, and ultimately into either apathy toward environmental issues, or commodification of the environment. For further discussion of the sublime and its relationship to environmentalism, see Oravec (1996).

REFERENCES

Aristotle. (350 BCE). *Rhetoric* (W. Rhys Roberts, Trans.). The Internet Classics Archive. Retrieved from http://www.classics.mit.edu//Aristotle/ rhetoric.html

Carson, R. (1941). *Under the Sea Wind: A Naturalist's Picture of Ocean Life.* New York: Oxford University Press.

———. (1951). *The Sea Around Us.* New York. New American Library.

———. (1955). *The Edge of the Sea.* Boston: Houghton Mifflin.

———. (1995). *Always, Rachel: The Letters of Rachel Carson and Dorothy Freeman, 1952–1964* (M. Freeman, Ed.). Boston: Beacon Press.

———. (2002). *Silent Spring* (fortieth anniversary edition). Boston: Mariner.

Flauto, F. (1999). Walking the Talk: The Relationship between Leadership and Communication Competence. *Journal of Leadership & Organizational Studies,* 6(1/2), 86–97.

Gardner, H. (1995). *Leading Minds: An Anatomy of Leadership.* New York: Basic Books.

Gartner, C. (2000). When Science Writing Becomes Literary Art: The Success of *Silent Spring.* In C. Waddell (Ed.), *And No Birds Sing: Rhetorical Analyses of Rachel Carson's* Silent Spring (pp. 103–125). Carbondale: Southern Illinois University Press.

Gore, A. (2006). *An Inconvenient Truth: The Planetary Emergency of Global Warming and What We Can Do about It.* Emmaus, PA: Rodale.

Keats, J. (1983). La belle dame sans merci. In A. Allison et al. (Eds.),*The Norton Anthology of Poetry* (pp. 658–659). New York: Norton.

Lear, L. (1997). *Rachel Carson: Witness for Nature.* Boston: Mariner Books.

Moser, S. (2007). More Bad News: The Risk of Neglecting Emotional Responses to Climate Change Information. In S. Moser & L. Dilling (Eds.), *Creating a Climate for Change: Communicating Climate Change and Facilitating Social Change* (pp. 64–80). Cambridge: Cambridge University Press.

Oravec, C. (1996). To Stand Outside Oneself: The Sublime in the Discourse of Natural Scenery. In J. Cantril & C. Oravec (Eds.), *The Symbolic Earth: Discourse and our Creation of the Environment* (pp. 58–75). Lexington: University Press of Kentucky.

Oravec, C. (2000). An Inventional Archaeology of "A Fable for Tomorrow." In C. Waddell (Ed.), *And No Birds Sing: Rhetorical Analyses of Rachel Carson's* Silent Spring (pp. 42–59). Carbondale: Southern Illinois University Press.

Oravec, C. (2001). The Sublime. In T. Sloane (Ed.), *Encyclopedia of Rhetoric* (pp. 757–761). Oxford: Oxford University Press.

Reading, A. (2004). *Hope and Despair: How Perceptions of the Future Shape Human Behavior.* Baltimore, MD: The Johns Hopkins University Press.

8 Artists as Transformative Leaders for Sustainability

Jill B. Jacoby and Xia Ji

INTRODUCTION

Much of the leadership literature focuses on people in positions of formal authority and with direct leadership roles (Heifetz, 1994). However, a hierarchical, top-down leadership style is insufficient to bring about significant and sustainable environmental change. Throughout the 20th century, command and control, notice and comment rulemaking, and hierarchical leadership were pervasive in environmental decision-making. However, the 21st century brings a host of significant environmental challenges that will require new forms of leadership and decision-making. Authors such as Lester Brown (2008) suggest that working together within community will be crucial as we confront challenges like climate change, resource depletion, species extinction, unbridled population growth, deforestation, and other such threats to the biosphere. In meeting such challenges, it will be vital to include those who have been previously excluded from the decision-making process.

We begin this chapter by sharing our passion and concern for water while stressing the fact that the world needs to become more water literate. We then examine artists as informal and indirect leaders with a focus on community-based eco-leadership styles that address environmental challenges. The chapter concludes with a case study of a collaborative decision-making technique called a *charrette* and analysis of the role that artists can play as transformative environmental leaders.

THE CENTRALITY OF WATER AND THE CRISIS OF LEADERSHIP

What is it about water that draws us to the banks of a river to hear and feel the thunder of a waterfall, or entices us to throw a stone into a pond and watch the ripples until they fade, or just to sit silently and watch a rising sun lift off of the edge of Lake Superior? Water is, quite simply, the element that sustains all life on our planet Earth, but water is more than biological nourishment for human life, water also replenishes the human spirit (France, 2003). Many cultures around the world treat water as sacred and often integrate water into rituals and ceremony (Garcia & Santistevan, 2008). Without a strong connection to water sources, many people in industrialized countries show a lack of respect for water and assume that it will always be available.

Despite the vital importance of water, one can look anywhere on our planet and find stressed water systems (Lohan, 2008; Brown, 2008; Gore, 2007; Marks, 2001). Glaciers that once replenished rivers, irrigated crops, and provided drinking water are now disappearing. Around the world, groundwater is being pumped for industrial agriculture at a rate far faster than precipitation can replenish. Global warming is reducing water levels of the Great Lakes, affecting shipping, recreation, and fish and plant populations alike. What water remains in our streams, lakes, rivers, and oceans faces ongoing threats from toxic discharges, stormwater runoff, and drought from climate change. The practice of water privatization in developing countries is forcing people to pay for water that they cannot afford, thus reducing water to a mere commodity to be sold and bought to satisfy a desire for profit. The following example illustrates an unsustainable approach to water management:

> If you want the perfect symbol for the high-consumption 21st century, look at a plastic bottle of water, fast replacing the SUV as the ultimate metaphor for our craziness. To take a product that is freely available to everyone in the West, and to turn it into a commodity, and to burn incredible amounts of energy shipping it around the world, and to create small mountain ranges of empty bottles—that is enough to tell you how out of control our consumer society has become. (McKibben, 2008, p. 10)

The imminent water catastrophe that is at our doorstep boils down to a crisis of leadership. The administrative procedures of the past have proven to be inadequate when it comes to solving current and future environmental problems. Wheatley (2005) observes the inadequacy of our current practices in public policy and engagement:

> Most public meetings, although originating from a democratic ideal, serve only to increase our separation from one another. Agendas and processes try to honor our differences but end up increasing our distance. They are 'public hearings' where nobody is listening and everyone is demanding airtime. Communities aren't created by such processes—they are destroyed by the increasing fear and separation that these processes engender. Such public processes also generate the destructive power dynamics that emerge when people feel isolated and unheard. (p. 53)

We don't need more public meetings of the type that Wheatley describes. What we need are new ways of listening as communities begin to turn towards localization and away from globalization, especially for energy and food resources (Brown, 2008). The realization that we are on the wrong path for humanity's long-term survival is a moment of great awakening to creativity and the envisioning of alternative paths. Democracy is becoming more deliberative, more meaningful, and more inclusive then ever before (Lappe, 2006). Likewise, leadership is beginning to look more like a form of collaboration than the agendas and commands of an authority figure. As we move into the uncharted territory of climate change and other complex environmental problems, we suggest that diversity is needed in our collaborative dccision-making efforts. We can't solve these problems by using the same kind of thinking that created the situation. Artists, as some of the most creative forces in society, have a crucial role to play in bringing out diversity, increasing a community's environmental awareness, developing common areas such as green space, and in being involved in the redesign of cities to create livable and sustainable communities.

THE TRANSFORMING LEADERSHIP ROLE OF ART AND ARTISTS

Dolman (2008) suggests that "[e]cological illiteracy is the single greatest global epidemic we face as a human species today" (p. 100). It is clear that humanity needs people who can bring both leadership and change quickly to our shattered and deteriorating environment, our common Earth home. We believe that one important yet neglected avenue of leading change is through art.

Many scholars have pondered the role of art and artists in society. In this chapter we define art in its broadest sense and include both the process and/or product of deliberately arranging elements in a way that appeals to the senses or emotions. Art serves to liberate human perception, challenge human creativity, and stir the human soul. Perhaps Eisner (2001) best captures the role of artists when he suggests that artists "invent fresh ways to show us aspects of the world we had not noticed; they release us from the stupor of the familiar" (p. 136). When artists connect what they do in various fields of the arts with emergent environmental and social issues in the community, there is real hope for restoring humanity to a more sustainable path. Humanity needs artists for their ability to reframe environmental issues so as to wake us up and shake us out of our complacency. What would change if communities invited members of their "creative class" (Florida, 2005) to sit at the table with the commonly invited stakeholders, and then were given free reign to create art with the goal of enhancing the dialogue and decision-making process?

The involvement of community-based artists (who place an emphasis on community, education, and collaborative production) into a decision-making process can increase the level of transformative power that is present in the process, along the lines of Burns's (1978) description of transforming leadership: "Leaders can also shape and alter and elevate the motives and values and goals of followers through the vital *teaching* role of leadership. This is *transforming* leadership" (p. 425). Transforming leadership focuses on "*end-values*, such as liberty, justice, equality" (p. 426), and as such mirrors the goals of community-based art, which attempts to increase a community's capacity for greater inclusion in decision-making and with a focus on shared power (Knight & Schwarzman, 2006, p. xvi). When we speak of artists as transformative leaders, we are talking about artists who teach and lead through their art and their presence by attempting to educate and even provoke the public to take action or make personal changes regarding social and ecological issues. This is not about art as a commodity, but about artists creating a transformative environment that raises public awareness, provides opportunity for community dialogue to occur, and encourages internal reflection and behavior change.

In addition to Burns's model of transforming leadership, the concepts of informal and indirect leadership also provide applications for artists as leaders. Heifetz (1994) provides a clear distinction between formal and informal authority by suggesting that formal authority is related to a position whereas informal authority is related to the ability to affect attitudes or behaviors (p. 101). Using Heifetz's framework, formal authority appears to be woven into one's employment and the power related to job status, whereas informal authority is about the personal integrity and influence that is necessary for leadership. Gardner (2004) talks about indirect leadership in a parallel fashion to how Heifetz discusses informal leadership. Gardner feels that indirect leadership is the ability to change minds indirectly through the use of scientific discoveries, scholarly breakthroughs, and artistic creations. Gardner uses Marx, Darwin, and artists like Pablo Picasso and poet T. S. Elliot as examples of indirect leaders because of the influence they have on events or the public. Both Heifetz and Gardner discuss the fact that although these types of leaders are more often found behind the scenes than direct leaders, they have an equally important impact on a community.

The artists we describe as transformative leaders are artists that emphasize the community-building, education, and social and environmental change dimensions of their art. These artists are clearly driven by different motives than commodity-oriented artists. At their core, community-based artists strive to raise community awareness about social and ecological issues and tend to work collaboratively with a diverse range of people from elementary school students to engineers, city planners, scientists, and other community members to effect positive social and environmental change.

The major implication of the preceding discussion is that certain artists can be transformative community leaders through informal and indirect means. With such a strong orientation towards community and working collaboratively, these artists also exhibit what are called "eco-leadership" skills. According to Western (2008), eco-leadership is "a new paradigm of leadership which takes an ecological perspective . . . it is about connectivity, interdependence and sustainability underpinned by an ethical and socially responsible stance" (p. 183; see also Chapter 2 in this volume). Western emphasizes that eco-leadership moves leaders away from individual control and towards collaboration in much the same way that Burns's (1978) transforming leadership is focused on the achievement of a higher collective purpose.

It is apparent that community-based artists rely heavily on collaborative and eco-leadership styles. The central idea behind artistic collaborative efforts is that artists work with other community members on public concerns, which in turn makes their communities stronger by building "social capital" (Putnam, 2000) and educating the public by addressing social or environmental concerns. This is a bit of an oversimplification, however, because collaborative and eco-leadership also challenge the commonly practiced hierarchical leadership methods and replace them with dialogue and affirming ways of working together. As Chrislip (2002) states:

> Working together entails a profound shift in the premises Americans hold for how public issues should be addressed. Instead of advocacy, collaboration demands engagement, dialogue instead of debate, inclusion instead of exclusion, shared power instead of domination and control, and mutual learning instead of rigid adherence to mutually exclusive positions. (p. 41)

The involvement of artists in collaborative decision-making challenges the status quo of who usually has the power to make decisions within a community. By involving artists from the very beginning of the decision-making process we are addressing the question of "who's missing from the dialogue?" (Linn, 2007; Wheatley, 2002) and broadening participation. (See Chapter 4 of this volume for in-depth analysis of both the promises and pitfalls of cross-sector community collaboration.)

Collaborative processes are also about building community by identifying skills, interests, and assets within a community. Simply through the introduction process of any group meeting, skills can be identified along with interests, past experiences, and other assets that strengthen collaboration. Identifying such assets helps to locate talents in a group that can assist in shaping the direction and success of collaborative efforts (Kretzmann & McKnight, 1993; Linn, 2007; Borrup, 2006).

In his community-oriented work, Borrup (2006) pays attention to identifying local assets and connecting them with the arts and culture. His premise is that through the use of the arts and culture, combined with identifying local assets, a community can build strong connections. Goldbard (2006) also speaks of building community through the arts by focusing on community cultural development projects that are built around educational experiences where participants learn more about their communities through others in the group or through their own research. Chrislip (2002) calls people who provide this type of community background information "content experts" (p. 53).

DULUTH'S PROPOSED BAYFRONT STORMWATER GARDEN

In light of our belief that artists can be transformative eco-leaders, and that many diverse voices need to be brought into community and environmental planning and problem solving, we hosted a collaborative design process in Duluth, Minnesota, that utilized the assets that local artists brought to the table. Neither of us are artists by training or profession but we have learned through our own experiences in working with artists that they bring with them the unique perceptions, creativity, and sense of humor that are essential elements for the transformation from Empire to Earth Community (Korten, 2006). In this section we provide a case study of a design *charrette* process that we facilitated in 2004 with artists in Duluth, Minnesota.

The city of Duluth is located at the headwaters of Lake Superior in northeastern Minnesota. Steep hills, an aging sewage infrastructure, and removal of natural wetlands have all contributed to the city's stormwater problems. In the urban and downtown areas, buildings and pavement cover the land surface and prevent rain and snowmelt from soaking into the earth. The city, like most developed areas, relies on storm drains to carry large amounts of runoff from roofs and paved areas to nearby rivers and Lake Superior. This stormwater runoff carries pollutants such as oil, sediment, a host of chemicals, and lawn fertilizers, and seriously degrades water quality. One of the greatest environmental challenges for cities is to balance natural resources with socioeconomic needs, but in doing so we often are not aware of the ecological losses sustained until after the damage is done. Such losses include the destruction of wetlands that once filtered pollutants out of stormwater and served as catchments for stormwater runoff. These losses become a threat to the health of both humans and ecosystems.

Sweetwater Alliance is a nonprofit organization in Duluth with a mission to build a more water-literate public through the arts and science. We have proposed to build a Stormwater Garden on Duluth's downtown waterfront. At the site of Slip 2 (currently an unused docking facility for large ships that is in disrepair) there is a visible stormwater pipe that drains Interstate 35 and the downtown area. The land surrounding Slip 2 is a vacant brownfield that has not been utilized since it housed industrial facilities. The site of our proposed project is located in the heart of the tourist district, on the far edge of the Bayfront Festival Park, and lies between the downtown area and the waterfront district, making it a highly visible and desirable site. In addition, the location is visible from Interstate 35 and from major downtown hotels and office buildings. The proposed Stormwater Garden will cleanse the stormwater that runs into Slip 2 and the St. Louis Bay and will educate the public about the ecological functions and values of wetlands, while doing so in artistically designed and constructed plant ponds. In this context we are embodying Alexandersson's (1990) notion that the "task of technology is not to correct nature, but to imitate it" (p. 34).

ENGAGING ARTISTS THROUGH A DESIGN *CHARRETTE*

The term *charrette* was created over 100 years ago at the Ecole des Beaux Arts in Paris (Condon, 1996). Students at the school worked hard to meet strict deadlines for their design assignments. When the deadline arrived, a small cart (in French a *charrette*) was wheeled past the students to collect their assignments. In contemporary use, a design *charrette* "collects" together the most talented architects and designers to develop creative proposals for difficult design tasks. The advantage of using a *charrette* is the ability to tap into the creative talents of many people at once; it allowed us to bring together visual artists who would not normally work together and to provide an atmosphere that allowed them to stimulate and learn from each other. The ideas that developed from this process provided a starting place for the next stage of design and engineering of the stormwater garden. Patricia Johanson, an internationally renowned ecological artist, was hired as the design consultant for the project. Ms. Johanson attended the design *charrette*, spoke with the artists about environmental art, worked with the artists throughout the *charrette*, and eventually took the artists' design elements and worked them into a 2-acre design.

People become excited about a project when they are included and believe their ideas are respected (O'Toole, 1996; Wheatley, 2005), and the way we utilized the *charrette* provided a way to encourage meaningful artistic involvement and collaboration. The participation of artists in a *charrette* allows a different level of communication to occur, one of "metaphor, cross reference, inclusiveness, and holistic thinking" and this level of creativity helps to "unclog a discourse that often finds itself mired in the narrow channels of technological and bureaucratic thinking" (Heartney, 1995, p. 143) in public hearings and feedback sessions.

CHARRETTE DAY

Sweetwater Alliance put out a call for artists to help design elements of the project in a daylong event that encouraged the artists to utilize elements of collaborative and eco-leadership. A regional mailing list of artists was used to recruit participants for the event. The *charrette* was held on December 11, 2004, at the Hartley Nature Center, which is located about 15 minutes from the downtown area of Duluth. The Nature Center offered a retreat-like atmosphere where artists could focus on various activities without outside interference.

The day began with an icebreaker type of activity that generated laughter and conversation and built trust among the participants. We discussed the goals for the day, showed photos of "green" stormwater projects, and described several scenarios (locations and size configurations) for our project. This was followed by a slide show of the site and the St. Louis River watershed (the St. Louis River enters Lake Superior near our proposed project site), as well as a discussion of previous environmental art projects created in Duluth. As facilitators, our role was to observe the *charrette* process, record information that was being created (we did this through audio recordings, note-taking, and from the artist's drawings), ask questions along the way, and summarize the discussions at the end of the day. One goal that we set for the day's activities focused on fostering a collaborative atmosphere where cooperation prevails over competition.

After gaining an understanding of the project, the goals surrounding the educational components of the project, and the ecology behind how wetlands cleanse stormwater, the participants broke up into small groups and discussed, brainstormed, and sketched ideas. We stressed to the participants that they were not necessarily designing the project, but helping us to identify design elements for the project. Most groups worked collaboratively, although some artists chose to draw individually but to discuss and work within a group. The participants were provided with paper, crayons, markers, food and beverages, and were encouraged to talk and share ideas. A high volume of background talk and laughter indicated that collaboration was occurring. Throughout the day the artists had access to Patricia Johanson, as well as a plant ecologist and the two authors, who have both been involved with similar projects in China and the United States.

At the end of the day, each small group reported back to the whole group about their ideas and shared their drawings. We summarized these ideas with the group and asked for feedback on the process. Several common themes came up as groups discussed their design elements.

Using recycled or reusable building materials came up in several of the groups. For example there was discussion of melting down old glass and using it in sculptures and mosaics and using old toilets for Flowforms (sculptures that aerate water) or scrap metal from ships for metal sculptures. Likewise the use of "green" energy sources came up in several groups: solar-powered water pumps, harnessing wind energy from Lake Superior, or even human-powered bicycles to pump and move water from one place to another. Many discussions occurred about how it was important for people to see the change in water quality from the dirty water coming into the stormwater garden to the clean water leaving.

The groups also shared interest in using native plants as well as teaching the visitors about identification of plants. Some suggested the creation of experiential learning environments where the public could get wet, walk across the water on stepping stones, see the water go over or under the pedestrian paths, and become immersed in the beauty of massive expanses of wetland plants. Getting the public involved by "taking something away or adding something" or by providing time for class or public projects, cleanups, or even having the public help make sculptures were all ideas that came out of the brainstorming sessions. Interactive ways for children to be involved were suggested such as ways to make water move from one place to another. Demonstrating to the public how they can build rain gardens and manage stormwater at their home was also discussed.

The most interesting discussions and design elements focused on the integration of the natural world into the stormwater garden. One group discussed human imprints on the Earth and suggested using hands and feet in a variety of ways: human footprints that transform into animal prints to show the interconnections of the four-legged and two-legged world; use of a child's hands pouring clean water back into the St. Louis Bay; and water flowing through fingers into a pool.

The image of turtles came up for several of the artists, perhaps because there was a turtle in a tank housed in the Nature Center that we met in. One group visualized an aerial perspective of a turtle shape or multiple turtles and suggested that the garden could be one big turtle shape and the scutes that make up the shell could be stepping-stones for people to walk on. Other turtle-related ideas included having water run between the scutes of the turtle to look like rivers. Many connected the turtle to local Ojibwa culture.

Another interesting topic of discussion focused on shapes in nature. In one group's words:

> We designed the creation of a spiral sculpture that goes up about 6 feet (to get the most out of the little piece of land). Water would be brought to the top by a bicycle pump and spiral or drip down into ponds, moving across musical instruments. Nature does cool things in small spaces to increase surface area and maximize efficiency. We visualize water pumped to the top of a big spiral, like an upside-down snail shell, then have the water spiral on its way down. The public could change gates and make the water routes change. By the time the water gets to the bottom it will be clean. We want the freeway traffic to see the big sculpture and to attract people to the site. It would be neat to have chimes that blow in the wind. The use of solar, wind, and a bike would supply the energy to pump the water all of the time. (See Figure 8.1)

SUMMARY OF THE DESIGN CHARRETTE

Our goal was to tap into the creative energy of community artists to help set the tone for the early stages of design. The design ideas and elements that came from the *charrette* provided a starting point for Patricia Johanson (lead designer) and Barr Engineering to elaborate upon during the following stages

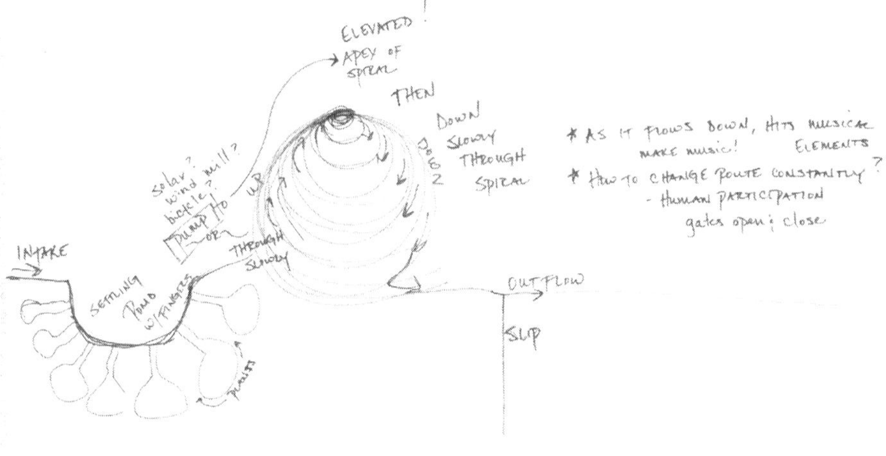

Figure 8.1 Drawing produced by a working group during *charrette* day.

of design. The design that Johanson created included many of the design elements that the artists developed. For example, the design for the 2-acre site starts with water being pumped up to a 10-foot tall turtle. The water runs down through the scutes and waters small pockets of ferns. There are stepping-stones for the public to walk out on as well as a dragonfly plaza that doubles as a bridge. There are cranks and levers where children can redirect water flows much like the locks and dams of the St. Lawrence Seaway. Solar panels will offset the energy required for the pumps and there will be ample opportunities for students and garden clubs to help with plant maintenance. Johanson's design is breathtaking from an aerial perspective (the interstate, office buildings, and other vantage points along the hillside), experiential from an on-the-ground vantage point, and a mass of color from a variety of native plants that bloom from early spring through late fall.

The day had several positive outcomes. First, we taught artists about stormwater concerns and water quality issues, and then we received the gift of the artists' visions and ways of interpreting an environmental issue to the public. In addition, the artists provided very creative design elements that were later worked into the project design. Some of the most significant dialogue that occurred was the artist's discussions about water quality and how to engage the public who would see the Stormwater Garden.

CONCLUSION: ARTISTS AS LEADERS FOR SUSTAINABILITY

The *charrette* provided an opportunity for unique community collaborations and a way to build partnerships with people who often do not work together. Engaging others in the Bayfront Stormwater Garden is multidimensional. Our initial intention was to expand on those voices that are asked to participate in the design of green space. The Bayfront area is the last undeveloped piece of waterfront land in downtown Duluth and previous proposed developments have been highly charged. By engaging some of the creative members of the local community, we hoped to build social capital while also engaging artists in their own environmental learning. Our design *charrette* event was just the first step toward engagement with art and artists in the hope to transform environmental leadership discourse. With a keener understanding of environmental issues, artists can truly help to create visionary projects that develop understanding and respect for the natural world, and hence serve as leaders for environmental sustainability.

The arts and artists can enhance and transform the environmental leadership discourse in the following ways. First, engagement with art and artists can bring out more diversity, which includes diverse participants, diverse forms of knowledge, and diverse ways of defining and solving problems. Our engagement with art and with artists in the Bayfront Stormwater Garden design *charrette* conveyed the message that we do not just need science and engineering, but also other forms of knowledge to face humanity's collective environmental challenges. Second, as a "creative force" in our society artists can serve as awakening, educating, and provoking agents as they themselves learn about the various social and environmental issues. Finally, artists can lead through connectivity and engagement—with themselves as well as with all other participants—which can lead to the inward transformation of leaders and followers. As environmental challenges surface each moment of our day we cannot afford to ignore the vital leadership force to be found in the arts and artists.

ACKNOWLEDGMENTS

The authors would like to thank the Beim Foundation for their support of the Design Charrette.

REFERENCES

Alexandersson, O. (1990). *Living Water.* Dublin: Gateway Books.

Borrup, T. (2006). *The Creative Community Builder's Handbook: How to Transform Communities Using Local Assets, Arts and Culture.* St. Paul: Fieldstone Alliance Publishing Center.

Brown, L. (2008). *Plan B 3.0: Mobilizing to Save Civilization.* New York: W. W. Norton and Company.

Burns, J. (1978). *Leadership.* New York: Harper and Row Publishers.

Chrislip, D. (2002). *The Collaborative Leadership Fieldbook: A Guide for Citizens and Civic Leaders.* San Francisco: Jossey-Bass.

Condon, P. (1996). *Sustainable Urban Landscapes: The Surrey Design Charette.* Vancouver: University of British Columbia.

Dolman, B. (2008). Watershed Literacy: Restoring Community and Nature. In T. Lohan (Ed.), *Water Consciousness: How We All Have to Change to Protect Our Most Critical Resource* (pp. 99–109). San Francisco: AlterNet Books.

Eisner, E. (2001). Concerns and Aspirations for Qualitative Research in the New Millennium. *Qualitative Research, 1*(2), 135–145.

Florida, R. (2005). *The Flight of the Creative Class: The New Global Competition for Talent*. New York: HarperCollins Publishers.

France, R. (2003). *Deep Immersion: The Experience of Water*. Sheffield: Green Frigate Books.

Garcia, P., & Santistevan, M. (2008). Acequias: A Model for Local Governance of Water. In T. Lohan (Ed.), *Water Consciousness: How We All Have to Change to Protect Our Most Critical Resource* (pp. 111–119). San Francisco: AlterNet Books.

Gardner, H. (2004). *Changing Minds: The Art and Science of Changing Our Own and Other People's Minds*. Boston: Harvard Business School Press.

Goldbard, A. (2006). *New Creative Community: The Art of Cultural Development*. Oakland: New Village Press.

Gore, A. (2007). *An Inconvenient Truth: The Crisis of Global Warming*. New York: Viking.

Heartney, E. (1995). Ecopolitics/Ecopoetry. In N. Felshin (Ed.), *But Is It Art? The Spirit of Art as Activism* (pp. 142–162). Seattle: Bay Press.

Heifetz, R. (1994). *Leadership without Easy Answers*. Cambridge, MA: Harvard University Press.

Knight, K., & Schwarzman, M. (2006). *Beginners Guide to Community-Based Arts*. Oakland: New Village Press.

Korten, D. (2006). *The Great Turning: From Empire to Earth Community*. San Francisco: Berrett-Koehler Publishers.

Kretzmann, J., & McKnight, J. (1993). *Building Communities from the Inside Out: A path toward Finding and Mobilizing a Community's Assets*. Skokie, IL: ACTA Publications.

Lappe, F. (2006). *Democracy's Edge: Choosing to Save Our Country by Bringing Democracy to Life*. San Francisco: Jossey-Bass.

Linn, K. (2007). *Building Commons and Community*. Oakland: New Village Press.

Lohan, T. (2008). *Water Consciousness: How We All Have to Change to Protect Our Most Critical Resource*. San Francisco: AlterNet Books.

Marks, W. (2001). *The Holy Order of Water: Healing Earth's Waters and Ourselves*. Great Barrington, MA: Bell Pond Books.

McKibben, B. (2008). Global Warming and Water Shortage: Different Faces of the Same Dilemma. In T. Lohan (Ed.), *Water Consciousness: How We All Have to Change to Protect Our Most Critical Resource* (p. 10). San Francisco: AlterNet Books.

O'Toole, J. (1996). *Leading Change: The Argument for Values-Based Leadership*. New York: Ballantine Books.

Putnam, R. (2000). *Bowling Alone: The Collapse and Revival of American Community*. New York: Simon and Schuster.

Western, S. (2008). *Leadership: A Critical Text*. London: Sage Publications.

Wheatley, M. (2002). *Turning to One Another: Simple Conversations to Restore Hope to the Future*. San Francisco: Berrett-Koehler Publishers.

Wheatley, M. (2005). *Finding Our Way*. San Francisco: Berrett-Koehler Publishers.

9 The Agrarian Mind and Good Leadership

Harvesting Insights from the Literary Field of Wendell Berry

Paul Kaak

INTRODUCTION

For more than 100 years, scholars of leadership have been harvesting their schemas from the soil of industrial thought. Our understanding of leadership has grown from ideas such as efficiency based on mechanization, the increase of speedy transportation and communication, and the extraction of natural resources for use as fuel. But as Rost (1991) suggests, while the prevailing school of leadership remains stuck in the industrial paradigm, "much of our thought and practice in other aspects of life have undergone considerable transformation to a postindustrial paradigm" (p. 100). In response to Rost, what could be more "postindustrial" than an agrarian farmer? What could do more for leaders and scholars who are "still caught up in the industrial paradigm" than to leave the factory and head back to the farm? Here is a metaphor, concrete and available to the imagination, that can inspire new thinking about leadership.

And the time is ripe. Today there is an outcry for leadership practices in all domains that will support the return to healthy land, resources, and communities. Leaders with a commitment to sustainability will have a different vision and a new set of values that run counter to their industrial forebears. While modern industry has tended to exploit resources (both natural and human) for economic gain narrowly defined, leaders with eco-awareness are realizing that such gain is secured by means of even greater losses. Farmer and author Wendell Berry has contributed to this renewed awareness. He suggests that:

> The costs are in loss of soil, in loss of farms and farmers, in soil and water pollution, in food pollution, in the decay of country towns and communities, and in the increasing vulnerability of the food supply system. The statistics of productivity alone cannot show these costs. We are nevertheless approaching a 'bottom line' that is not on our books. (1987, p. 128)

Berry is considered by many to be the 20th century's major spokesperson for the agrarian mind (Wirzba, 2003; Peters, 2007). In this chapter, I call upon Berry as a mentor to leaders of the emerging postindustrial paradigm. His mind-set, methods, and well-considered agrarian worldview will serve as seedlings for a harvest of rich insights about good leadership.

WHO IS WENDELL BERRY?

"I seem to have been born with an aptitude for a way of life that was doomed" (Berry, 2004, p. 172). Wendell Berry is a farmer-author from Kentucky, where he has lived his entire life, except for a few short years when he was a student on the west coast. He grew up in a farm family that stewarded the land in the same rural community where Berry, his wife Tanya, and their children have lived and worked for over 40 years.

Berry has written more than 40 books of poetry, essays, and fiction. Via their own unique literary voice, each genre retains his essential message. While his agrarian essays are the clearest articulation of his point of view, the stories in Berry's fiction illustrate how a small rural community has coped with enormous change over the last 100 years. His poetry is not romantic and sentimental. Rather, it is focused on what is real. His land and home are the primary sources for his verse in which he occasionally takes up the alternative persona of the "mad farmer."

In a published letter, Berry's Stanford University writing teacher Wallace Stegner (1991) comments that Berry has been "apparently immune to the Angst" of his times and therefore writes books that are "revolutionary" (p. 49). He adds that Berry's books "fly in the face of accepted opinion and approved fashion. They reassert values so commonly forgotten or repudiated that, re-asserted, they have the force of novelty" (p. 50). "He is," says David Orr, "widely admired for his literary gifts and wisdom, yet much dismissed" (2003, p. 171). Early in his career as a writer, Berry accepted this dismissal as part of his calling. In his poem "The Contrariness of the Mad Farmer" (1970) he says: "I am done with apologies. If contrariness is my inheritance and destiny, so be it. If it is my mission to go in at exits and come out at entrances, so be it" (p. 44).

As an outsider to both the academic and applied scholarship of leadership, Berry's voice offers insights found nowhere else, insights that are highly critical of what is and boldly idealistic regarding what should be. In a recent collection of essays dedicated to Berry, philosopher Stanley Hauerwas (2007) comments on "an oft-made criticism that Berry's agrarianism is utopian." He responds that "it is clear Berry's life and work are not utopian but as real as the dirt he farms" (pp. xi–xii). David Orr (2003) speaks to the extensive significance of Berry's essays in noting: "Agrarianism . . . is no small whittled-down philosophy for rural folks. It is a full-blown philosophy rooted in the realities of soil and nature as 'the standard' by which we also come to judge much more . . . The logic of agrarianism, in Berry's work, unfolds like a fractal through the division and incoherence of the modern world" (p. 184). The sum total of his body of work is "an incisive critique of industrial, corporate capitalism and the concepts of autonomy and freedom it rests upon, as well as a provocative blueprint for an alternative, ecologically sensitive agrarian society based on the value of stewardship," according to political philosopher Kimberly K. Smith (2003, p. 3).

AGRARIANISM AND INDUSTRIALISM IN CONTRAST

American history is rooted in agrarianism. Although modern society sees progress in the transition from agriculture to industrial culture, Berry and his literary kin continue their bellwether cry to not forget the agrarian way. Norman Wirzba (2003) states, "there are good reasons to suggest that a culture loses its indispensable moorings, and thus potentially distorts its overall aims, when it foregoes the sympathy and knowledge that grows out of cultivating (*cultura*) the land (*ager*)" (p. 1). Wirzba, an advocate of Berry's perspective, offers agrarianism as an alternative, describing it as "a deliberate and intentional way of living and thinking that . . . is not simply the concern or prerogative of a few remaining farmers, but it is rather a comprehensive worldview that holds together in a synoptic vision the health of land and culture" (pp. 4–5). In his essay "The Whole Horse," Berry (2003b) seeks to persuade the reader of the value of agrarianism over against industrialism. He states:

> The fundamental difference between industrialism and agrarianism is this: Whereas industrialism is a way of thought based on monetary capital and technology, agrarianism is a way of thought based on land. Agrarianism . . . is a culture at the same time that it is an economy. Industrialism is an economy before it is a culture. Industrial culture is an accidental by-product of the ubiquitous effort to sell unnecessary products for more than they are worth. (p. 116)

In "The Agrarian Standard" Berry (2003a) says, "What we [agrarians] have undertaken to defend is the complex accomplishment of knowledge, cultural memory, skill, self-mastery, good sense, and fundamental decency—the high and indispensable art—for which we probably can find no better name than 'good farming'" (p. 24).

The connections to leadership become more apparent in noticing that good leaders and true agrarians carry the same general objective: to work for increased probability that people, places, and products will be sustainable, healthy, and life-giving. True empowerment for leaders and cultivators is manifested in the development of followers and fields that have the capacity to produce what is good in independent and proper ways. Leaders interested in sustainability may have much to learn, therefore, from farmers and visionary agrarian thinkers like Berry, whose single-minded commitment is to the agrarian worldview and its moral implications. As K. B. Miller (1971) suggests, "Moral value . . . is not separable from other values. An adequate morality would be ecologically sound; it would be esthetically pleasing. But the point I want to stress here is that it would be practical" (p. 165).

What does Berry's particular form of agrarianism contribute to leadership that is good in both moral and practical terms, resulting in sustainability? To answer this question, recall that sustainability is more than simply delaying, for example, the increase in global warming and dependence upon fossil fuels. Calhoun and Cortese (2005) note: "Sustainability is not just about the environment. All challenges are interdependent and must be addressed in order to create a healthy, just, and sustainable society" (p. 1). Seen in this light, Berry's writings connect the agrarian standard to important concerns in the work good leaders do. Three of these issues—vision, values, and virtue—will now be considered in turn.

LEADERSHIP AND THE AGRARIAN VISION

Bennis and Nanus (1985) give what has become the standard definition of vision: "a mental image of a possible and desirable future stage of the organization." Such a vision is "a condition that is better in some important ways than what now exists" (p. 89). Berry's agrarian vision, as we shall see, is not limited to organizations. In fact, it is this specialization of vision that results in unsustainable communities and consequently implores leaders to consider Berry's proposed better way.

Berry (1972) defines his vision at the conclusion of one of his longest essays, "Discipline and Hope." He says, "What I have been preparing at such length to say is that there is only one value: the life and health of the world" (p. 164). Upon reading such a simple statement, the thoughtful reader may wonder about the many other issues that might be folded into a leader's vision. Berry's reply is that "[m]oral, practical, spiritual, esthetic, economic, and ecological values are all concerned ultimately with the same question of life and health" (p. 164). He is advocating a vision for the care of physical places and the communities of people that reside and work within them. Berry takes pains in his writings to show that when this vision is compromised, the consequences do not limit themselves to the declining farm communities:

> In a national and increasingly international industrial economy, the land-dependent people who do the actual work of production are served last; their places and communities are served not at all . . . The catch is that this is bad for everybody. Even the richest beneficiaries of the present economy cannot prosper indefinitely in a country, or a world, of devastated landscapes populated by the poor, the exploited,

> and the unemployed. Finally, the bills will be delivered, and everyone will pay. (Berry, 2003b, p. 138)

Here he is doing visionary work as defined by Max De Pree, former CEO of the Herman Miller furniture company. De Pree (1989) contends, "The first responsibility of a leader is to define reality" (p. 9). Kimberly Smith (2003) points out that Berry's "starting point is always our current social and political situation" (p. 122). She unpacks Berry's vision of current reality as:

> a complex combination of cultural, ecological, and economic practices and institutions that are, he claims, resulting in ecological and cultural decay. He compares this state of affairs with his own richly imagined alternative, a set of social practices that embody a different moral vision. (p. 122)

To illuminate his vision, Berry articulates what one might call the "interconnectedness" of local life within an interlocking system of systems. Individuals live within a community, the community is situated upon a particular place, and so on:

> The definitive relationships in the universe are thus not competitive but interdependent. And from a human point of view they are analogical. We can build one system only within another. We can have agriculture only within nature, and culture only within agriculture. At certain points these systems have to conform with one another or destroy one another. (Berry, 1997, p. 47)

He offers the picture of "a system of nested systems: the individual human within the family within the community within agriculture within nature" (1983, p. 46; see Figure 9.1).

Berry (1983) believes that: "So long as the smaller systems are enclosed within the larger, and so long as all are connected by complex patterns of interdependency, as we know they are, then whatever affects one system will affect the others" (p. 46). This vision goes far beyond the self-centeredness of a person or an entity such as an organization. Whereas Peter Drucker (1994) acknowledges that "organizations in the post-capitalist society . . . constantly upset, disorganize, and destabilize the community" (pp. 60–61), it is Berry's hope that this anthropocentric audacity be transformed into religious humility and mutually beneficial cooperation.

Unfortunately, the modern worldview is not set up to abide by Berry's recommendations in either the largest or the smallest applications. The rule of the day is specialization, which mitigates against sustainable behaviors in the lives of people and institutions. While Berry (1997) recognizes the benefits that specialization brings to the larger social system, he suggests

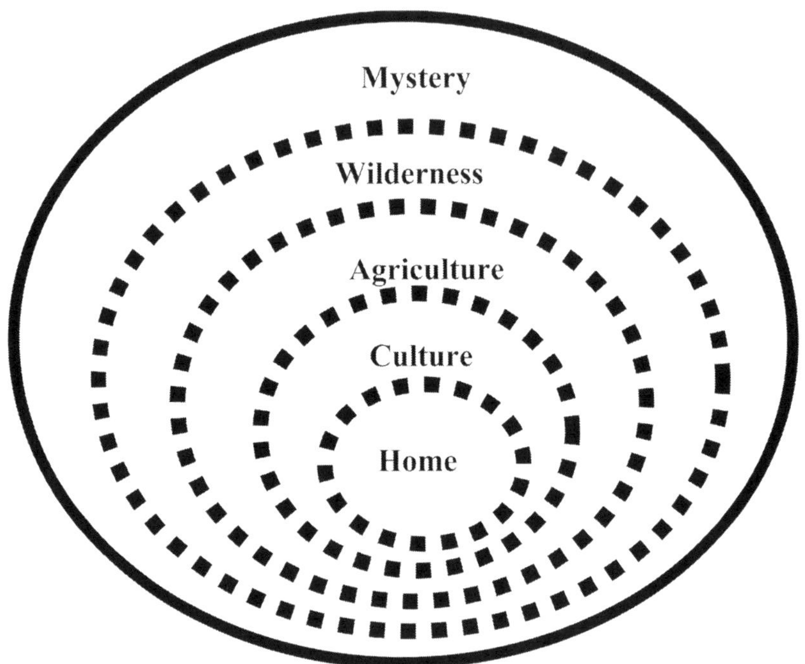

Figure 9.1 Wendell Berry's "system of nested systems."

that when we consider specialization from the point of view of individual persons:

> We . . . begin to see the grotesquery—indeed, the impossibility—of an idea of community wholeness that divorces itself from any idea of personal wholeness . . . Specialization is thus seen to be a way of institutionalizing, justifying, and paying highly for a calamitous disintegration and scattering-out of the various functions of character: workmanship, care, conscience, responsibility. (p. 19)

In response, it seems likely that Berry (1983) would advise leaders to apply what he calls "the unspecialized imagination":

> The winged imagination, the imagination free and unfettered, is the specialized imagination. The unspecialized imagination [on the other hand] may imagine a farm, a favor, a community, a marriage, a family, a household, a city, a poem—but only as a first step. Having imagined one, it will then strive to imagine the relation of that one to all the rest. It is, thus, a disciplined imagination. It is a formal imagination. It is

> concerned with relation, dependence, propriety, proportion, balance. (pp. 89–90)

This view of the imagination can be illustrated from a scene in Berry's fictional book *A World Lost*. Berry envisages Andy Catlett recalling a farm that "was beautifully laid out, so that all the rows followed the contours of the ridge . . . The design of the field would have been my father's work: a human form laid lovingly upon the natural conformation of the place" (Berry, 2002b, p. 317). Andy then recalls something of a vision he had, a point of awareness as he looked over the field: "I saw how beautiful the field was, how beautiful our work was. And it came to me all in a feeling how everything fitted together, the place and ourselves and the animals and the tools, and how the sky held us" (p. 318). The agrarian vision is communal, necessarily complex, and comprehensive. Postindustrial leaders will apply these ideals to their work of clarifying the current reality and cultivating a hopeful image of the future.

LEADERSHIP AND AGRARIAN VALUES

Agrarians are concerned with values such as "well-tended land, good food, honest work, beauty, neighborliness" (Donahue, 2003, p. 37). The concept of values, however, is problematic in that the starting point for evaluating worth is not always clear. Anthropocentric philosophers utilize a subjective approach: something is a value if it has positive benefits for the one making the valuation. Ecocentric thinkers, on the other hand, grant intrinsic value to, for example, land, air, and water. For the former, values are instrumental. For the latter, values are linked to identity and purpose. Berry (1987) explains industrial values from an agrarian perspective, saying such values are based on three assumptions:

> Value equals price—that the value of a farm, for example, is whatever it would bring on sale . . . all relations are mechanical. That a farm, for example, can be used like a factory, because there is no essential difference between a farm and a factory . . . The sufficient and definitive human motive is competitiveness—that a community, for example, can be treated like a resource or a market, because there is no difference between a community and a resource or a market. (p. 168)

For most modern organizations, something has value, or is a value, if it leads to lucrative financial results, even if those results bring damage to a community. If the accumulation of monetary capital is a primary value held by a leader or organization, then treating topsoil unkindly may be deemed excusable (consciously or unconsciously) for the attainment of the benefits that this value accrues. For agrarians like Berry, good land is recognized as being valuable when its primary ontological purpose (supplying a healthy harvest) is viable. This perspective does assign land an instrumental value. But far from being presumptuous, this is an expectation that is dependent on agricultural land's *raison d'être*: to sufficiently feed those who steward it well. If this premise is accepted, the practice of nurture—not damage—will be in order.

When the essence of good land and its need to be treated in a way that sustains its health is not a value, exploitation becomes the accepted method and destruction the inevitable result. A leader who is working within the worldview of consumption will be tempted to think of nature as a resource warehouse for increasing short-term financial gain. Berry's agrarian diagnosis offers keen guidance to any leader whose value orientation does not make the spoils of conquest their fundamental reward.

Although he is pleading for a reexamination of industrial values, Berry doesn't reject economic values. Rather, he links them to another value that he calls "the practice of neighborhood." He states: "In a viable neighborhood, neighbors ask themselves what they can do or provide for one another, and they find answers that they and their place can afford" (Berry, 2003b, p. 74). Such neighborly practice "must be, in part, charitable, but it must also be economic, and the economic part must be equitable; there is significant charity in just prices" (pp. 74–75). Responding to the globalists' accusation that this is "protectionism," Berry retorts, "That is exactly what it is. It is protectionism that is just and sound, because it protects local producers and is the best assurance of adequate supplies to local consumers" (p. 75). In another place Berry (1990) notes:

> A good community . . . is a good local economy. It depends on itself for many of its essential needs and is thus shaped, so to speak, from the inside—unlike most modern populations that depend on distant purchases for almost everything and are thus shaped from the outside by the purposes and the influences of salesmen. (p. 158)

Berry's neighborly economic values can help leaders committed to sustainability set the course for reevaluating what is important in local contexts. This is precisely what Ronald Heifetz (1994) calls adaptive work, which attempts:

> to close the gap between reality and a host of values . . . This adaptive work involves not only the assessment of reality but also the clarification of values . . . To make progress, not only must invention and action change circumstances to align reality with values, but the values themselves may also have to change. (pp. 31, 35)

Usually such talk suggests "new values" for a new day. Berry would suggest that the values of yesterday are the values of tomorrow. For him, the goal is not to create new values, but to reactivate forgotten ones as we move into the impending future.

Berry (2001) does recognize, however, that a focus upon values alone is insufficient to produce either personal or societal change. He says:

> The danger . . . is that people will think they have made a sufficient change if they have altered their 'values', or had a 'change of heart' . . . The trouble . . . is that a proper concern for nature and our use of nature must be practiced, not by our proxy-holder [such as the corporations and government], but by ourselves. A change in heart or of values without a practice is only another pointless luxury of a passively consumptive way of life. (p. 13)

This insight leads to the conclusion that leaders committed to achieving sustainability must themselves be committed to practical virtue, a topic to which we now turn.

LEADERSHIP AND AGRARIAN VIRTUE

Berry's commentator Kimberly K. Smith (2003) asserts that his "form of moral reasoning belongs to a branch of philosophy known as virtue ethics, so called because it asks not only which actions are justified but what sort of persons we should strive to be, what virtues we should seek to cultivate" (p. 117). She suggests that "we read Berry's novels and essays as offering contextual justifications for his moral and social theories" (p. 122). In this way, the moral dimensions of agrarianism emerge.

In America it was Thomas Jefferson who first crafted a social vision that described "those who labor in the earth" as "the chosen people of God" and the nation's "most valuable citizens" (Koch & Peden, 1998, p. 259, 351). For him, farm life was about two things that would affect both individual and nation: economics, in which the farmer and nation avoid external dependence; and virtue, since farm life incorporates the disciplines of industry, humility, and frugality (Smith, 2003, p. 21). In order to extol agrarian work, Jefferson describes those who do no such work but are instead reliant upon others to feed them:

> Corruption of morals in the mass of cultivators is a phenomenon of which no age nor nation has furnished an example. It is the mark set on those, who, not looking up to heaven, to their own soil and industry, as does the husbandman, for their subsistence, depend for it on casualties and caprice of customers. Dependence begets subservience and venality, suffocates the germ of virtue, and prepares fit tools for the designs of ambition. (p. 259)

Berry's is a Jeffersonian vision (Berry, 1995, p. 49) with a postindustrial twist: "Jefferson hoped a republic of yeomen famers could avoid the political corruption stemming from concentration of wealth. Berry hopes that a republic of good farmers (and other responsible citizens) will sustain the environmental conditions necessary for a fully human life" (Smith, 2007, p. 50).

This is not to say that all good people, or good leaders, are farmers (Berry, 2003b). Berry is not so narrow. The greater concern is that proper disciplines, or practices, be devoted to the development of practical virtue for which agrarianism offers a promising framework. Berry (1972) the moral philosopher emerges when he says, "The discipline of ends is not discipline at all. The end is preserved in the means" (p. 131). Berry adds: "the closer we come to correct discipline, the less concerned we are with ends, and with questions of futurity in general. Correct discipline brings us into alignment with natural process, which has no explicit or deliberate concern for the future" (p. 138).

That is why Smith (2003) argues that in Berry, "Practices and virtues are thus mutually constitutive" (p. 161) and that this results in graceful work that "creates order and enriches the world, both materially and spiritually" (p. 162). Berry (1987) crafts a picture for our imagination as he writes:

> When the virtues are rightly practiced within the Great Economy [the interlocking system of systems mentioned earlier], we do not call them virtues: we call them good farming, good forestry, good carpentry, good husbandry, good weaving and sewing, good homemaking, good parenthood, good neighborhood, and so on. The general principles are submerged in the particularities of their engagement with the world . . . The work of the small economy, when it is understandingly placed within the Great Economy, minutely particularizes the virtues and carries principle into practice. (p. 74)

Right virtue is measured against right standards. To illustrate how standards and virtue are linked, Berry (1990) makes use of the word *amateur* as one who loves, contrasting this with typical professional standards, which are, he says:

> the standards of ambition and selfishness [and] are always sliding downward toward expense, ostentation, and mediocrity. They tend to always narrow the ground of judgment. But amateur standards, the standards of love, are always straining upward toward the humble and the best. They enlarge the ground of judgment. The context of love is the world. (p. 90)

Love, not selfishness; humility, not presumptuousness; contentment, not greed; propriety, not carelessness. These are the virtues that Berry believes will lead to a sustainable world. I maintain that Berry is practicing leadership as he helps readers and leaders see that becoming virtuous in the way he imagines will lead to a more sustainable world. In turn, leaders committed to sustainability must work to reorient people's paradigm regarding what is good and successful. Ethics professor Bill Shaw (1997) explains, "Virtuous behavior is identified with, and advances, a balanced and coherent notion of the good, and economic well being is only part of that good, not its entirety. It follows," he adds, "that virtuous behavior may advance some non-material aspect of the good even though that behavior is not efficient in the economic sense" (p. 36).

Upon hearing this kind of rhetoric, some leaders—whether in business, education, politics, or even religion—will disavow the priority of virtue in favor of more narrowly construed "results." And while that disavowal may allow for short-term effectiveness, we now live in an age when we must address the question of whether rejecting ultimate good will not lead us to social, ecological, and even economic self-destruction.

CONCLUSION

Ira Jackson (2008), the dean of the Peter F. Drucker Graduate School of Management, explains what he believes are Drucker's two main responsibilities of leaders: "1) They are responsible and accountable for the performance of their institutions and 2) They are also responsible for the community as a whole." Jackson says, "it's the second part that concerns me," and it is Berry's concern, too.

From Berry, leaders can learn that vision must be unspecialized, seen completely, the connections being clear, and having the health of the whole community as its ultimate concern. The vision is out there, beyond the leader's own particular institutional boundaries. Sustainability will result when the institution's vision and the community's vision are mutually dependent upon each other but not manipulatively codependent.

In *On Leadership*, John Gardner (1990) says, "A vision relevant for us today will build on values deeply embedded in human history and in our own tradition" (p. xi). Berry's values are deeply traditional and deeply relevant. And they are deeply concerned for communities since values are lived out in community. Leaders must mobilize people for problem solving that will inevitably involve a reassessment of values (Heifetz, 1994). Establishing sustainable communities is adaptive work, not technical work, and as such, leaders and followers need each other to clarify what is important. Burns (1978) believes that the result of this kind of leadership will be transforming for leaders, citizens, organizations, and neighborhoods.

Virtue, on the other hand, puts its focus on individuals. Virtue ethicists suggest that: "The virtuous person [finds] . . . no struggle to act on his view of the requirements of the situation. And, because there is no struggle, there may in fact be no actual 'balancing': he may just see what is called for, and do it" (Crisp & Slote, 1997, p. 14). Leaders are judged by how explicit the links are between their stated convictions and their actions. When leaders "go first" in terms of linking the virtues of sustainability to sustainable practice they "serve their constituents' desire to know more about the unknown; constituents can learn from their leaders' experiences and feel more comfortable knowing that they are not alone" (Kouzes & Posner, 1993, pp. 187–188). Virtuous leaders are trusted leaders and trusted leaders are agents of change.

And so, can Wendell Berry offer help to leaders interested in a sustainable world? Law Professor Eric Freyfogle (2007), one of Berry's most ardent supporters, says that to abide by Berry's ideal persons as found in his fiction may make it difficult to see his agrarian dreams realized. "The quiet leaders whom Berry admires most—the Mat Feltners and Wheeler Catletts, who display exceptional moral fiber . . . remain disengaged from public power . . . Berry's fictional leaders remain outsiders. They cope with change but do not shape it." Freyfogle goes on to advise, however: "We need Berry more than ever . . . At the same time, we need to attach his criticism to a realistic understanding of structural change and how it might come about" (2007, p. 191).

Yet Berry's vision *is* prophetic. Orr (2003) notes, "We don't much like prophets because they make us feel uneasy. They see things most prefer not to see, and say things many wish went unsaid" (p. 176). Here one wonders if even Berry has hope that his work is worth continuing. "I will not be altogether surprised to be told," Berry (2002a) states, "that I have set forth a line of thought that is attractive but hopeless . . . My aim is not hopelessness. I am not looking for reasons to give up. I am looking for reasons to keep on" (p. 317). Perhaps there is a cadre of leaders who are willing to see and hear uneasy truths. Perhaps a generation of citizen leaders—though not planting the seeds, tending the fields, and harvesting the crops—will rise up to share Berry's agrarian vision, values, and virtues. This would give Berry, and the rest of us, reasons to keep on.

REFERENCES

Bennis, W., & Nanus, B. (1985). *Leaders: The Strategies for Taking Charge*. New York: Harper and Row.

Berry, W. (1970). *Farming: A Handbook*. New York: Harcourt Brace Jovanovich.

Berry, W. (1972). *A Continuous Harmony: Essays Cultural and Agricultural*. San Diego, CA: Harcourt Brace and Company.

Berry, W. (1983). *Standing by Words*. San Francisco: North Point Press.

Berry, W. (1987). *Home Economics*. San Francisco: North Point Press.

Berry, W. (1990). *What Are People For?* San Francisco: North Point Press.

Berry, W. (1995). *Another Turn of the Crank*. Washington, DC: Counterpoint.

Berry, W. (1997). *The Unsettling of America: Culture & Agriculture*. San Francisco: Sierra Club Books.

Berry, W. (2001). *In the Presence of Fear: Three Essays for a Changed World*. Great Barrington, MA: The Orion Society.

Berry, W. (2002a). Hope. In A. Kimbrell (Ed.), *The Fatal Harvest Reader: The Tragedy of Industrial Agriculture* (pp. 317–321). Washington, DC: Island Press.

Berry, W. (2002b). *Three Short Novels*. Washington, DC: Counterpoint.

Berry, W. (2003a). The Agrarian Standard. In N. Wirzba (Ed.), *The Essential Agrarian Reader: The Future of Culture, Community, and the Land* (pp. 23–33). Lexington: University Press of Kentucky.

Berry, W. (2003b). *Citizenship Papers*. Washington, DC: Shoemaker and Hoard.

Berry, W. (2004). *The Long-Legged House*. Washington, DC: Shoemaker and Hoard.

Burns, J. (1978). *Leadership*. New York: Harper and Row.

Calhoun, T., & Cortese, A. (2005). *We Rise to Play a Great Part: Students, Faculty, Staff, and Community Converge in Search of Leadership from the Top*. Ann Arbor, MI: Society for College and University Planning.

Crisp, R., & Slote, M. (1997). *Virtue Ethics*. New York: Oxford University Press.

De Pree, M. (1989). *Leadership Is an Art*. New York: Doubleday.

Donahue, B. (2003). The Resettling of America. In N. Wirzba (Ed.), *The Essential Agrarian Reader: The Future of Culture, Community, and the Land* (pp. 34–51). Lexington: University Press of Kentucky.

Drucker, P. (1994). *Post-Capitalist Society*. New York: HarperBusiness.

Freyfogle, E. (2007). Wendell Berry and the Limits of Populism. In J. Peters (Ed.), *Wendell Berry: Life and Work* (pp. 173–191). Lexington: University Press of Kentucky.

Gardner, J. (1990). *On Leadership*. New York: Free Press.

Hauerwas, S. (2007). Foreword. In J. Peters (Ed.), *Wendell Berry: Life and Work* (pp. xi, xii). Lexington: University Press of Kentucky.

Heifetz, R. (1994). *Leadership without Easy Answers*. Cambridge, MA: Harvard University Press.

Jackson, I. (2008). We Must Recommit Ourselves to Working for the Common Good. *Inland Valley Daily Bulletin* (November 2). Retrieved from http://www-druckerinstitute.com/ShowPage.aspx?Section=RP&PageID=56

Koch, A., & Peden, W. (1998). *The Life and Selected Writings of Thomas Jefferson*. New York: Random House.

Kouzes, J., & Posner, B. (1993). *Credibility: How Leaders Gain It and Lose It, Why People Demand It*. San Francisco: Jossey-Bass.

Miller, K. (1971). *Ideology and Moral Philosophy: The Relation of Moral Ideology to Dynamic Moral Philosophy*. New York: Humanities Press.

Orr, D. (2003). The Uses of Prophecy. In N. Wirzba (Ed.), *The Essential Agrarian Reader: The Future of Culture, Community, and the Land* (pp. 171–187). Lexington: University of Kentucky Press.

Peters, J. (2007). *Wendell Berry: Life and Work*. Lexington: University Press of Kentucky.

Rost, J. (1991). *Leadership for the Twenty-First Century*. New York: Praeger.

Shaw, B. (1997). Sources of Virtue: The Market and the Community. *Business Ethics Quarterly*, 7(1), 33–50.

Smith, K. (2003). *Wendell Berry and the Agrarian Tradition: A Common Grace*. Lawrence: University Press of Kansas.

Smith, K. (2007). Wendell Berry's Political Vision. In J. Peters (Ed.), *Wendell Berry: Life and Work* (pp. 49–59). Lexington: University Press of Kentucky.

Stegner, W. (1991). A Letter to Wendell Berry. In P. Merchant (Ed.), *Wendell Berry* (pp. 47–52). Lewiston, ID: Confluence Press.

Wirzba, N. (2003). *The Essential Agrarian Reader: The Future of Culture, Community, and the Land*. Lexington: University Press of Kentucky.

10 Leadership from Below

Farmers and Sustainable Agriculture in Ethiopia

Ezekiel Gebissa

INTRODUCTION

In recent years the Ethiopian government has introduced several policy initiatives aimed at environmental rehabilitation, natural resource management, and conservation measures (Keeley & Scoones, 2000). Nyssen et al. (2004) claim that these policies have achieved some success by helping to restore the degraded environment and enhancing agricultural productivity. However, looking at the history of the last several decades, Bassi (2002) argues that the country's capacity to cope with environmental fluctuations has been steadily decreasing and the relationship between human communities and their living environment is now characterized by a "crisis in livelihood." Despite formal claims that particular policies are succeeding, what has not changed is that Ethiopia's poor farmers are highly dependent on natural resources for subsistence (Abegaz, 2004, p. 314). Although leaders in some developing countries have demonstrated a capacity to attend simultaneously to development concerns and environmental priorities (Steinberg, 2001), circumstances that contributed to success elsewhere have not yet obtained in Ethiopia.

In fact, the quest for food self-sufficiency in the face of diminishing resources and a high rate of population growth in Ethiopia has been adversely affected by a policy culture in which a network of experts in agricultural and related sciences, along with government officials, establish a dominant discourse intended to inform and shape policies. As successive regimes have struggled with food production amidst cyclical famines (Abegaz, 2004), they have exhibited a persistent tendency toward an authoritarian and centralized bureaucratic culture that is antithetical to bottom-up or decentralized practices and learning (Keeley & Scoones, 2000, pp. 53–54).

The Ethiopian experience illustrates the challenges that confront government officials trying to solve natural resource and other environmental problems from the top down. C. S. Holling (1995) suggests that policies aimed at managing ecosystems focus their attention narrowly on the crisis they intend to manage, mobilizing technological, economic, and administrative resources to reestablish control. But such successes gradually reduce the system's overall resilience, increase its vulnerability to disturbances that were once absorbed, and divert attention from the gathering crisis. Such outcomes are invariably the result of the fact that human institutions are not flexible enough to cope with the complexities of ecosystems (Holling, 1995, p. 8). However, as Holling suggests, the usual pattern could be broken by adaptive learning that creates new opportunities for the human inhabitants of the system. This kind of approach to policymaking seeks broad understanding of ecological, economic, and social behavior in order to prepare for inevitable shocks and surprises.

In this chapter I make use of Holling's perspective to argue that policymaking that presumes the certainty of scientific knowledge and policy implementation that ignores the need for adjustments are unlikely to initiate sustainable growth and to result in ecosystems recovery. On the other hand, a participatory approach, such as the one that the current Ethiopian government is said to have recently employed, which integrates local knowledge and farmer initiative into the policies that aim to achieve food self-sufficiency and environmental recovery, is more promising (Nyssen et al., 2004). At least with respect to Ethiopia, environmental leadership should take the form of adaptive leadership (Heifetz, 1994, 2006) that employs strategies that have shown tangible results in achieving food self-sufficiency and attaining a higher level of income while enhancing the natural environment.

This chapter will show that in contrast to the failed top-down leadership approach and agricultural policies of Ethiopian governmental leaders, farmers in the Harer highlands (Harerge province) in eastern Ethiopia have been able to develop environmentally responsible farming and resource management strategies that farmers elsewhere in Ethiopia have now adopted. They have led by the example of their success, but their leadership is rarely, if ever, recognized due to the fact that they do not occupy visible or acknowledged positions of authority. To understand the "leadership from below" that Harerge's farmers have provided, we need to redefine leadership, turning attention away from top-down patterns of authority in a political hierarchy and the common assumption that the leader–follower dyad is an immutable structure of leadership. Instead, we need to develop a wide-angle perspective that brings into focus the innovative methods of everyday men and women across different levels of society who find creative solutions to difficult and demanding problems, and influence others to follow their example (Heifetz, 2006; Badaracco, 2002). The example set by innovative actors at the grassroots levels affects outcomes so dramatically that the behavior of these actors, who are the farmers themselves, constitutes effective adaptive leadership for environmental sustainability in Ethiopia.

THE FAILURE OF LEADERSHIP FROM ABOVE

In the past half century, the failure of state-sponsored rural development strategies to create favorable circumstances for agricultural productivity and sustainable rural livelihoods and ecosystems has led not only to worsening conditions of life, but also to ecological degradation in the highlands of Ethiopia. With an ever-growing population and diminishing resources, per capita production has declined precipitously, resulting in a crisis of subsistence characterized by episodic food shortages and cyclical famines (McCann, 1990, pp. 389–390).

Defining the crisis as a technical problem that could be addressed successfully with existing know-how and current managerial and authoritative expertise, successive governments implemented agricultural policies that consistently focused on augmenting productivity by expanding state-owned or privately operated mechanized commercial farms and increasing the capacity of smallholder farmers. The modernization of agriculture of the imperial regime (1941–1974), the socialist agriculture championed by the military regime (1974–1991), and the Agriculture Led Development Industrialization (ADLI) of the current regime are all guided by the belief that the crisis of livelihood that farmers face would only be alleviated through the application of modern scientific and technical knowledge. However, far from resolving the crisis of subsistence, such policies have exacted severe human costs and resource depletion, rendering agriculture environmentally dissonant and socially destructive (Abegaz, 2004).

There is a fundamental reason why these policies failed. It is simply that to make decisions that could work at the farm level requires, above all, an understanding of the nature of the challenge at the local level. Planning decisions that are made centrally are rarely based on an understanding of the complexities and sophistication of highly diversified agricultural knowledge and practices. This occurs not because decision-makers deliberately ignore the local situation, but because they simply do not see it. And they don't see it because they are, in James C. Scott's (1998) phrase, "seeing like a state," that is, they are influenced by a planning mentality that tends to exclude consideration of local knowledge, interests, and technical know-how. However, according to Scott (1998), it is precisely this tendency to ignore the local level that explains why so many state-sponsored schemes for the improvement of human welfare fail. Put another way, it is "leadership from above" that failed.

THE INNOVATION OF FARMERS

The subsistence crisis in Ethiopian agriculture was in fact the type that Ronald A. Heifetz would describe as an "adaptive challenge" that cannot be met by existing approaches, current expertise, or proven decision-making methods. Adaptive challenges, Heifetz argues, "require solutions that lie outside the current way of operating" and call for "leadership that can engage people in facing challenging realities and then changing at least some of their priorities, attitudes, and behavior in order to thrive in a changing world" (Heifetz, 2006, p. 76). Put simply, the crisis was one that required farmers to make adjustments to their livelihood systems and change some of their long-held beliefs, priorities, attitudes, and behaviors (Heifetz & Laurie, 1999).

Rather than waiting for someone who is presumed to have the technical knowledge to solve their problems, ordinary farmers in the densely populated Harer highlands responded to food shortages by deploying strategies based on indigenous knowledge of the ecosystem, cultural farm management practices, and the ability to quickly respond to external economic opportunities. Realizing that the crisis of subsistence they faced required a fundamental change in their agricultural practices and cropping patterns, they made several modifications to their farming system and eventually adopted the cultivation of a high-value cash crop. These initiatives allowed them to achieve sufficient capital to move to nonfarming occupations, thus relieving the demographic pressure on land resources and, at least temporarily, resolving the crisis of subsistence they faced. The farmers adopted a new paradigm of farming that has helped them cope with, and in some cases, thrive, in a constantly changing demographic, biophysical, and socioeconomic environment (Mulatu & Kassa, 2001).

Their innovations were gradually adopted by farmers in southern and central Ethiopia (Anderson, 2007; Dessie & Kinlund, 2008). Today, even farmers in the northwestern highlands of Ethiopia, long known for its cereal cultivation (McCann, 1995), have adopted the farming strategies applied in the Harerge highlands, which are based on noncereal cash crops (Anderson, 2007, pp. 30–32). Where political leadership had failed to envision and communicate long-term strategies, farmers themselves led the way in achieving food security as well as income and environmental sustainability through a variety of innovations (Gebissa, 2008; Tefera, Perret, & Kristen, 2004; Feyissa & Aune, 2003). It is to these innovations that we now turn.

INTERCROPPING, MULTICROPPING, AND DIVERSIFICATION

To cope with the crisis more effectively, Harerge's farmers needed to learn a new set of priorities and habits and take responsibility for their own future, rather than perpetually expecting the authorities to deliver solutions. Harerge's smallholder farmers realized that government policies emphasizing modernization of farm implements and agricultural inputs were neither available nor effective. The innovation that the farmers eventually introduced was a culmination of experimentation and improvisation—the art of distinguishing what is precious and essential from what is expendable, combined with the courage to take the best from history and leave behind that which is no longer serviceable in order to thrive in the new environment (Heifetz, 2006).

At the heart of the crisis of subsistence was the problem of arable land scarcity caused by high population density and rate of growth, which farmers initially defined as a technical problem that could be addressed by making minor modifications to the farming system. In the 1940s and 1950s, they responded to the problem by increasing the cultivated fields through clearing vegetation (Brooke, 1956, pp. 171–172); reduction of the fallow areas (Risoud, 1987, p. 22); increased inputs of manure, fertilizers, or labor; or changes in farming practices, augmenting yield through irrigation, and bringing marginal lands under cultivation. In the long view, the measures were essentially temporary tactical responses to a long-term problem. By the late 1960s, the agrarian system remained under severe demographic pressure, despite the overall augmentation of the land area, reduction of fallowing time, and improvements in farming techniques.

The most effective innovation proved to be the shift to high-value perennial cash crops. Coffee, the main cash crop before World War II, had enjoyed favorable market conditions during the 1940s. It experienced the postwar price slump in the early 1950s and never recovered its status as the premier cash crop in the Harerge highlands. For the areas close to main highways leading to large urban centers, khat—a stimulant whose leaves are typically chewed—became the cash crop of choice for most farmers. Increasing demand for khat from the Horn of Africa and the Arabian Peninsula stimulated production, but the shift to khat cultivation was one in a series of decisions that farmers made at the farm level in response to the limitations imposed by population pressure on the agrarian system. A study of the cropping patterns of farming households in selected villages of the Harer highlands shows that the area covered by khat increased by an average of between 36 and 55 percent between the 1940s and the 1980s (Wibeaux, 1986, pp. 22–44; Risoud, 1987, p. 38). In the region as a whole, the acreage devoted to khat production in Harerge more than doubled between 1954 and 1961, from 7,400 to 17,300 acres (Getahun & Krikorian, 1973, pp. 370–373).

Khat provided an answer to the problem of severe land shortages that had dogged the agrarian production system for a long time. The primary reason for its increase was the shrub's proven ability to provide long-term yields (Peters, 1952, p. 16). The second reason for khat's success was related to the agrarian system's labor allocation patterns. Basically, khat needed little maintenance, taking little labor away from other crops during the annual crop calendar (Langlais, Weill, & Wibeaux, 1984). Thirdly, khat exhibited the characteristics of a classic cash crop. It was easily sold and often fetched high profits throughout the year (Getahun & Krikorian, 1973, p. 357). The fourth advantage of cultivating khat was the shrub's adaptability to a wide range of soil conditions and rainfall patterns. Khat could be cultivated on terraced hillsides interspersed with coffee trees. On lands that sloped rather gradually, khat was intercropped with sorghum, allowing for more productive land use in a way that is consistent with the overall farming strategy of maximizing cash income while maintaining food self-sufficiency. Finally, khat had a remarkable capacity to resist diseases and drought (Peters, 1952, p. 16).

Despite the surge in the khat production in 1960s, food crop production remained the dominant agricultural activity. Arable land consequently grew extremely scarce in the early mid-1970s. The average family had between 0.5 to 1.5 hectares. The farmers of Harer highlands believed that they could use their land to the best advantage and provide some crop insurance by growing several food crops together. One study, based on research conducted in 1968–1969, noted, "It is not uncommon to see as many as five kinds of crops interplanted in a field. The most usual crops that are found interplanted are sorghum, corn, [khat], beans and sweet potatoes" (Mekonnen, 1974, p. 8). The planting of diverse crops indicates the premium placed on food self-sufficiency. Sorghum occupied 33 to 53 percent of most families' farmland, followed by corn and khat. Most of the farming households maintained khat orchards in their cropping system, usually intercropped with other food crops (Miller & Mekonnen, 1965, pp. 18–19).

The common theme in all large and smallholdings' cropping systems was that most farming families exhibited the practice of maintaining food self-sufficiency and avoiding monoculture (Davis, Mohammed, & Wayt, 1965, pp. 12–16). Diversification was adopted as an insurance against land scarcity, disease, and pest infestations, but it was also evident that the smaller one's holding, the greater the tendency to increase the production of khat (Davis et al., 1965, pp. 25–26). As part of a diversified cropping system, khat not only fit well into the environment and the agricultural cycle of small-farm households, but also provided a regular source of income to meet household expenditure with a comparatively low labor investment (Miller, 1965, pp. 42–43). Khat also consistently maintained a price advantage over other crops (Gebre Michael, 1974; Birke, 1965).

Khat's relative profitability did not render other cash crops unattractive. While potential incomes were high, there were significant elements of risk in expanding the cultivation of khat. The leaves must be consumed within 48 hours of being cut. Consequently, not only were prices volatile but the market itself was unpredictable. In an effort to even out price fluctuation and retain more value from their own labor, producers diversified the cash crops they cultivated on their farms. From the mid-1960s on, there was increasing cultivation of vegetables, particularly of potato, especially in areas where irrigation was possible (Arity, 1969, p. 56). By the late 1960s vegetable production was the second highest cash earner for farming households, a logical response to the uncertainties of the khat market. Vegetables, particularly potatoes, enjoyed a much longer "shelf life" than khat. If market prices happened to be low, the tubers could remain in the ground for a few weeks. In this way, the potato provided income the whole year round because it could be harvested at any time if irrigation was available. In providing a continuous cash flow, potatoes possessed the characteristic that farmers appreciated in khat (Wibeaux, 1986, p. 50).

In observing the farming strategy of the period before the mid-1970s, one can only conclude that the subsistence imperative of the family comes first when farmers make decisions about selecting crops, allocating land, and deciding how much of the produce to sell. In the decade that followed the Ethiopian revolution of 1974, the production and marketing of khat assumed new patterns and significance. The cultivation of khat continued to increase, owing perhaps to the policy of land redistribution adopted by the revolutionary government, which initially gave farmers plots of their own over which they maintained usufructuary rights. However, although the farming households were entitled to make cropping decisions, the holdings they were granted were in some cases insufficient to sustain a household.

The revolutionary government's redistribution of land did not provide a lasting remedy for arable land shortage, but the ending of tenancy removed structural constraints on the region's agriculture in the sense that farmers were free to make decisions regarding the cropping patterns on their individual plots. The fact that land reform did not solve the main problem of Harerge's agriculture stimulated farmers to pursue new strategies for increasing production. One farmer summed up the new dynamics of agrarian change in Harerge quite succinctly: "One who possesses large tracts of land, relies on his land to produce enough for his family's sustenance. One who has less land, innovates to overcome his predicament" (interview with Mume Ahmed, Fala'ana, June 8, 1994).

Many farming families took up the production of marketable commodities by using irrigation to increase productivity and the levels of dry season production. However, not every area in Harerge was endowed with water resources and there was not enough irrigable land to distribute equally among all farmers. In the 1980s, after more than a decade of effort, the highest proportion of irrigated areas was just under 25 percent of the arable lands in Harerge (Storck, Bezabih, Berhanu, Andrzejo, & Shimelis, 1991). Farmers dealt with water scarcity by building new reservoirs, collection basins, and canals. Some farmers used whatever profits they made from the irrigated crops to purchase pumps for their own use and to rent out. In that sense, it is possible to say mechanical irrigation revolutionized the use and management of land and water, the scarcest resources of the agrarian system.

The high returns on investment and the perception of farmers described earlier indicate a marked change in the logic of production that informed farmers' decisions in regard to cropping patterns and the use of the available resources for production purposes. Before the Ethiopian revolution, the logic of production was to maintain self-sufficiency while progressively increasing cash crop production without jeopardizing food crop production. The new logic of production of the 1980s was to increase cash crop production as long as there was sufficient food in the market and the crops yielded sufficient cash (Gebissa, 2004, pp. 180–181). In both cases, the food security of the farming household was paramount in driving their cropping strategies. Even the commitment to cash crop production was premised on the basic assumption of maintaining a secure source of food. While khat cultivation may not prove to be a permanent panacea for Harerge's crisis of subsistence, the khat phenomenon explains how the commercialization of agriculture sustained the region's demographic weight of more than 400 inhabitants per square kilometer (Wakjira, 1989, p. 89).

EFFECTS OF KHAT PRODUCTION

The switch from the age-old, grain-dominated, cereal-coffee-livestock complex described in McCann (1995) to the cash crop–dominated mixed cropping regime was an adaptive decision. The conversion of khat to a high-value commodity created an opportunity for Harerge's farmers to improve their standard of living when most rural Ethiopians were experiencing a decline. The increase in financial prosperity has brought a number of commodities, including mattresses, blankets, clothing, household utensils, and building materials, to the villages and towns of farming communities and made them available at an affordable price. Electrification has reached some homes, and appliances such as tape players and television sets were found in small-town shops and even in some farmer's homes (Gebissa, 2004, pp. 179–186). These commodities have made life easier, more comfortable, and healthier for those who derive their livelihood from khat. High income from cash cropping proved to be the best strategy for achieving food security by allowing farmers to purchase food from grain surplus areas such as the neighboring Arsi province.

Using a different set of indicators, such as farmers' ability to send their children to school, having a kitchen for cooking, and a separate structure from the main dwelling for keeping livestock, studies have confirmed that khat producers enjoy a better quality of life than nonproducers (Tefera et al., 2004; Mulatu & Kassa, 2001). By the late 1980s, many farmers had become owners of minibuses, pickup trucks, and taxis, dominating the transport business in Harerge. The staple food of ordinary people also changed. Instead of the traditional bread made of sorghum, people ate rice, pasta, and canned food. Some families reabsorbed people who had gone to the cities but had not been able to succeed, hiring them as drivers for their commercial vehicles. Farmers generally radiated self-confidence, although some were unsure of the sustainability of the market for the leaf. The majority of farmers benefited from the high price of their khat, the only commodity whose price kept ahead of inflation and, during the command economy years of the late 1970s and 1980s, evaded government price controls (Gebissa, 2004, p. 181).

In addition to the improved cash income and its effects on food security, khat has positive agronomic consequences. As a tree crop, it halts the rate of erosion and land degradation. The integration of khat into the farming system has also benefited farmers directly by providing a temporary solution for the apparently intractable problem facing Harerge's agriculture—shortage of arable land. In Harerge, particularly in the eastern and central districts, as much as 90 percent of the land is cultivated and the average household land size had dwindled to an average of 0.84 hectares in 1990 compared to 1.1 hectares in 1980 and 1.5 hectares in 1965. In the 1980s, the average yield per hectare for sorghum was 19 quintals. Since it is impossible to survive on this quantity of sorghum, farming households must maximize the productivity of the available land. No other crop that the farmers adopted kept the price differential and profit margins of khat (Mulatu & Kassa, 2001, p. 99).

The most enduring impact of khat was the fact that its trade provided badly needed investment capital required for individuals to leave their farms in order to look for and develop nonagricultural opportunities elsewhere. Using khat-generated capital, many farmers have joined nonfarm occupations such as transport businesses, brick factories, filling stations, and small retail stores. These ventures have enabled farmers to extricate themselves from land that had become extremely scarce and had threatened the possibility of self-sufficiency. In this regard, khat did what policy planners would have never imagined they could do for farmers: move them to nonagricultural occupations, thereby easing demographic pressure on land and agricultural resources. It is interesting to note that farmers pursued diversified occupational strategies to cope with the challenges of agriculture, whereas policymakers sought to fix the existing problems of agriculture by perpetuating smallholder farms.

CONCLUSION

Too often studies of agrarian change are oriented to look at the development of governmental policies and to assess the relative success or failure of the attempts to implement those policies. These approaches regard rural producers as either supporters or resisters of state actions, but rarely as initiators of actions that affect their own lives. Government policies that centered on prescribing the strategies farmers must follow, without taking into account the views of farmers themselves, have not succeeded in bringing about agrarian transformation. It seems Harerge's farmers have identified a successful rural development strategy of using their cash wealth to enter nonfarm life. Their success has inspired farmers elsewhere in the country to follow their "lead," shift to a high-income cropping regime, and thrive in a changing world. Significantly, it has compelled scholars of agricultural development and environmental management to recognize the wisdom of local knowledge (Klingele, 1998; Mulatu & Kassa, 2001; Feyissa & Aune, 2003) and forced policymakers to leave them alone.

While I have argued that the Harerge farmers' strategic activity represents an informed, conscious, and forward-looking adaptive response to changing market situations, political adversities, environmental challenges, and family considerations, khat production alone cannot be the basis of sustainable rural development. Neither should a policy strategy that envisions nearly 90 percent of Ethiopia's population to continue to earn its livelihood from farming in a country where the farming resource is under severe demographic pressure be considered adaptive or forward-looking. The essence of the farmers' "leadership from below" lies in the diversification of the regional economy and moving away from rural development strategies guided by the doctrinaire assumption that farmers must be helped to become better farmers. Indeed, they need to be able to move to nonfarm economies and cease to be farmers.

The experience of Harerge farmers has important implications for environmental leadership and policymaking. Acknowledging the potential of traditional knowledge for improving agricultural productivity without endangering environmental sustainability is an important step in the right direction. The activities of Harerge's farmers initiated a social process that might be described as adaptive leadership whose particular aspects included learning from mistakes, understanding the unpredictability of nature in society, and delving down to the root of the problem rather than avoiding it (Heifetz, 1994). In that sense, the farmers themselves might not be aware of it, but they are leading by example. Positional leaders must acknowledge the pivotal role played by those on the "leading edge" of change in finding solutions to the problems they face. Political leaders and policymakers, rather than dismissing farmers as conservative opponents of progress, should incorporate such "leadership from below" in their own leadership and decision-making. Policymakers in Ethiopia must regard the development of diversified agriculture and, beyond that, the diversification of the overall economy in Harerge as a success. To allow and even to encourage farmers to be involved in the continual experimentation, adaptation, and transformation of the structures in which they live will ensure that the solutions devised by the present generation will enhance rather than irreparably damage the ability of future generations to meet their needs (World Commission on Environment and Development, 1987).

REFERENCES

Abegaz, B. (2004). Escaping Ethiopia's Poverty Trap: The Case for a Second Agrarian Reform. *Journal of Modern African Studies, 42*(3), 313–342.

Anderson, D. (2007). *The Khat Controversy: Stimulating the Debate on Drugs (Cultures of Consumption).* Oxford: Berg.

Arity, L. (1969). *A Regional Study of Hara Maya Based on the Studies of the Alemaya College of Agriculture.* BA essay, Department of Agricultural Economics, Haile Sellassie I University.

Badaracco, J. (2002). *Leading Quietly: An Unorthodox Guide to Doing the Right Thing.* Cambridge, MA: Harvard University Press.

Bassi, M. (2002). The Making of Unsustainable Livelihoods: An On-Going Tragedy in the Ethiopian Drylands. *Policy Matters, 10,* 7–10.

Birke, L. (1965). *A Survey of the Marketing Methods and Facilities in Alemaya District Imperial Ethiopian College of Agricultural.* Dire Dawa: Haile Sellassie I University.

Brooke, C. (1956). *Settlements of the Eastern Galla, Hararge Province, Ethiopia.* PhD dissertation, Department of Geography, University of Nebraska.

Davis, K., Mohammed, A., & Wayt, W. (1965). *Farm Organization of Terre and Galmo Villages: Harer Province, Ethiopia. Imperial Ethiopian College of Agricultural and Mechanical Arts, Experiment Station Bulentin No. 42.* Alemaya: Imperial Ethiopian College of Agriculture and Mechanical Arts.

Dessie, G., & Kinlund. P. (2008). Khat Expansion and Forest Decline in Wondo Genet, Ethiopia. *Geografiska Annaler: Series B, Human Geography, 90*(2), 187–203.

Feyissa, T., & Aune, J. (2003). Khat Expansion in the Ethiopian Highlands: Effects on the Farming System in Habro District. *Mountain Research and Development*, 23 (2), 185–189.

Gebissa, E. (2004). *Leaf of Allah: Khat and the Transformation of Agriculture in Harerge, Ethiopia, 1875–1991.* Oxford: James Currey.

Gebissa, E. (2008). Scourge of Life or an Economic Lifeline: Public Discourses on Khat (catha edulis) in Ethiopia. *Substance Use and Misuse, 43*(6), 784–802.

Gebre Michael, D. (1974). *The Kottu of Harerge: An Introduction to the Eastern Oromo. Imperial Ethiopian College of Agriculture Experiment Station Bulletin (62).* Dire Dawa: Haile Selassie I University, College of Agriculture.

Getahun, A., & Krikorian, A. (1973). Khat: Coffee's Rival from Harar, Ethiopia, I. Botany, Cultivation and Use. *Economic Botany, 27*(4), 353–377.

Heifetz, R. (1994). *Leadership without Easy Answers.* Cambridge, MA: Harvard University Press.

Heifetz, R. (2006). Anchoring Leadership in the Work of Adaptive Progress. In F. Goldsmith (Ed.), *The Leader of the Future 2: Visions, Strategies, and Practices for the New Era* (pp. 73–84). New York: Jossey-Bass.

Heifetz, R., & Lauire, D. (1999). Mobilizing Adaptive Work: Beyond Visionary Leadership. In J. Conger (Ed.), *The Leader's Change Handbook* (pp. 55–86). New York: Jossey-Bass.

Holling, C. (1995). What Bridges, What Barriers? In L. Gunderson, C.

Holling, & S. Light (Eds.), *Barriers and Bridges to the Renewal of Ecosystems and Institutions* (pp. 3–34). New York: Columbia University Press.

Keeley, J., & Scoones, I. (2000). Knowledge, Power and Politics: The Environmental Policy Making Process in Ethiopia. *Journal of Modern African Studies, 38*(1), 89–120.

Klingele, R. (1998). *Harerge Farmers on the Crossroad between Subsistence and Cash Economy.* Unpublished report, UNDP-Emergency Unit for Ethiopia, Addis Ababa, Ethiopia, United Nations Emergency Unit for Ethiopia.

Langlais, C., Weill, M., & Wibeaux, H. (1984). *Farming Systems Research: Preliminary Report and Future Programme.* Alemaya: Alemaya University of Agriculture.

McCann, J. (1990). A Great Agrarian Cycle? Productivity in Highland Ethiopia, 1990 to 1987. *Journal of Interdisciplinary History, 20*(3), 389–416.

McCann, J. (1995). *People of the Plow: An Agricultural History of Ethiopia, 1800–1990.* Madison: University of Wisconsin Press.

Mekonnen, T. (1974). *Economic and Sociological Characterstics of Peasant Families at Alemaya: The Cherch Highland.* Dire Dawa: Department of Agricultural Economics and Business, College of Agriculture, Haile Sellassie I University.

Miller, L. (1965). *Input-Output Data for Chat and Sorghum Production, Harer Highlands, Ethiopia. Experiment Station Bulletin.* Alemaya: Imperial Ethiopian College of Agriculture and Mechanical Arts.

Miller, L., & Mekonnen, T. (1965). *Organization and Operation of Three Ethiopian Case Farms. Experiment Station Bulletin.* Alemaya: Imperial Ethiopian College of Agriculture.

Mulatu, E., & Kassa, H. (2001). Evolution of Smallholder Mixed Farming Systems in the Harar Highlands of Ethiopia: The shift towards Trees and Shrubs. *Journal of Sustainable Agriculture, 18*(4), 81–112.

Nyssen, J., Haile, M., Moeyersons, J., Poesen, J., & Deckers, J. (2004). Environmental Policy in Ethiopia: A Rejoinder to Keeley and Scoones. *Journal of Modern African Studies, 41*(1), 137–147.

Peters, D. (1952). Khat: Its History, Botany, Chemistry and Toxicology. *Pharmaceutical Journal, 169*, 16–18, 36–37.

Risoud, G. (1987). *Evolution of Peasant Agriculture in the Eastern Harerge Highlands: Development Prospects. Farming Systems Research.* Alemaya: Alemaya University of Agriculture.

Scott, J. (1998). *Seeing Like a State: How Certain Schemes to Improve the Human Condition Have Failed.* New Haven, CT: Yale University Press.

Steinberg, P. (2001). *Environmental Leadership in Developing Countries: Transnational Relations and Biodiversity Policy in Costa Rica and Bolivia.* Cambridge, MA: MIT Press.

Storck, H., Bezabih, E., Berhanu, A., Andrzejo, B., & Shimelis, W. (1991). *Farming Systems and Farm Management Practices of Smallholders in Harerge Highlands. Farming Systems and Resource Economics in the Tropics 11.* Kiel: Wissenschafts Verlag.

Tefera, T., Perret, S., & Kristen, J.(2004). Diversity in Livelihoods and Farmers' Strategies in the Harerge Highlands, Eastern Ethiopia. *International Journal of Agricultural Sustainability, 2*(2), 133–146.

Wakjira, M. (1989). *An Economic Analysis of the Development for the Alemaya Lake Sub-Watershed with Special Reference to Soil and Water Conservation Methods.* MSc thesis, Department of Agricultural Economics, Alemaya University of Agriculture.

Wibeaux, H. (1986). *Agriclture in the Highlands of Harerge, Kombolcha Area: Study of Six Farms.* Dire Dawa: Farming Systems Research, Alemaya Univerisity of Agriculture.

World Commission on Environment and Development. (1987). *Our Common Future.* Oxford: Oxford University Press.

11 The League of Nations and the Problems of Health and the Environment

Leadership for the Common Good in Historical Perspective

Michael D. Callahan

INTRODUCTION

The idea that nations and peoples share certain interests across national boundaries and should cooperate in achieving common objectives is an old one in the history of international relations (Iriye, 2002; Kennedy, 2006) and historians since Herodotus have studied leaders. More recently, the field of leadership studies has examined the role of leadership in confronting specific global problems, including those concerning the interdependent relationship between human health and the environment. In *Leadership for the Common Good: Tackling Public Problems in a Shared-Power World*, Barbara C. Crosby and John M. Bryson note: "Today's citizens live in a world where no one is in charge, where the needed resources for coping with the most important public problems extend well beyond the capacity of any group or organization, and often beyond the scope of national governments" (2005, p. xiv). As a consequence, "shared and widespread leadership is required for dealing with the effects of global complexity and interdependence, from economic shifts to climate change to terrorism" (Crosby & Bryson, 2005, p. xiv).

Crosby (1999) identifies the types of leadership that can best promote the forms of "global citizenship" and build the "transnational community" needed in this "shared power, no-one-in-charge world" (p. 5). She argues that "leaders in the global commons need to think systematically and holistically about the process of tackling public problems that spill beyond national boundaries" (p. 175). Understanding the nature of shared power within an international context and the forms of leadership required for a multipolar world will help "global citizens" of a "transnational community" achieve common aims.

Equally important is understanding the limitations and dangers of leadership in such a "shared-power world." In *Bad Leadership: What It Is, How It Happens, Why It Matters* (2004), Barbara Kellerman reminds us that there are no leaders without followers and that both interact within a larger social, political, and economic context. She also contends that not only are the concepts of leadership and power interconnected, but "we must come to grips with leadership as two contradictory things: good and bad" (2004, p. 14). While some leaders and followers are effective and ethical, others are incompetent, rigid, callous, insular, or evil. Above all, Kellerman argues that the single best explanation for why leaders lead and followers follow is self-interest. If followers want better leaders, it is up to the followers to demand change from leaders (Kellerman, 2004, p. 243; see also Kellerman, 2008).

Combining Crosby and Bryson's arguments with those of Kellerman provides a general analytical framework for assessing the role of leadership for the common good within an international context. What is missing is a broad historical perspective that tests these theoretical models against the documentary evidence. A study of the League of Nations offers such a perspective. Nearly a century ago, the League became the first international organization designed to preserve peace by means of a system of sovereign states working collectively. Established in Geneva as a consequence of the First World War, the member states of the League promised "to promote international co-operation and to achieve international peace and security" by accepting the rule of international law, promoting justice, and respecting treaty obligations (Scott, 1973, pp. 407–418). Throughout the 1920s and 1930s, the League was responsible for addressing a wide range of global problems such as controlling the international arms trade, aiding refugees, protecting ethnic minority groups, promoting human rights, fostering intellectual cooperation, encouraging economic cooperation, and supervising the administration of peoples in Africa, the Middle East, and the Pacific (Walters, 1952). Such tasks marked what one historian calls "the world's first sustained and consequential experiment in internationalism" (Pedersen, 2007, p. 1116). With the collapse of the Soviet Union and the reemergence of a multipolar global order in the early 1990s, the world of the League of Nations is remarkably similar to that of today.

Among the many issues the League grappled with were those concerning health and nature. According to the Covenant of the League of Nations, member states pledged "to take steps in matters of international concern for the prevention and control of disease." They also agreed to cooperate in mitigating "suffering throughout the world." The Covenant made no direct reference to environmental issues. However, while organized efforts to protect the environment date from the 19th century, there were a number of new international nongovernmental organizations promoting cross-border environmental cooperation during this period. For example, the International Council for Bird Preservation was founded in London in 1922. The International Office for the Protection of Nature was created in 1928 (McCormick, 1989, pp. 22–23). Such groups appealed to public opinion and pressed the League to consider problems affecting wildlife.

This chapter first examines how the international community addressed specific problems of health and environment in the interwar period, and then analyzes the impact of two leaders who championed the aims and actions of the League in very different ways. It concludes that the League achieved important objectives as a result of a form of leadership that encompassed a shifting mix of scientists, technical experts, activists, diplomats, and politicians working with nongovernmental organizations, private foundations, business groups, national governments, and the permanent staff and officials in Geneva. Many of these achievements were tentative, imperfect, and incomplete. The League also failed in several crucial respects and illustrates what may not work as nations and peoples continue to confront serious global challenges in the 21st century. In particular, the history of the League does not support the optimistic conclusion that "almost anything is possible with enough leadership for the common good" (Crosby & Bryson, 2005, p. 363). Nonetheless, the League's relative successes in the 1920s and 1930s prove that Crosby and Bryson's concept of "leadership for the common good" in a "shared-power world" can be both effective and ethical.

LEAGUE LEADERSHIP ON HEALTH AND THE ENVIRONMENT

An international organization is unlike other organizations. The League of Nations was a product of international law. This type of law, which generally refers to the rules that govern the relations between sovereign states, is different from domestic or municipal law since there is no ultimate authority higher than the individual state (Boyle, 1999, pp. 7–24; Chen, 2000). The League relied on voluntary cooperation and the promises of governments to uphold their international obligations "in good faith." Yet this is not to suggest that international law had no binding force. International law was important to states since it established greater predictability in foreign relations, decreased potential international conflicts, and addressed problems that were beyond the control of any single state. The ultimate sanction for international law was public opinion and moral suasion, or what one contemporary legal scholar called the "mobilization of shame" (Zimmern, 1939, p. 472). In short, Geneva relied on various national interests, reinforced by the threat of public criticism, to encourage member states to act collectively for the common good (Rubin, 1997).

Using these powers, the League successfully combated epidemic disease and dramatically increased international health cooperation (Weindling, 1995; Ostrower, 1996, pp. 101–104). The First World War transformed international public health agencies. The spread of smallpox, cholera, dysentery, and typhus killed tens of thousands while many of the existing health care systems collapsed. A worldwide influenza pandemic from late 1918 to 1920 killed at least 50 million people. The League created an Epidemics Commission to help reorganize national health offices for controlling such diseases (Balińska, 1995). In addition to an office in Geneva that acted as a clearinghouse for information concerning global outbreaks of disease, the

League also opened the "Far-Eastern Epidemiological Intelligence Office" in Singapore that collected, standardized, and disseminated information concerning epidemics in Asia (League of Nations, January 1925, p. 9). A new "Maritime Quarantine Station" in Latvia helped to combat epidemics in Eastern Europe.

The League also established a Health Committee, later renamed the League of Nations Health Organization. It was a permanent body of experts drawn from around the world. The Health Organization supervised specialized agencies and technical commissions composed of governmental officials, medical specialists, and representatives from several private agencies. It enjoyed widespread approval including the active support of Americans despite the U.S. never formally joining the League. Two of the members were Americans, one of whom was the U.S. surgeon general, and the Rockefeller Foundation awarded over two million dollars to the League's health programs (Dubin, 1995, p. 72; Farley, 1995, pp. 203–221). The League's Health Organization saved or improved countess lives and had an impact on every continent. It distributed medicines and vaccines, sponsored educational campaigns, trained local health care providers, and established clinics for pediatric care. It subsidized campaigns to reduce sleeping sickness in colonial Africa (Callahan, 2004, pp. 38, 72, 130). The League also provided assistance to reorganize or establish public health services, most notably in China where it virtually took over the entire public health system. Iraq, Iran, Liberia, and countries in the Balkans also received direct technical assistance. As a result, there were declines in reported cases of malaria and tuberculosis as well as a greater global awareness of public hygiene and nutrition (League of Nations, February 1926, p. 43; League of Nations, 1936).

Another success with implications for human health and the environment was the League's work to eliminate the use of white lead paint from residential applications. By the early 1920s, many within the scientific and medical community were convinced of lead's toxicity (Warren, 2000, pp. 1–43). In particular, it was known that workers in the lead-using industries suffered from the often acute and chronic effects of lead poisoning (Hamilton, 1929; Aub, 1926). In 1921, 400 delegates from 40 nations went to Geneva to discuss regulating the lead trades. The United States, however, refused to participate. America's rejection was due partly to the economic interests of paint manufacturers, particularly the National Lead Company, which owned the "Dutch Boy" trademark and the Sherwin-Williams Company whose slogan boasted that their paints "cover the earth." Powerful American painters' associations also opposed new regulations and praised lead paint's durability and performance. According to historian Christian Warren, "Trade unions and big business alike feared internationalism. Smug feelings of American superiority were largely to blame" (2000, p. 62). Nonetheless, American intransigence did not prevent the League of Nations from drafting an international convention to ban or restrict the use of lead paint for interior use. The agreement stipulated that interior paint could contain no measurable amount of lead while exterior paint was not to exceed 2 percent lead by weight (Warren, 2000, pp. 285–286). By the early 1930s, a number of European and Latin American countries were signatories, including the United Kingdom, France, Sweden, Spain, and Cuba (League of Nations, 1933).

The U.S. government did not adopt the ban until 1977. Warren estimates that between 1910 and 1977 over 4,000 tons of lead pigments were applied to millions of American homes and products (Warren, 2000, p. 63). One result was a dramatic increase in lead poisoning among children with a disproportionate number from poor and black families. Lead is especially dangerous to children and can cause nervous system damage, stunted growth, hearing loss, kidney damage, and delayed development (Reich, 1992; Richardson, 2005). The League's reforms undoubtedly saved or protected thousands of lives outside of the United States.

In addition to the dangers of lead paint, the League was responsible for increasing public awareness about the importance of safe drinking water, clean air, and green space in urban planning. One of the technical commissions the League's Health Organization supervised was the Housing Commission. In 1936, the Commission adopted a three-year plan to cooperate with the International Labor Organization to establish the "definition of the principles of modern hygiene as regards urban and rural housing, national urban and rural planning, and the placing of all the experience resulting from these studies at the disposal of administrations and legislative bodies" (League of Nations, March 1937, pp. 133–134). The Commission insisted on "essentially practical aims" and that "all the research work and all the technical effort must aim at the improvement of the living conditions" of individuals. Among the subjects it agreed to examine were natural and artificial lighting, water supply, sewage, waste and garbage disposal, and "density of the population, 'zoning,' and open spaces (gardens, parks, playgrounds, etc.)." Another issue was "noise and public health" since "[i]n noise, we are faced with an environmental problem which has markedly increased in significance in recent years with the development of mechanised civilisation" citing "radio sets," motor traffic, and road construction in urban areas as contributing to this problem. Overall, the project sought to foster collaboration between engineers, architects, town planners, biologists, clinicians, and medical experts on national noise levels while "establishing extensive and rational co-operation in the *international* sphere" as well (League of Nations, March 1937, pp. 133–134).

A problem of particular concern to the Housing Commission was what it called the "campaign against smoke and air pollution." In 1939 the Commission reported that it had spent nearly a year "working on the question of man's *outdoor* environment, both individual and collective." While risks to human health were the primary concern, the Commission stated:

> Smoke, toxic gases and dust result in the pollution of the atmosphere and it has been estimated in England that the total cost to the country of the smoke nuisance alone is at least eighty million pounds a year. The Commission examined methods of measuring the degree of pollution in the air, the effects of smoke, toxic gasses and dust and method[s] now available for combating these evils. (League of Nations, June 1939, pp. 248–249)

Thus, the League of Nations not only identified air pollution as a serious environmental danger, but was studying specific ways to control it for the common good.

In comparison to the global problem of human health, the League's efforts to protect wildlife or the natural world as ends in themselves were more limited. The modern environmental movement was in its infancy during the interwar period, with only a handful of states agreeing to preserve African game, protect migratory waterfowl, or suppress ivory smuggling (Hayden, 1942, pp. 21–113). The concept of protecting nature also meant different things to different groups, if it mattered at all. Still, the League of Nations did debate a proposal for the creation of a World Commission for Nature Protection in the early 1920s (Wöbse, 2003). In territories in Africa supervised by the League, corporate monopolies of the natural resources were prohibited (Callahan, 1999/2008, p. 195). During the Great Depression, the League created a special committee to study "the question of equal commercial access for all nations to certain raw materials" (Heald & Wheeler-Bennet, 1938, pp. 773–774). One purpose of the committee was to respond to complaints that states with overseas colonies were unfairly exploiting their natural resources (Crozier, 1988, pp. 210–215; Callahan, 2004, pp. 82, 87, 135). Among other ideas, the committee considered creating "an international mines and forests trust to be administered by the League of Nations, with the twofold object of guaranteeing joint control and free circulation of raw materials, and also their conservation" in these colonies (League of Nations, March 1937, p. 54). The trust would foster more open markets, but also place the conservation of natural resources under international supervision.

In the late 1920s, the League declared that whales needed "urgent international measures" to protect them from extinction and set up a committee of experts to find a solution (League of Nations, July 1929, p. 243). Representatives from Britain, Germany, Norway, Japan, the United States, and other principal whaling states participated (League of Nations, April 1930, p. 75). The result was an international convention, signed at Geneva in 1931, that prohibited the killing of several species of whales and required new controls over the whaling industry (League of Nations, September 1931, pp. 278–280; Hayden, 1942, pp. 148–172). It was signed by 26 states, ratified by 17, and applied throughout the entire world.

Throughout the 1920s, many were also aware of the problem of oil pollution (Hayden, 1942, pp. 106–113). It was still common for ships to flush out their empty oil tanks after a voyage, dumping the waste oil into coastal waters and streams. In 1934, Great Britain, a leading maritime power and the most influential member of the League, complained to Geneva about the effects of oil pollution on wildlife by pointing out "the suffering caused to sea birds whose bodies are covered with grease, which renders them incapable of movement and exposed them to death by starvation" (League of Nations, September 1934, p. 220). After noting the damage also done to fish and seaside resorts, the British government declared "it was ready to agree to any international measures for remedying the situation." The League quickly asked a committee of experts to draft a convention (League of Nations, January 1935, pp. 17, 238, 267). It was completed in late 1935 and the League agreed to convene an international conference to invite nations to sign it (League of Nations, October 1936, p. 302; November 1936, pp. 1196–1197, 1391–1395).

The conference, however, never occurred. Despite reports that "[t]he situation is obviously getting worse," three major maritime powers refused to cooperate (League of Nations, March 1937, p. 178; September 1938, p. 246). Italy, Germany, and Japan increasingly abandoned the League and its principles, making any meaningful agreement impossible. Still, Geneva's efforts were not in vain. The United Nations later used the League's text when drafting the International Convention for the Prevention of Pollution of the Sea by Oil in 1954, the first international treaty designed to protect the oceans from oil pollution (McGonigle, 1979).

TWO INTERNATIONAL LEADERS: WOODROW WILSON AND ALICE HAMILTON

Identifying a leader who, using Crosby's terms, could "think systematically and holistically about the process of tackling public problems" and who understood the need for building a "transnational community" is relatively easy when examining the League of Nations. The most prominent example is American president Woodrow Wilson who proposed the creation of the League and then convinced nations and peoples around the world to support it. Historian John W. Coogan offers perhaps the best assessment of Wilson's leadership:

> By 1917 [Wilson's] analysis of the roots of international conflict as extraordinarily sophisticated. He was the first world leader to recognize that the old world order could not be rebuilt, that to restore the system of uncontrolled nationalism and the balance of power would condemn humanity to continue an endless cycle of conflict. He sought to create a new system of international relations, one based on a League of Nations united under the democratic, progressive leadership of the United States and the British empire. The fact that the League, in the absence

> of American participation, fell short of Wilson's expectations does not detract from the genius of his vision. (1994, p. 86)

Wilson won the Nobel Peace Prize in 1919 for visionary and ethical leadership for the common good. Even though the United States never joined the organization he inspired, America's determination to remake the League after the Second World War into the current United Nations and establishing it in the city of New York owes much to Wilson. In many profound and long-lasting ways, Wilson's leadership succeeded, and continues to succeed, in ways that he could not have imagined or understood.

By the same token, Wilson fits Kellerman's definition of a "bad" leader in equally profound and long-lasting ways. While brilliant, Wilson was often erratic, rigid, and ineffective. Coogan rightly contends that "historians cannot allow the glory of the vision to distract attention from the consequences of Wilson's failure to achieve it. Noble failure in the highest cause remains failure" (Coogan, 1994, p. 86). While largely due to unintended consequences rather than by design, Wilson did not construct a lasting peace and in significant ways made conditions in the world worse, not better. He undermined the international organization he inspired, left Europe divided and weak, and angered many when he did not produce the changes he promised.

Yet, the measurable effective and ethical reforms the League did achieve required much more than Wilson's leadership. Geneva depended on others who shared the American president's broad ideals and values, but who cooperated and shared power in smaller ways to confront specific public problems over time. Discounting the role of such individuals not only distorts the historical significance of the League in general, but obscures the complex nature of the leader–follower relationship within the context of an international organization in particular.

An example of the type of person who cooperated with others to transform some of the League's stated aims into practical results was Dr. Alice Hamilton (Hamilton, 1943; Sicherman, 1984). One recent scholar contends that Hamilton "was this country's first great urban/industrial environmentalist" (Gottlieb, 2005, p. 83). After earning a medical degree in 1893, Hamilton worked in Chicago as a champion for progressive reforms to improve the lives of the immigrant poor. She was most concerned about workers being exposed to toxins, particularly lead dust. Her research proved that lead accumulated in the bones and was a serious danger to public health. In 1919, she was hired as the first woman on the faculty of Harvard Medical School.

Hamilton expanded her public influence nationally in the 1920s. She was an advocate for the so-called "radium girls," the women who were dying of cancer from exposure to the radium used to manufacture "glow-in-the-dark" watches and dials. She also fought the decision of General Motors, DuPont, and Standard Oil of New Jersey (now Exxon) to put poisonous tetraethyl lead into gasoline in the 1920s (Rosner & Markowitz, 1989). Charles F. Kettering, vice president for research at General Motors, and his assistant, Thomas A. Midgley, Jr., insisted that the new additive not only prevented "engine knock" and increased fuel efficiency, but was safe despite reported fatal refinery accidents and dozens of workers suffering from acute lead poisoning (Kovarik, 1999). The discovery also promised to make many, including Kettering, rich. Both Kettering and Midgley claimed that no alternatives existed to tetraethyl lead, something denied by other engineers. According to one historian, Midgley, who also later helped Kettering discover "Freon," a chlorinated fluorocarbon (or CFC), "had more impact on the atmosphere than any other single organism in earth history" (McNeil, 2000, p. 111).

Protests by Hamilton as well as medical experts, labor groups, the press, and the public forced the Ethyl Gasoline Corporation, created by General Motors and Standard Oil in 1924 to manufacture the new additive, to voluntarily suspend sales. GM abruptly replaced Kettering as president of Ethyl after the U.S. surgeon general called for a conference on tetraethyl lead in Washington DC in 1925 (Robert, 1983, p. 124). During the conference, Hamilton was a prominent critic. She told a reporter for the New York newspaper *The World* that "it is foolish to talk of the industrial value of tetraethyl lead when there is a health hazard involved. Men who could discover the fuel value of tetraethyl certainly could invent or discover something equally efficient and in no way dangerous. American chemists can do it if they will" (*The World*, May 22, 1925, p. 1). The representative for Standard Oil disagreed and declared that "our continued development of motor fuels is essential in our civilization" and tetraethyl lead was an "apparent gift of God" (U.S. Public Health Service, 1925, p. 105). The corporations cited their own scientific studies that suggested that leaded gasoline posed little risk to the public.

The U.S. government ultimately sided with the corporations and did not impose restrictions on the sale of leaded gasoline until the early 1970s (Warren, 2000, pp. 117–133, 221–223). The tangible economic benefits for the automobile industries combined with the public's demand for high-performance cars outweighed any long-term environmental hazards, especially since it appeared that scientists differed about the significance of those hazards. The Ethyl Corporation went on to produce 6.6 million tons if tetraethyl lead over the next six decades (Warren, 2000, pp. 127–128). While the company did issue new safety regulations for the manufacture and distribution of the product, "Faith in industry's science produced an ill-informed public whose untroubled indifference allowed hundreds of thousands of children to die or be permanently disabled" from exposure to lead as "consumers confidently burned ethylized gasoline and relished the enhanced automotive performance that resulted from the newest lead product" (Warren, 2000, pp. 117, 132).

While Hamilton failed to prevent the use of leaded gasoline, she remained convinced that empirical evidence, democratic institutions, and public opinion could combine to produce progressive, albeit incremental, reforms for the common good. She later cited the improved safety procedures in the manufacture of tetraethyl lead as an example (Hamilton, 1943, pp. 415–416). She put these convictions into practice as a "global citizen" to foster a "transnational community" as well. In 1924 the U.S. government appointed her to the League of Nations Health Organization. She served two consecutive three-year terms and was the only woman on the commission. For the rest of the decade, Hamilton continued to fight what she called the "dangerous trades" in lead and other toxins at home, but also gave numerous speeches on the work of the League, supervised Geneva's programs to combat epidemic diseases, and increased public awareness of the League's reports on the impact of poverty and bottle-feeding on infant morality rates. With funding from the Rockefeller Foundation, she helped the League train men and women from countries around the world who had returned home and entered the public health service. Writing during the Second World War, she insisted that the League "was in principle an international organization devoted to the welfare of all" and:

> The task that will face us after this war will be far, far heavier and more widespread than in 1919. But we know that the task that will face us can be done; we can point to the work of the Health Committee of the League of Nations as a proof, and we can go forward on the path it blazed. (1943, pp. 315–317)

CONCLUSION: INTERNATIONAL LEADERSHIP FOR THE COMMON GOOD

The United Nations did go forward on the path the League of Nations blazed. After 1945, the League's Health Organization became the World Health Organization, an agency of the UN. Yet, like the Covenant of the League, the UN Charter contains no mention of environmental protection. As with the League, political and ideological conflicts often dominated and restricted the activities of the UN, particularly during the Cold War (Roberts & Kingsbury, 1993). Unlike the interwar period, however, the public now seems more aware of the impact of human activity on the environment and there have been an increasing number of international conferences dedicated to the issue since the first UN Conference on the Human Environment (UNCHE) was held in Stockholm in 1972 (Birnie, 1993, pp. 337–341). There is also a more advanced international cooperative structure in place for understanding and confronting the global environmental challenge (Mingst & Karns, 2007, pp. 211–238). Still, the gap between the UN's ambitious goals and modest accomplishments remains wide. Leaders concerned about the growing ecological crisis still "cannot allow the glory of the vision to distract attention from the consequences" of their inability to resolve this crisis since "noble failure in the highest cause remains failure." As historian Paul Kennedy (2006) observes, "Whether the globe can ever really be protected from our capacity to damage it remains an open question. Taken overall, the post-1945 record is not an encouraging one" (p. 165).

Recent work in leadership studies and an analysis of the League of Nations offers a useful basis for understanding the role of leadership in confronting environmental issues within a global context. There were at least four principal reasons for the relative successes of the League. One was leaders like Woodrow Wilson and Alice Hamilton who were dedicated to democratic and progressive principles while advocating informed ethical choices based on reason and human compassion. Such "global citizens" illustrate how Crosby's conceptions of visionary and ethical leadership for the common good are possible in a "shared-power world." A second reason was the League's ability to bring some of the best minds of the world together to study issues and disseminate knowledge. By the late 1930s, the League was a genuine "transnational community" of scientists, technical experts, and activists examining a range of topics from urban planning to oil pollution. A third was when Geneva convinced states that it was in their long-term national interests to accept certain constraints on their domestic liberty in order to serve the greater good. Lastly, the League proved that the awareness of public health and "the mobilization of shame" could save lives and improve conditions in measurable ways worldwide. Taken together, the leaders and followers who supported the League's ideals created an effective shared system that identified and confronted important common problems.

The League's failures are equally as instructive and substantiate Kellerman's analysis of the contradictory nature of leadership as well as the limitations of "global citizenship" within a "shared-power world." By the late 1930s, nationalism proved more powerful than internationalism. A few determined dictators convinced their followers to first challenge and then destroy an international organization founded on democratic concepts and shared obligations. Economic motives also outweighed environmental concerns, particularly after the global financial system began to collapse in 1929. Corporations and governments resisted or skirted international regulations. Advocacy groups for wildlife were weak and divided. The slaughter of whales, for example, actually increased in the late 1930s and one expert concluded that "while much has been put on paper little really has been accomplished to protect the whale, indeed the entire effort has been close to ineffectual" (Hayden, 1942, p. 169). In democratic states, the public was often uninformed or ambivalent while their political leaders failed to sustain effective foreign policies or were unable to adapt to changing global events. In nondemocratic states, public opinion mattered even less as leaders either ignored their followers or manipulated their fears and hatreds. In the end, war and the threat of war paralyzed the League and undermined many of its accomplishments.

There are other lessons as well. The history of the League of Nations demonstrates not only how difficult it is for the global community to combat threats to public health and the environment, but how long it can take to attain even the most incremental and pragmatic reforms. In the "shared-power world" of the League, debates ended without resolution, reports went unread, and projects were abandoned before completion. Even leaders with the best intentions could not comprehend all the complexities of every problem, treaty obligations were not always clear or enforced, the general public was largely ignorant of the activities of the League, and a universal system for defending the common interests of all states proved illusory. Many, if not most, of these problems continue to plague the United Nations today.

Despite these many flaws and failures in the international response to environmental challenges, there were those who understood that the international community could at least begin to confront some of the most important problems concerning the relationship between human beings and the natural world. In 1934, John Phillips, an early American environmentalist, wrote:

> Agreements among nations in the field of conservation, whether based on economics or not, help to build up a unified cultural background, to develop an aesthetic response to nature which ought to be part of the common inheritance of mankind. (Hayden, 1942, p. 176)

The record of the League of Nations proves that while such agreements are extraordinarily difficult, they are not impossible. As Crosby and Bryson contend, leadership for the common good is essential. It is equally essential that followers take Kellerman's advice and develop their own sources of information, take collective action, and hold leaders to account. "It is up to us to insist on change from leaders, or that they stop being leaders" (Kellerman, 2004, p. 242).

REFERENCES

Aub, C. (1926). Lead Poisoning. *Baltimore, MD: The Williams and Wilkins Co.*

Balińska, M. (1995). Assistance and Not Mere Relief: The Epidemic Commission and the League of Nations. In P. Weindling (Ed.), International Health Organisations and Movements, 1918–1939 (pp. 81–108). Cambridge: Cambridge University Press.

Birnie, P. (1993). The UN and the Environment. In A. Roberts & B. Kingsbury (Eds.), *United Nations, Divided World: The UN's Roles in International Relations* (pp. 237–383). Oxford: Clarendon Press.

Boyle, F. (1999). *Foundations of World Order: The Legalist Approach to International Relations, 1898–1922*. Durham & London: Duke University Press.

Callahan, M. (1999/2008). *Mandates and Empire: The League of Nations and Africa, 1914–1931*. Brighton & Portland: Sussex Academic Press.

Callahan, M. (2004). *A Sacred Trust: The League of Nations and Africa, 1929–1946*. Brighton & Portland: Sussex Academic Press.

Chen, L. (2000). *An Introduction to Contemporary International Law: A Policy-Oriented Perspective*. New Haven, CT: Yale University Press.

Coogan, J. W. (1994). *Wilsonian Diplomacy in War and Peace*. In G. Martel (Ed.), *American Foreign Relations Reconsidered 1890–1993* (pp. 71–89). London: Routledge.

Crosby, B. (1999). *Leadership for Global Citizenship: Building Transnational Community*. Thousand Oaks, CA: Sage Publications.

Crosby, B., & Bryson, J. (2005). *Leadership for the Common Good: Tackling Public Problems in a Shared-Power World*. San Francisco: Jossey-Bass.

Crozier, A. (1988). *Appeasement and Germany's Last Bid for Colonies*. New York: St. Martin's Press.

Dubin, D. (1995). *The League of Nations Health Organization*. In P. Weindling (Ed.), *International Health Organisations and Movements, 1918–1939* (pp. 56–80). Cambridge: Cambridge University Press.

Farley, J. (1995). *The International Health Division of the Rockefeller Foundation: The Russell Years, 1929–1934*. In P. Weindling (Ed.), *International Health Organisations and Movements, 1918–1939* (pp. 203–221). Cambridge: Cambridge University Press.

Gottlieb, R. (2005). *Forcing the Spring: The Transformation of the American Environmental Movement*. Washington, DC: Island Press.

Hamilton, A. (1929). *Industrial Poisons in the United States*. New York: Macmillan and Co.

Hamilton, A. (1943). *Exploring the Dangerous Trades: The Autobiography of Alice Hamilton*, M.D. Boston: Little, Brown, and Co.

Hayden, S. (1942). *The International Protection of Wild Life: An Examination of Treaties and Other Agreements for the Preservation of Birds and Mammals*. New York: Columbia University Press.

Heald S., & Wheeler-Bennet, J. (Eds.). (1938). *Documents on International Affairs 1937*. London: Oxford University Press.

Iriye, A. (2002). *Global Community: The Role of International Organizations in the Making of the Contemporary World*. Berkeley: University of California Press.

Kellerman, B. (2004). *Bad Leadership: What It Is, How It Happens, Why It Matters*. Boston: Harvard Business School Press.

Kellerman, B. (2008). *Followership: How Followers Are Creating Change and Changing Leaders*. Boston: Harvard Business School Press.

Kennedy, P. (2006). *The Parliament of Man: The Past, Present, and Future of the United Nations*. New York: Random House.

Kovarik, B. (1999) *Charles F. Kettering and the 1921 Discovery of Tetraethyl Lead in the Context of Technological Alternatives*. Retrieved from http://www.radford.edu/~wkovarik/papers/kettering.html

League of Nations. (1920–1939). *The Monthly Summary of the League of Nations*. Geneva.

League of Nations. (1933). *Report of the International Labor Office upon the Working of the Convention Concerning the Use of White Lead in Painting*. Geneva.

League of Nations. (1936). *The Problem of Nutrition. Interim Report of the Mixed Committee on the Problem of Nutrition* (3 vols.). Geneva.

McCormick, J. (1989). *The Global Environmental Movement: Reclaiming Paradise*. London: Belhave Press.

McGonigle, M. (1979). *Pollution, Politics, and International Law: Tankers at Sea*. Berkeley: University of California Press.

McNeil, J. (2000). *Something New under the Sun: An Environmental History of the Twentieth-Century World*. New York: Norton.

Mingst, K., & Karns, M. (2007). *The United Nations in the 21st Century*. Boulder, CO: Westview Press.

Ostrower, G. (1996). *The League of Nations from 1919 to 1929*. Garden City Park, NY: Avery Publishing Group.

Pedersen, S. (2007). *Back to the League of Nations*. American Historical Review, 112(4), 1091–1117.

Reich, P. (1992). *The Hour of Lead: A Brief History of Lead Poisoning in the United States over the Past Century and of Efforts by the Lead Industry to Delay Regulation*. Washington, DC: Environmental Defense Fund.

Richardson, J. (2005). *The Cost of Being Poor: Poverty, Lead Poisoning, and Policy Implementation*. Westport, CT: Praeger.

Robert, J. (1983). *Ethyl: A History of the Corporation and the People Who Made It*. Charlottesville: University Press of Virginia.

Roberts, A., & Kingsbury, B. (Eds.). (1993). *United Nations, Divided World: The UN's Roles in International Relations*. Oxford: Clarendon Press.

Rosner, D., & Markowitz, G. (Eds.). (1989). *Dying for Work: Workers' Safety and Health in the Twentieth Century*. Bloomington: Indiana University Press.

Rubin, A. (1997). *Ethics and Authority in International Law*. Cambridge: Cambridge University Press.

Scott, G. (1973). *The Rise and Fall of the League of Nations*. London: Hutchinson and Co.

Sicherman, B. (1984). *Alice Hamilton: A Life in Letters*. Cambridge, MA: Harvard University Press.

U.S. Public Health Service. (1925). *Proceedings of a Conference to Determine Whether or Not There is a Public Health Question in the Manufacture . . . of Tetraethyl Lead Gasoline*. PHS Bulletin, 158(August).

Walters, F. (1952). *A History of the League of Nations*. London: Oxford University Press.

Warren, C. (2000). *Brush with Death: A Social History of Lead Poisoning*. Baltimore & London: The Johns Hopkins University Press.

Weindling, P. (Ed.). (1995). *International Health Organisations and Movements, 1918–1939*. Cambridge: Cambridge University Press.

Wöbse, A. (2003). *Der Schutz der Natur im Völkerbund—Anfänge einer Weltumweltpolitik*. Archiv für Sozialgeschichte, 43, 177–190.

Zimmern, A. (1939). *The League of Nations and the Rule of Law, 1918–1935*. London: Macmillan and Co.

12 Protest, Power, and "Political Somersaults"[1]

Leadership Lessons from the German Green Party

Heather R. McDougall

INTRODUCTION

Rising from a fringe protest group to prominent political power, the German Green party (*Die Grünen*) celebrates its 30th anniversary in 2010. The Greens have drafted some of the most stringent environmental protection policies in the world (Markovits & Silvia, 1997, p. 127). The party draws its strength from its progressive and inclusionary approach to leadership. The party's path to political success was filled with numerous twists and turns—starting as a grassroots outsider, becoming one of the first "green" parties to enter national politics, experiencing an embarrassing loss in 1990, and finally reemerging as a secondary coalition partner from 1998 to 2005. The Greens' tumultuous and in many ways extraordinary path is well known to political scientists. There is ample research from scholars who analyze the Greens from the perspective of party formation (Papadakis, 1984; Rothacher, 1984; Kitschelt, 1989), Inglehartian post-materialism (Burklin, 1985; Kolinsky, 1989; Frankland & Schoonmaker, 1992), ideological formation (Kvistad, 1987; Heywood, 2003; Markovits & Gorski, 1993), and as a new type of social movement (NSM) (Rohrschneider, 1993; Dalton, Recchia, & Rohrschneider, 2003). The Greens are typically credited with creating an "alternative model" for party formation (Frankland & Schoonmaker, 1992, p. 118), lending voice to previously excluded groups. However, the Greens' story has yet to be assessed by scholars of leadership. What does this "alternative model" and "outsider" mentality mean in the realm of leadership?

From a leadership studies vantage, the Greens began as "citizen leaders" (Cronin, 1995; Couto, 1995; Mabey, 1995). Citizen leaders are educated and active citizens who emerge when traditional leaders are not acting in the best interests of society. The Greens exemplify the attempted crossover from citizen leadership into formal political leadership, allowing the group to move from "outsider" with restricted political impact to "insider" with national legislative authority. Within this alternative model, the Greens sought to emphasize the role of citizen participation and bottom-up organizational structure (what they termed *Basisdemokratie*). Of particular note, the Greens transformed the typical party system to include women as equal members in the party leadership.

Unfortunately, the Greens' extreme measures to restrict the formation of strong leaders within the party led to intraparty fighting and disorganization. From this case study students of leadership can learn two things: (a) the complexity, difficulty, and perhaps, at times, incompatibility of citizen leadership with the political realm; and (b) how a group can successfully create policies and practices to increase women's representation. Furthermore, given the Greens' continued struggle to define its "alternative" identity, I propose that the Greens and others like them can learn from the Relational Leadership Model (Komives, Lucas, & McMahon, 2007), which seeks to combine ethics, empowerment, purpose, and inclusion to create positive change in society. This model, I contend, is highly applicable to the Greens, considering their move from the periphery to a key player in society and their need to move past an "outsider" mentality.

HISTORY

The formation of the Green party must be understood in the context of the protest movements of the 1960s (Frankland & Schoonmaker, 1992; Langguth, 1986). As Frankland and Schoonmaker (1992) contend, the Greens are the "institutional form of many of the ideals and organizational practices" of this era (p. 30). The mid-1960s was a turbulent time around the world as a series of political and social wars raged. Still recovering from the destruction caused by the Nazi regime, the German people were particularly resistant to, and critical of, power and authority. The Federal Republic of Germany became a hotbed of protest and dissent, particularly amongst its youth. One of the most prominent movements of the period, the German Socialist Student Association (SDS), captured the angst of young persons and channeled their anger into fervent protest. The SDS philosophy, influenced by Herbert Marcuse, called for a "new human being" who could live in a "culture without suppression" and "without repressive mechanisms" (Langguth, 1986, p. 2). The group criticized the middle class for its materialism and vapid morals. The SDS organized a series of successful demonstrations in the late 1960s—the climax being the Easter disturbances of 1968 in protest of the attempted assassination of protest leader Rudi Dutschke. Soon after, the movement waned, eventually dissolving itself in 1970. The failure of the movement stemmed in part from the diverse and often conflicting ideologies of its members—communists, terrorists, anarchists, subculture advocates, and reformers. Perhaps the most infamous movement of this time, the Red Army Faction (later known as the Baader-Meinhoff Gang) embarked on a path of violence escalating into terrorism throughout the 1970s.

Although the SDS appeared to wither away, the underlying frustrations and antiauthoritarian sentiments remained. A second wave of the protest movements eventually resurfaced in a somewhat milder tone. In contrast to the continued path of destruction and chaos of the Red Army Faction, the new movements emphasized alternative lifestyles, asceticism, communal harmony, and grassroots democracy. In other words, rather than "dropping out" of society, the second wave decided to "drop in" with its own style of democracy (Frankland & Schoonmaker, 1992, p. 32). The Greens initially formed as local citizen groups to work on environmental initiatives and to oppose atomic power. This eclectic group of leftists, feminists, pacifists, environmentalists, and other grassroots activists needed an umbrella to connect the groups together. Quoting Detlef Murphy and Roland Roth, Frankland and Schoonmaker (1992) argue that ecology served as "a diverse and more flexible concept which allowed various political positions a chance to express political opposition and encourage wider participation and pragmatic compromise" (p. 34).

In 1980 the Greens formed a national party around the platform of ecology, grassroots democracy, social justice, and nonviolence. While the Greens articulated a clear ecological platform, they found themselves unable to rally general support. Although they achieved successes on the local and state levels, the party failed to capture enough votes in the 1980 election to meet the minimum 5 percent threshold for federal office. Economic and security issues dominated the election, leaving little room for the Greens (Irving & Paterson, 1981). Tactical decisions saved the group from falling into the periphery (Condrat, 2003; Frankland & Schoonmaker, 1992). Joining forces with peace movement activists allowed the Greens to widen their support base and to gain experienced political members who could help the party articulate its platform and win seats in the 1983 election. As a result, the Greens won 5.6 percent of the votes in that year, enough to send 27 representatives to the *Bundestag*.

Despite forming an official party, the group retained a counterculture persona (de facto leader Joschka Fischer regularly wore sneakers to public events) and continued to label themselves as "outsiders" to the system. The Preamble to the Greens' Constitution proclaimed: "The Greens are the fundamental alternative to conventional parties" (Kolinsky, 1987, p. 243). Protest remained the defining character of the Greens: criticism of society, capitalism, gender inequality, environmental destruction, and traditional political institutions was its hallmark. The party's structure matched its alternative persona. Unlike typical parties, the Greens rejected charismatic leaders, hierarchical structures, and representative democracy. Similar to a social movement (Gundelach, 1982; Offe, 1985), the Greens retained a grassroots system (what they termed *Basisdemokratie*), emphasizing participatory and inclusive democratic decision-making practices. The Greens went to great efforts to ensure a transparent and open organizational environment. For example, almost all party meetings, at all levels, were open to the members; party assemblies reserved space for minority viewpoints; and the party often enlisted outside experts and interested activists to join special working groups on the local, state, and national levels.

Highly skeptical of "professional politicians," the Greens implemented a series of policies to protect its grassroots democracy against top-down and authoritarian leadership styles and to prevent the establishment of "elite leaders." Firstly, party leaders did not receive salaries; secondly, party leaders could be removed at any time; thirdly, federal (*Bundestag*) representatives rotated leadership positions every two years; fourthly, no person could serve consecutively as a party officer and then party representative; and, finally, each top leadership position had two co-leaders. The idea behind these policies was that leaders in the party should not be viewed as more important than the people (*die Basis*). A decentralized party was viewed as a necessary check on power and its abuse. In this respect, the Greens continued to maintain the antiauthoritarian character of the 1960s.

CITIZEN LEADERSHIP: SUCCESSFUL INTEGRATION OR INTERNAL DESTRUCTION?

In leadership theory terms, the Greens began as "citizen leaders" (Cronin, 1995; Couto, 1995; Mabey, 1995). Underlying citizen leadership is a critique of the relationship between leaders and citizens: the malaise in society is a result of the mentality and actions (or inaction) of leaders and followers. In particular, the current relationship between citizens and leaders is based on distrust and separation (Cronin, 1995). Leaders view themselves as disconnected—and in some instances superior—to citizens; and citizens are passive, unknowledgeable, and disinterested. Leadership should not simply be a small group of individuals imposing views from the top down and a passive group of citizens idly watching from the side. Citizen leadership supports an active and engaged citizenry that recognizes its duties and obligations to society (Mabey, 1995). Couto (1995) describes citizen leaders as persons who work on local levels to protect the needs and rights of community members. These leaders are "transforming leaders who engage others in efforts to reach higher levels of human awareness and relationship" (p. 13). Often emerging in "the cauldron of conflict and crisis" (Mabey, 1995, p. 317), they fight against the system to ensure that liberties are being upheld. It is important to emphasize that citizen leaders do not seek formal leadership positions. On the contrary, they are often the "reluctant warriors" who step in when traditional leaders fail to act in the best interests of society. Uncomfortable being in the spotlight, "often they intend to make some public action, to achieve their purpose quickly, and then to return to private matters" (Couto, 1995, p. 13).

The Greens' story appears to reflect the path of citizen leadership. As previously described, the Greens arose as a protest movement, calling for a fundamental change in government. In particular, the Greens felt that

German leaders were unresponsive to the needs of their people. The Greens regularly embarked on a series of protests calling for the end to nuclear expansion, opposition to U.S. and NATO military policies, and the rebirth of citizen action. In many ways, the Greens exemplify the desire to transform the problems with current-day leaders and followers. Members of the Greens movement felt that they *could* make changes and it was their duty to do so. As Kolinsky (1989) explains:

> Where their parents and grandparents were inclined to underestimate the role the individual could play in political life and would expect the state or the relevant authorities to define the issues and prescribe acceptable actions, the young generation have been more confident that each citizen could contribute to the agenda of policy issues and styles and influence events and decisions. (p. 1)

Through the initial citizen initiative groups, the Greens could ensure that the citizens' voices were heard. In turn, leadership would be more accountable to the people.

Yet, the Greens present an interesting variation on citizen leadership. Citizen leaders are often temporary leaders—their intention is not to obtain or retain formal leadership power or to become part of the system. At first glance, the Greens exemplify the successful crossover from citizen leadership into formal political leadership—allowing the group to move from "outsider" with limited political impact to "insider" with national legislative authority. As stated in their 1980 Federal Program Preamble, it was necessary for the Greens to transition from a movement into a formal party so that actual policies could be achieved. "In this way we will open a new possibility for citizens' and grassroots initiatives to put their concerns and ideas into practice" (Kolinsky, 1987, p. 240). The party would create a formal space for grassroots democracy to flourish. The Preamble clearly outlined that the structure of the party would remain primarily in the hands of the citizens. The basis for grassroots democracy (*die Basis*) is to ensure that the party is responsive to the needs and concerns of its people. It must be open to and decentralized so that new ideas can be heard and incorporated. Inherent in the Greens' formation was the notion that citizens were the source of power, not individual leaders. The national organization served as an umbrella to tie all of the local and national entities together. Nevertheless, primary control was to remain with the people. In this sense, the Greens sought to achieve the new type of leadership Couto, Mabey, and Cronin advocate.

PROBLEMS

The actual leap from "outsider" to "insider" turned out to be far more complicated. The dual identity gave the Greens a unique identity and, at the same time, plagued its development (Langguth, 1986; Kitschelt, 1989; Kolinsky, 1989; O'Neill, 1997). As O'Neill (1997) elucidates, "The origins of the Green movement in the new left, libertarian and anarchist politics of the 1960s have burdened the Greens with an unhelpful ideological baggage and organizational quandaries that have constrained their political efforts" (p. 51). Delving further, the party's dual identity led to four main problems:

counterproductive confrontational tactics
distrust of leaders
disorganization
party infighting

Firstly, the party entered the political arena fixated on maintaining its "extraparliamentary" and "political critic" persona. Initial confrontational tactics included moderate forms such as disregarding dress and speech protocol, while more radical ones included displaying large protest banners and presenting the newly elected Chancellor Kohl in 1983 with a dead evergreen branch in response to his inaction on acid rain (Frankland, 1988, p. 111). The tactics, while intended to shake up the government, verged on becoming counterproductive. The Greens were initially dismissed by some as "not ready to accept the responsibility of governing" (Langguth, 1986, p. 108).

Secondly, the quest to inhibit the development of a "professional party elite" translated into drastic limits on the leaders. As previously mentioned, restrictions included: short limits on the length of party office, rotation every two years in the *Bundestag*, prohibition of individuals from consecutively holding party offices and party seats, no salaries for party officers, and co-leaders in each top position. Leaders in the party began to resent the policies. At the same time, Green members became distrustful and unsupportive of party leaders. The unconventional structures and policies for its leaders led to a "disjointed framework party" that was unable to adequately respond to the needs of its constituents or its fellow party members; and furthermore led to a power vacuum in the party (Frankland & Schoonmaker, 1992, p. 118).

The third problem of disorganization led to the most dangerous problem: party infighting. Kitschelt (1989) attributes the lack of strong leadership, unaccountability, and weak organization to the struggle that emerged between the fundamentalists (*fundis*) and the realists (*realos*), which plagued the party for years (p. 274). Similar to Michels's 1962 notion of the "iron law of oligarchy,"[2] the Greens fell susceptible to struggling factions within the party that threatened to destroy it. The main conflict centered on this "insider" versus "outsider" identity—should the party professionalize and become more mainstream in its leadership policies or continue its emphasis on being a radical "outsider"? The realists (*realos*), led by Joschka Fischer and Otto Schily, wanted to professionalize the party and widen its voter appeal. In order to do so, it needed to demonstrate to voters that the Greens could enact political change. Thus the *realos* supported a coalition with the Social Democrats (SPD). The *fundis* (fundamentalists) led by Petra Kelly and Jutta Ditfurth, on the other hand, wanted to remain a decentralized "anti-party" unwilling to make policy compromises, let alone coalitions—any change would be counter to the beliefs of *Basisdemokratie*.

Thus a fundamental value crisis existed: what were the Greens and what did they stand for? Already in an identity crisis, the Greens faced the difficult task of merging with East Germany's Alliance 90 after the reunification of Germany. The Greens presented themselves as a disorganized mess in the 1990 election, resulting in an embarrassing failure to meet the 5 percent minimum threshold.

But out of chaos emerged a stronger party. Fischer realized that in order to move forward, the Greens had to reorganize themselves and focus attention on making actual contributions to policy. The reorganization entailed key initiatives, including abolishing the rotation policy, reducing the size of the executive committee, and the addition of a political manager. Defection by some hard-line *fundis* helped to transition the new organization. With improved organization and communication, the Greens were ready to merge with the East's Alliance 90. The process was not entirely smooth as the two did not agree on gender policy or how to confront the past. Despite these potentially divisive issues, they paled in comparison to previous battles between the *realos* and *fundis*. The "super election year" of 1994 showcased the newly unified Alliance 90/Greens into one party, earning 7.3 percent of the vote. The new Greens abandoned much of the anti-party and anti-capitalism rhetoric that dominated the 1980s, proving to voters that the once "motley collection of protestors and antipoliticians" could be a "normal" actor in politics (Betz, 1995, p. 203). Calls for human rights, social and economic liberty, a healthy environment, and education became the central focus. The party had transitioned to a more centrist (albeit still left-leaning) party. The Greens used the renewed legitimacy to push forward new citizenship, asylum, and immigration laws.

A TRANSFORMED LEADER

The Greens' successful reemergence is due in part to the leadership of Joschka Fischer—a drastic change for a party that previously disallowed any strong leader to emerge. Fischer was the radical activist accused of throwing rocks at police officers in 1968 and who entered the Green party ministry in 1983 wearing sneakers. Fifteen years later, he became the vice-chancellor in a tailored suit in the SPD-led coalition party of 1998. His personal transformation symbolized a maturing of the Greens' identity and values. Fischer exemplified the charisma and strong leadership needed at the time of crisis. In 2005 *Der*

Spiegel heralded, "only [Fischer] could display [the] persuasive power" needed to take the Greens in a new direction (Malzahn, 2005).

As foreign minister, Fischer made the controversial decision to join Allied Forces in Bosnia. The decision helped the Greens to take a more nuanced stance on nonviolence, which it had previously held as sacrosanct. At the same time, the movement sought to protect the human rights of individuals. The Greens, Fischer argued, would be promoting a new type of fascism if it did not stand up for Bosnia; the Greens' soul would be tainted. The Greens' value of nonviolence came into conflict with its value of human rights. In this case, human rights must be protected. Under conditions of genocide, the Greens had a moral obligation to intervene. Assessing his leadership style, Markovits and Silvia (1997) describe Fischer as "brilliant strategist, a superb tactician and a 'Realpolitiker' par excellence" (p. 124). To date, Fischer remains one of the most popular politicians in Germany. Since leaving the party, no other strong leader has emerged.

There is debate as to whether or not the party made a necessary change or sold out. Tranter (2009) and Pakulski, Tranter, and Crook (1998) warn that "routinization" can stifle the innovation of environmental movements, and can furthermore result in declining support and membership. In the case of the Greens, the change helped the party move from pending implosion to viable coalition partner. Looking back at the party and its decision, *Der Spiegel* writer Malzahn (2005) argues:

> Over the years, the Greens have sacrificed almost all of their sacred cows to the political process. Critics insist they have sold their environmentally-friendly souls for power and have lost their idealism. To this, there is but one truthful retort: Thank God.

Burchell (2002) further explains that the change, rather than being a sign of weakness, was necessary to regain the party's credibility amongst claims that it had simply become "impractical" (p. 167).

CONTRIBUTION: GENDER EQUALITY

The Greens are known as the champions of the "underdogs" (Markovits & Silvia, 1997). Up to this point, this chapter has focused on the Greens as "outsiders" to leadership. Yet within the movement is another minority group that has remained an "outsider" in all parties: women. In its effort to create a more inclusionary form of politics, the German Greens made substantial strides to equalize women's representation. Considering the current state of women in leadership, it is important to briefly assess the Greens' accomplishments.

Presently, women hold only 16 percent of the seats in parliamentary bodies. At this rate, it would take 100 years for women to have equal representation in political leadership (Kellerman & Rhode, 2007, pp. 2–3). Some question whether numbers really matter; perhaps the number of women in office does not truly influence policy or perceptions. Yet according to a 1995 UN Development report, 30 percent female representatives is the minimum necessary for women to make meaningful contributions to politics—most countries fall drastically short (United Nations, 1995). Political parties are often part of the problem. Research shows that most political parties in democracies are less likely to encourage women to run for office (United Nations, 1997; Ford, 2006; Fox & Lawless, 2005; Harrison, 2003). Since parties are typically led by males, male "in-groups" form, leaving women out of decision-making processes and without the same access to resources. Exacerbating the situation, there are not enough female mentors to cultivate a new generation of female leaders (Kellerman & Rhode, 2007, p. 22). In sum, the practices of most parties help to perpetuate the stereotypes of women in leadership.

Environmentalists, on the contrary, are more likely to support female candidates in political office (Ford, 2006, p. 156). Part of the reason is environmental groups' progressive and inclusionary leadership style. The case of the German Greens is a clear example. From the beginning the Greens provided an arena for feminists who wanted to not only counter hierarchical structures, but also "the aggressive, manipulative 'masculine' political style" (Frankland & Schoonmaker, 1992, p. 108). As part of its platform to increase the rights of individuals, the Greens criticized the discrimination of women in the workforce, the reduction of women to being seen solely as mothers, and the underrepresentation of women in all areas of society. Many women became involved with the Green party after being disenchanted with the way in which the SDS excluded them from leadership roles and treated women as merely "little women" whose "liberation" was conceived as occurring in sexual mores rather than political and social equality (Kolinsky, 1987, p. 194).

But rather than merely voicing women's concerns, the Greens' organizational structure echoed a participatory and inclusive model that countered the traditional hierarchical and often patriarchical structure of typical parties. On a smaller scale, the party developed a series of seminars that explored female styles of communication and the most effective ways to articulate their perspectives. Beginning in the 1980s, the party required at least 50 percent of its electoral candidates to be female and required that the top slot be held by a woman. Although the beginning had a rocky start, by 1987 the Greens' gender quotas were achieved, giving the public confidence in its commitment to a "cohesive women's policy" (Kolinsky, 1989, p. 200). This initiative increased female representation in the *Bundestag* from 10 to 15.4 percent (Deutsch, 1999). While such initiatives do not necessarily lead to more women in office—they can simply put the women at the bottom 50 percent, thus making it unlikely that a woman will actually be placed in office—the Greens used the "zipper system," which requires the list to be female, male, female, male, etc., and applied it to all party offices. The policy influenced the Social Democrats, one of the largest parties, to adopt a similar policy after women began defecting to the Greens.[3]

Two other policies are noteworthy. On a national level, the party led the repeal of Paragraph 218 of the German Judicial Code—a law that made abortion illegal and allowed for legal action against women who had abortions and the doctors who performed them. Within the party, the Greens expanded parental leave policy to include both men and women, and unmarried couples. The policy is a crucial step in addressing the work–family conflicts that often impede women's ability to obtain and retain leadership positions. Surveys by Hewlett and Luce, in 2005, and Wellington and colleagues, in 2003, reveal that between two-thirds and four-fifths of high-achieving women cite work–family relationship as both the greatest obstacle and solution for women's advancement (cited in Kellerman & Rhode, 2007, p. 29). Furthermore, parental leave rights for both men and women allows for more females to remain in leadership positions (Ford, 2006; Harrison, 2003; Kellerman & Rhode, 2007). Interviews with one couple currently working for the Green party credited the Greens' parental leave policies as instrumental in their ability to balance work and family. Career advancement, they stated, would be extremely difficult without family-friendly policies. No other party in Germany provides such a favorable environment (Interview 1, 2008).[4]

It is certainly not the case that the Green's policies have completely closed the gender gap in leadership. Important distinctions remain, including a discrepancy between male and female political ambition—meaning one's desire or drive to run for political office (Davidson-Schmich, 2008). Nevertheless, the Greens have created a culture of inclusion backed by effective policies. The Greens have the opportunity to continue to be forerunners in women's leadership. Too many organizations and parties are content to maintain the status quo. The Greens have demonstrated a true commitment to women's leadership on both a philosophical and organizational level.

MOVING FORWARD: THE RELATIONAL LEADERSHIP MODEL

Thus, despite making substantial changes to the party's structure, the Greens did not abandon their goal of creating an inclusionary party. Burchell (2002) argues that the party retained its "distinctive approach to party organization, participation and democracy" (p. 126). In interviews with current party workers and advisers, the perceived strength of the party continues to be its emphasis on inclusion and protection of human dignity. One worker described the party favorably as "very democratic from the roots" (Interview 2, 2009), while another praised the nonhierarchical structure that allows easy access to everyone in the organization. As he explained, "We can easily approach everyone in the organization. It is a very pleasant working environment. The small size does have benefits" (Interview 3, 2009).

Given the Greens' strong emphasis on inclusion, ethics, and positive change, it may be more productive to frame its leadership style within the Relational Leadership Model, as developed by Komives, Lucas, and McMahon (2007) and others. Komives et al. (2007) assert that relationships are the central component of leadership and that leadership theories must take into consideration the dynamic relationship between leader and follower while at the same time retaining an ethical dimension. They define leadership as "a relational and ethical process of people together attempting to accomplish positive change" (Komives et al., 2007, p. 74).

Their model depicts leadership as an inclusive, empowering, ethical, and purposive process. The purpose should be vision-driven rather than position-driven. At the same time, the means to achieve the purpose—the way in which the group recruits its members, makes decisions, and accomplishes tasks—are just as important as the purpose itself. By opening the arena up to all members, the unique talents and potential of members are opened and cultivated (Manz & Sims, 1989; McGill & Slocum, 1993). Empowerment helps to motivate individuals to work towards the goals of the organization. It also helps to counter the formation of "in-groups" and "out-groups," which often results in one group excluding the other from decision-making processes (Kohn, 1992). Supporting the model, studies show that individuals prefer a collaborative rather than competitive environment (Johnson, Maruyama, Johnson, Nelson, & Skon, 1981; Kantor, 1989; Spence, 1983; Tjosvold & Tjosvold, 1991).

Assessing the Greens within the Relational Leadership Model provides a framework for understanding the Greens' values and goals. The model "supports positive change—that is, change that improves the human condition and that does not intentionally harm others" (Komives et al., 2007, p. 84). At the heart of the Greens' Preamble are the individual and the cultivation of his or her moral development:

> Only the self-determination of those affected can avert a complete ecological, economic, and social crisis. Because we favour self-determination and the free development of every human being and think that people should be able to lead their lives creatively and in harmony with their natural environment [and] their own desires and needs, we radically advocate human rights and extensive democratic rights for everyone. (Kolinsky, 1989, p. 241)

Within the Greens' platform is an emphasis on the importance of inclusivity that values diversity and seeks to involve all members of the group. By allowing a forum for expression, the Greens provide an arena in which minority views can be heard. Frankland and Schoonmaker (1992) contend that the Greens succeeded in making a political culture change in German society by refocusing attention from elite party members to the citizens, thereby cultivating a more participatory citizenry (p. 177). The party sought to create a culture in which personal accountability and leadership along with tolerance of others' viewpoints were essential to a thriving community. Particularly in the case of women, the Greens developed a culture of inclusion and actual policies to support it, empowering individuals to take on new leadership roles. Emphasizing the importance of the means to their ends, the Greens' grassroots vision demanded that its members become active contributors within ethical boundaries.

Despite their accomplishments, the Greens still have room for improvement. The party could learn from the Relational Leadership Model's alternative view of power. The Greens have always maintained skepticism of power, particularly in the hands of individuals. The notion of "professional politicians" has been horrifying to them. What the Greens need to develop is a better sense of how power is shared among leaders and followers, and that the use of power does not necessarily need to be negative. In the model, persons in formal leadership positions understand that the source of their power and effectiveness comes from the relationship with their group members (Kouzes & Posner, 2002). The Relational Leadership Model emphasizes the difference between personalized vision and socialized vision (Howell, 1988). Personalized vision is developed by a leader in a top-down manner and directed to the group members. In contrast, socialized vision is developed by the members. The idea is that individuals will have a vested interest in goals that they participated in creating and will be more motivated to its completion. According to Bennis and Thompson (2002), socialized vision fosters a partnership between leaders and group members (p. 137). This idea models that of grassroots democracy. As Nanus (1992) explains, "There is no more powerful engine driving an organization toward excellence and long-range success than an attractive, worthwhile, and achievable vision of the future, widely shared" (p. 3).

The Greens' strength comes from its socialized vision. Strong leaders need not destroy this; on the contrary, strong leaders can help the vision grow and prosper. Although the party did ease some of the restriction on leaders, it retains a double leadership structure: for top leadership positions, there are two people (one man and one woman). This practice serves to foster inclusion and diffuse the leadership structure; however, it is this diffusion that may be the problem. While the vision of the party is clear, interviews with party workers and advisers indicated a potential leadership "vacuum" in the party (Interview 4, 2009). Workers identified former leaders Petra Kelly and Joschka Fischer as the two most important leaders of the party, but did not name a current leader as having the same importance or influence. Although the workers and advisers pointed out the positive benefits of double leadership positions (more access for more individuals, less hierarchical structure), a clear direction seemed lacking. One worker called double leadership "a disaster" (Interview 4, 2009) and another argued "with so many people, trying to lead, the result is no leadership at all" (Interview 3, 2009).

It may thus be time for the party to rethink its view of leadership. Done correctly, leadership can foster and strengthen the values of an organization—providing a path towards their accomplishment. By invigorating the moral commitment of their members, leaders cultivate a strong sense of duty and obligation among members, as well as provide necessary direction (Gardner, 1990, p. 191). Reframing the Greens' approach within the Relational Leadership Model can help the party to focus its attention on its policy goals and values rather than on its fear of leadership.

CONCLUSION

Amidst "political somersaults and twists" (Henning, 2001), the Greens reemerged from impending internal destruction to become one of the most influential green parties in the world. From the Greens, students of leadership—including particularly those who are concerned about leadership for environmental sustainability—can learn about the precarious relationship between citizen leadership and political leadership, and that the two are not so easy to reconcile. Crossing the realm from citizen activist movement to political party, the Greens attempted to maintain a dual identity of "outsider" and "insider"—what Fischer called "both a power factor and a nuisance factor" (Langguth, 1986, p. 111). At first, the party seemed to demonstrate a successful transition from citizen to political leadership. However, maintaining the balance was certainly not without its difficulties. For the Greens, the entrenched sense of "outsider" led to antagonistic behavior and unwillingness to compromise—both of which are often counterproductive in the political realm. Facing a power vacuum, the party entered the path towards professionalization and extended more power to leaders by relaxing some of the office rotational limitations and seeking coalitions with other parties.

Although the party's internal struggles seemed at times to overshadow its original goals, the Greens' accomplishments are not to be underestimated. The party's Four Pillars (ecological wisdom, social justice, grassroots democracy, and nonviolence) are now becoming the foundation for political parties worldwide. The Greens' emphasis on inclusion paved the way for gender equality both in their policies and their culture. For obvious reasons, the Greens are praised for their contribution to environmental policy, including their Nuclear Exit Law to end nuclear power in Germany by 2020 and the Renewable Energies Act. In addition, the party initiated a new eco-tax system on private households and businesses in order to encourage the reduction of energy consumption. The Greens have not only successfully articulated a vision of environmental protection but also transformed that vision into mainstream rhetoric. As Markovits and Silvia

(1997) explain, the Greens have "succeeded in transforming the mainstream and the establishment of German politics into a locus of ecological awareness, even vigilantism. Everybody in Germany claims to be at least environmentally-conscious (*umweltbewusst*) if not in fact environmentally-active (*umweltfreundlich*), and a surprising percentage actually are" (p. 127). The Greens brought the natural environment—previously a marginalized topic—to the mainstream. In doing so, the Green party has accomplished its goal of giving voice to minority views.

What is next for the Greens? In the September 2009 elections, the Greens received 10.7 percent of the popular vote. Although this was an increase of 2.6 percent from the previous election, the party was hoping for a higher percentage. Talks of a coalition with the Christian Democrats circulated but did not materialize. For the time being, the party will remain one of the minority parties in the *Bundestag*. As an oppositional party in Parliament, it will be essential for the Greens to find ways to have their voice heard and influence policy. Looking forward, the party would be better served by emphasizing their strength of inclusion and empowerment rather than antagonism. Utilizing the Relational Leadership Model can help the Greens create a more positive framework and, perhaps, space for new and stronger leadership to emerge.

NOTES

1. Henning (2001).
2. Michels's famous theory argued that all organizations need leaders or experts who can manage and give direction to the followers. The leaders are extolled as heroes and soon the followers become passive and remissive. Left to their own devices, the leaders follow their own interests, ignoring the interests of the followers. As the leaders compete for control, the followers are left powerless to intercede.
3. The Social Democrats currently require that there can be no less than 40 percent and no more than 60 percent of one gender; while the Christian Democratic Union includes a 33 percent "women's quorum" (Davidson-Schmich, 2008, p. 6).
4. The names of interviewees cited in this chapter have been kept anonymous. Notes of interviews are in the author's possession. Interviews are listed numerically in the References by date.

REFERENCES

Bennis, W., & Thompson, R. (2002). *Geeks and Geezers: How Era, Values, and Defining Moments Shape Leaders*. Boston: Harvard Business School Press.

Betz, H. (1995). Alliance 90/Greens: From Fundamental Opposition to Black

Green. In D. Conradt, G. Kleinfeld, G. Romoser, & S. Christian (Eds.), *Germany's New Politics: Parties and Issues in the 1990s* (pp. 203–220). Providence, RI: Berghahn Books.

Burchell, J. (2002). *The Evolution of Green Politics: Development and Change within European Green Parties.* London: Earthscan.

Burklin, W. P. (1985). The German Greens: The Postindustrial Non-Established and the Political System. *International Political Science Review,* 6(4), 463–481.

Conradt, D. (2003). *German Polity.* Upper Saddle River, NJ: Prentice Hall.

Couto, R. (1995). Defining a Citizen Leader. In J. Wren (Ed.), *The Leader's Companion: Insights on Leadership through the Ages* (pp. 11–17). New York: Free Press.

Cronin, T. (1995). Leadership and Democracy. In J. Wren (Ed.), *The Leader's Companion: Insights on Leadership through the Ages* (pp. 303–309). New York: Free Press.

Dalton, R., Recchia, S., & Rohrschneider, R. (2003). The Environmental Movement and the Modes of Political Action. *Comparative Political Studies, 36*(7), 743–771.

Davidson-Schmich, L. (2008). *Gender Quotas and Political Ambition: Evidence from Germany.* Paper presented at the MPSA Annual National Conference, Chicago, IL. Retrieved from http://www.allacademic.com/meta/p266714_index.html

Deutsch, R. (1999). 90 Years of Votes for Women. Goethe-Institute e. V. Retrieved from http://www.goethe.de/ges/pok/zdk/en4206290.htm

Ford, L. (2006). *Women and Politics: The Pursuit of Equality* (2nd ed.). Boston: Houghton Mifflin.

Fox, R., & Lawless, J. (2005). *It Takes a Candidate: Why Women Don't Run for Office.* Cambridge: Cambridge University Press.

Frankland, E. (1988). The Role of the Greens in West German Parliamentary Politics, 1980–87. *The Review of Politics, 50*(1), 99–122.

Frankland, E., & Schoonmaker, D. (1992). *Between Protest & Power: The Green Party in Germany.* Boulder, CO: Westview Press.

Gardner, J. (1990). *On Leadership.* New York: Free Press.

Gundelach, P. (1982). Grass-Roots Organizations, Societal Control and Dissolution of Norms. *Acta Sociologica, 25*(1), 57–65.

Harrison, B. (2003). *Women in American Politics: An Introduction.* Belmont, CA: Wadsworth.

Henning, D. (2001). German Green Party Leaders Suppress Protests against Transport of Nuclear Waste. *Synthesis/Regeneration: Magazine of Green Social Thought Online, 25*(Summer). Retrieved from http://www.greens.org/s-r/25/25-13.html

Heywood, A. (2003). *Political Ideologies: An Introduction.* New York: Palgrave Macmillan.

Howell, J. (1988). Two Faces of Charisma: Socialized and Personalized Leadership in Organizations. In J. Conger & R. Kanungo (Eds.), *Charismatic Leadership: The Elusive Factor in Organizational Effectiveness* (pp. 213–236). San Francisco: Jossey-Bass.

Interview 1. (2008). August 10. Berlin, Germany. Notes are in the author's possession.

Interview 2. (2009). May 28. Berlin, Germany. By telephone. Notes are in the author's possession.

Interview 3. (2009). June 9. Berlin, Germany. By telephone. Notes are in the author's possession.

Interview 4. (2009). June, 9. Berlin, Germany. By telephone. Notes are in the author's possession.

Irving, R., & Paterson, W. (1981). The West German Election of 1980: Continuity Preferred to Change. *Parliamentary Affairs, 334*(2), 191–209.

Johnson, D., Maruyama, G., Johnson, R., Nelson, D., & Skon, L. (1981). Effects of Cooperative, Competitive, and Individualistic Goal Structures on Achievement: A Meta-Analysis. *Psychological Bulletin, 89*(1), 47–62.

Kantor, R. (1989). *When Giants Learn to Dance*. New York: Simon and Schuster.

Kellerman, B., & Rhode, D. (2007). Women and Leadership: The State of Play. In B. Kellerman and D. Rhode (Eds.), *Women and Leadership: The State of Play and Strategies for change* (pp. 1–62). San Francisco: Jossey-Bass.

Kitschelt, H. (1989). *The Logics of Party Formation: Ecological Politics in Belgium and West Germany*. Ithaca, NY: Cornell University Press.

Kohn, A. (1992). *No Contest: The Case against Competition*. Boston: Houghton Mifflin.

Kolinsky, E. (1987). *Opposition in Western Europe*. London: Croom Helm.

Kolinsky E. (1989). *The Greens in West Germany*. New York: Berg.

Komives, S., Lucas, N., & McMahon, T. (2007). *Exploring Leadership: For College Students Who Want to Make a Difference* (2nd ed.). San Francisco: Jossey-Bass.

Kouzes, J., & Posner, B. (2002). *The Leadership Challenge* (3rd ed.). SanF r a n - cisco: Jossey-Bass.

Kvistad, G. (1987). Green Political Ideology in the mid-1980s. *West European Politics, 10*, 211–228.

Langguth, G. (1986). *The Green Factor in German Politics: From Protest Movement to Political Party*. Boulder, CO: Westview Press.

Mabey, C. (1995). The Making of a Citizen Leader. In J. Wren (Ed.), *The Leader's Companion: Insights on Leadership through the Ages* (pp. 310–317). New York: Free Press.

Malzahn, C. (2005). Happy 25th Birthday Greens. What's the Plan Now? *Der Spiegel*, January 13.

Manz, C., & Sims, H. (1989). *Superleadership: Leading Others to Lead Themselves*. New York: Berkley Books.

Markovits, A., & Gorski, P. (1993). *The German Left: Red Green and Beyond*. New York: Oxford University Press.

Markovits, A., & Silvia, S. (1997). The Identity Crisis of Alliance '90/The Greens: The New Left at a Crossroad. *New German Critique, 72*, 115–135.

McGill, M., & Slocum, J. (1993). Unlearning the Organization. *Organizational Dynamics, 22*(2), 67–79.

Michels, R. (1962). *Political Parties*. New York: Macmillan.

Nanus, B. (1992). *Visionary Leadership: Creating a Compelling Sense of Direction for Your Organization*. San Francisco. Jossey-Bass.

Offe, C. (1985). New Social Movements: Challenging the Boundaries of Institutional Politics. *Social Research, 52*(4), 817–868.

O'Neill, M. (1997). New Politics, Old Predicaments: The Case of the European Greens. *Political Quarterly, 68*(1), 50–67.

Papadakis, E. (1984). *The Green Movement in West Germany*. London: Croom Helm and St. Martin's Press.

Pakulski, J., Tranter. B., & Crook, S. (1998). The Dynamics of Environmental Issues in Australia: Concerns, Clusters and Carriers. *Australian Journal of Political Science*, 33(2), 235–252.

Rohrschneider, R. (1993). New Party versus Old Left Realignments: Environmental Attitudes, Party Policies, and Partisan Affiliations in Four West European Countries. *The Journal of Politics, 55*(3), 682–701.

Rothacher, A. (1984). The Green Party in German Politics. *West European Politics, 7*(3), 109–116.

Spence, J. (1983). *Achievement and Achievement Motives: Psychological and Sociological Approaches*. San Francisco: Freeman.

Tjosvold, D., & Tjosvold, M. (1991). *Leading the Team Organization*. New York: Macmillan.

Tranter, B. (2009). Leadership and Change in the Tasmanian Environment Movement. *The Leadership Quarterly, 20*(5), 708–724.

United Nations. (1995). *Report of the Fourth World Conference on Women*. Beijing, China, September 4–15, Paragraph 182. Retrieved from http://www.un.org/esa/gopher-data/conf/fwcw/off/a—20.en United Nations. (1997). *Committee on the Elimination of Discrimination against Women. General Recommendation 23, Political and Public Life*. U.N. Doc. A/52/38/Rev.1 at 61.

13 Religion, Leadership, and the Natural Environment

The Case of American Evangelicals

Calvin W. Redekop

INTRODUCTION

There can be little doubt that religious beliefs help structure the way human beings relate to the natural world, and that achieving environmental sustainability will depend in no small part on the degree to which religious groups make the cause their own. This chapter analyzes the intersection between religion, leadership, and the environment, with a focus on American Evangelicalism. Traditional evangelical theology arguably presents special challenges to environmental concern, yet evangelicals are beginning to play a role in the environmental movement, due largely to the efforts of some key evangelical leaders. What are the challenges faced by religious leaders when it comes to concern for the natural world, and by evangelical leaders in particular? Who are these leaders, and what have they done to heighten environmental concern and action among evangelicals? And what is the best way to understand the nature of leadership that is exercised in this context? In order to answer these and other pertinent questions, we must begin by considering the general relationship between religion and nature.

RELIGION AND NATURE

Many early religions have been characterized as "encouraging harmonious and sustainable relations with the environment" (York, 2005, p. 1259). According to Wach (1942), "Cosmologies of traditional and indigenous societies invoke respect for the sacred and the spiritual essence of all forms of existence, to keep a balanced coexistence among the parts comprising the total whole of the cosmos" (p. 422). However, the myths, legends, ceremonies, and rituals of traditional religions suggest an increasing differentiation, over time, of religion from nature. Doctrines emerged purporting to define the divine or transcendent as distinct from nature (Wach, 1942, p. 37). One of the differentiating forms was the emergence of "god" or deity. This took several forms, including theism, pantheism, and panentheism.

Pantheism "ascribes divinity to the cosmos or simply identifies god with the world." Panentheism "wishes to place the divine beyond nature as much as within it," while theism proposes that "god and nature are ontologically separate and distinct" (York, 2005, pp. 1257–1258).

Theistic religions tend to be dualistic, seeing the life of the "spirit" in conflict with the material, mundane, and temporal aspects of human existence. Self-denial, or transcendence, and debasement of physical reality and earthly existence are features of most theistic religions. Dualistic theologies lay out varying degrees of separation between nature and spirit, elevate the value of transcendent deity over nature, and consequently tend to place the natural world in a subordinate position. On the other hand, it has often been asserted that monistic eastern religions are more eco-friendly than western dualisms (Oelschlaeger, 2005, p. 1256; Knopf, 1987, p. 785). Kalland (2005) concludes, "Whether looking at indigenous traditions or Asian religious creeds, scholars of such worldviews have almost invariably stressed that they are what Christianity allegedly is not, namely ecocentric and monistic, promoting a sense of harmony between human beings and nature." Christianity "is portrayed as anthropomorphic and dualistic, promoting a relation of domination rather than harmony" (p. 1368).

A form of environmental leadership among traditional religions was exercised by the shaman, diviner, medicine man, or chief. Such figures would express, via rituals and other means, "individual and collective responsibility to monitor the state of biosocial systems and to redress socio-environmental imbalances" (Wach, 1942, p. 422). This implies that the relationship between human beings and nature could become imbalanced, and the need of the shaman (leader) to help redress the imbalance. Furthermore, early cosmologies "explained" natural events such as droughts, floods, famines, etc., with evil spirits and other forces that were the province of the shaman. Thus although nature was thought to be basically dependable and friendly, the shaman helped restore the "harmonious" order when it was lacking.

CHRISTIANITY AND CREATION

Christianity, as a monotheistic religion, has had a problematic cosmology when it comes to the treatment of nature. In spite of valiant efforts to posit an ontological role for nature in God's plan (see, for example, Chapter 8 of the Apostle Paul's Letter to the Romans), the Christian community has wrestled with this issue right up to the present day. Theologians such as Paul Tillich (Protestant) and Teilhard de Chardin (Catholic) have tried to define and attenuate the tensions between divinity and nature, but the issue is far from settled (Tillich, 1963, pp. 141–143; Tucker, 2005, pp. 1627–1629).

Christianity's relation to nature involves interpreting God's goal for the creation, based on interpretation of the Old and New Testaments. According to Wiebe (2005), "Nature has two dominant fates in the New Testament books. It either passes away to be replaced by a new creation, or is transformed anew. In either case, tension exists between nature's current state and its future form." Wiebe proposes, "The dominant New Testament view of nature's fate is restoration (from a fallen state), alongside human restoration" (p. 437). But because the Bible does not clearly describe the relationship, a variety of Christian understandings of nature has emerged.

The three major Christian groups, namely, Greek Orthodox, Roman Catholic, and Protestant, have developed diverse (although at times overlapping) understandings of the Creation. For example, the Greek Orthodox believed "the presence of God in the world is neither one of illusion (a-theistic) nor of identification (pantheistic) but would espouse pan-entheism" (Chryssavgis, 2005, p. 337). Although Martin Luther (1483–1546) felt similarly, saying that God "is in, with, and under the whole created world, with all creatures, flowing and pouring into them, filling all things," both Luther and John Calvin (1509–1564) placed overwhelming emphasis on the human–divine relationship to the exclusion of the human–nature relationship (Santmire, 2005, pp. 341–342). To this day evangelical Protestants emphasize being in a "right relationship" with Jesus Christ rather than with the creation. The Earth is seen as a temporary abode for the soul that will at some point in time either be destroyed or transformed with the second coming of Christ. Other Protestant groups that place less emphasis on salvation tend to be more open to seeing nature as a (divinely created) good in itself, although without much spiritual significance. St. Francis of Assisi (1181–1226) was famously sensitive to plants and animals as expressions of the divine (see Chapter 14 of this volume), but the Roman Catholic view was never totally affirming of nature since "it accommodated itself to potent Platonic and neo-Platonic philosophical systems emphasizing the transcendence of the spiritual realm over the world of embodied reality" (French, 2005, p. 328).

THE RECOVERY OF NATURE

An influential critique of Christian views of nature is found in an essay by Lynn White, Jr., entitled "The Historical Roots of our Ecological Crisis," written in 1967. White linked the "ethos of medieval Christianity to the emergence of . . . an 'exploitative' attitude toward nature in the western world during the Middle Ages" (Whitney, 2005, p. 1735). White pointed to the broad elements within the Judeo-Christian tradition (e.g., the biblical mandate of Genesis 1:28 to exercise "dominion over the earth," and the notion of matter as inert material), which led "ultimately not only to Western technological dominance but also to the continuing impact on the environment of an aggressive stance toward nature" (Whitney, 2005, p. 1735).

The response to this thesis was dramatic and sensational, embraced by some and vigorously attacked by others. Many defenders of Christianity maintained that some Christians may have "exploited" nature, but cited numerous examples of the deep respect for nature expressed by many influential Christian groups and individuals. But whether or not White overstated the case against Christianity, "White's ideas, and the range of responses to them, is an essential chapter in contemporary discussion about the relationship of religion and attitudes toward nature" (Whitney, 2005, p. 1735), and thus became a major force in the development of the Christian environmental movement (Womersley, 2005, p. 1159).

It was thus only during the second half of the 20th century, when nature was increasingly seen to be in crisis, that the theological importance of nature came to the fore.

> The multidimensional ecological crisis, covering a range of problems from species extinction to climate change, has created a theological and ethical crisis in contemporary Christianity . . . theologians and ethicists discovered that the conventional theological and ethical interpretations of the faith often did not fit ecological realities. (Nash, 2005, p. 372)

Modern Protestant thinkers who have taken the environment seriously include Paul Tillich, Joseph Sittler, Juergen Moltmann, and John Cobb, among others (Santmire, 2005, p. 342). In 1990 Pope John Paul II promulgated an address titled "The Ecological Crisis: A Common Responsibility," in which he stated "Catholics have a 'serious obligation to care for all of Creation'" (French, 2005, p. 331).

The recent awakening of thinking and action regarding nature has been dubbed "environmental theology" or "eco-theology" (Van Wensveen, 2005, p. 354). It has included revisiting Christian teachings about God, Creation, the Fall, the Covenant, Christ, the Church, and Eschatology. The results expressed themselves in the formation of organizations promoting stewardship, conservation, recycling. and even political action. For example, Protestant seminaries have formed "The Green Seminary Initiative" to encourage "creation care" in the curriculum, worship, ministry, and lifestyle of church members (www.webofcreation.org).

Probably the most important actions were promoted by the North American Conference on Christianity and Ecology. Formed in 1986, it was an early effort to bring together Christian environmental groups and is considered an important milestone in the emergence of the Christian environmental movement (Kearns, 2005a, p. 1213). James Nash believes, "The ecological reformation is firmly established in contemporary Christianity." Its success will "depend on a number of factors, including the reformers' capacities to make theological and ethical cases for their cause, their strategic skills in influencing Christian churches, and their persistence in the hope and affections that first inspired the movement" (2005, p. 375). Clearly, the Christian "recovery of nature" has been instigated by a variety of leaders within the various branches of the Christian church, foregrounding the importance of leadership as Christians confront the growing environmental crisis.

RELIGIOUS LEADERSHIP

It is generally accepted that "the endless accumulation of empirical data has not produced an integrated understanding of leadership" (Bass, 1990, p. vii). In fact, it is questioned "whether a [grand theory of leadership] is desirable or possible" (Sorenson & Goethals, 2004, p. 873). The issue becomes even more complicated when religion is added to the mix: "Leadership is claimed, exercised, and contested in religious groups in many of the same ways that it is in other social situations. But religion also has distinctive features, particularly its appeal to supernatural forces for unsurpassable legitimization" (Gallagher, 2004, pp. 1307–1308).

Traditional theories of leadership, such as trait, behavioral, charismatic situational, contingency, transactional/transformational, and cognitive can all contribute to an understanding of religious leadership. But the leadership literature pays little attention to religion as a major field of study, and the concept of religious leadership remains relatively undeveloped (Lindt, 1986; McClymond, 2001). Thus, Heifetz (1994) does not include religion as a context in which leaders operate. Nevertheless Heifetz's contention that leadership is value-based is irrefutable and has special relevance for religion (p. 14). This position, along with Heifetz's notion of leadership as adaptive work (discussed further in the following), provides a useful foundation upon which to understand environmental leadership in a religious context.

To understand religious leadership it is necessary to situate it in the specific and well-defined beliefs and values of religious communities or traditions, as opposed to the larger social context. Several axioms seem appropriate: (a) religious leaders "achieve and maintain their status through a variety of interactions with specific audiences"; (b) the cosmology or value system of the "specific audience" is narrowly defined and bound together by a system of norms, values, and practices; (c) the claims to leadership in this context are evaluated by audiences who "themselves may be well versed in the specific issues of contention because of their personal experiences, familiarity with [the] tradition, or intellectual and moral acuity"; and (d) this "contention pertains to the larger milieu in which the specific religion struggles to prosper, and to organize its forces for evangelizing 'the world'" (Gallagher, 2004, p. 1308).

Other social systems in the larger environment, such as economic institutions, express more secular values and norms, with little if any direct reference to the sacred realm. It is consequently the disconnect between sacred and secular cosmologies that causes some of the most virulent conflicts within religious communities, and between those communities and the wider world. For example, maintaining and defending biblical Creationism in the context of an increasingly aggressive and convincing scientific cosmology (and the theory of evolution in particular) is a source of great tension between evangelicals and the wider society. As long as the sacred Christian biblical cosmology and secular scientific cosmologies are kept relatively separate, religious leadership tends to be more maintenance-oriented. But tensions—and the call for leaders to become defenders of traditional beliefs or brokers between conflicting cosmologies—are most prone to emerge when sacred and secular belief systems interact most intensely.

The religious communities most vulnerable to conflict are those whose members participate in the secular educational institutions and organizations. It is there that beliefs and truths that make up sacred cosmologies are most likely to be challenged, and consequently it is where leadership is most likely to emerge, as when a Dover, Pennsylvania, school board member held out for including coverage of Creationism in textbooks, and in the process became a local leader among evangelicals on the issue (Irons, 2007, p. 286).

Here Heifetz's notion of leadership as "adaptive work" becomes relevant. According to Heifetz (1994), "Leadership means influencing the community to face its problems," and requires "a change in values, beliefs or behavior" (pp. 14, 22). Leaders help groups confront complexities "that demand trade-offs in their ways of working or living . . . a gap between a desired state and reality that cannot be closed using existing approaches alone" (Heifetz, 2004, p. 9). Heifetz does not devote much attention to sacred belief systems in his adaptive work schema but strongly insists on the central significance of values:

> Typically, a social system will honor some mix of values, and the competition within this mix largely explains why adaptive work so often involves conflict. People with competing values engage one another as they confront a shared situation from their own point of view. (Heifetz, 1994, p. 32)

This stress on values makes Heifetz's theory particularly pertinent for understanding the dynamics of religious leadership, since most religious groups share a strong focus on values that very often conflict with the values of other groups and/or the dominant social, scientific, and political cultures that surround them.

EVANGELICALISM AND THE ENVIRONMENT

For the evangelical community, a major adaptive challenge involves the need to reconcile a belief system that often identifies "evil" with natural impulses and processes (e.g., sexual drive), with the growing need to foster and protect nature as a "good" with at least some intrinsic value. For many traditionally minded evangelicals, this latter begins to sound like "nature worship" and secular humanism: better leave it to God to decide the ultimate fate of the Earth and its creatures. As we shall see, however, the challenge is not merely to adapt evangelical beliefs and values to the need for environmental protection, but to do so in the context of mainstream environmentalism and modern secular beliefs and values pertaining to the natural world, some of which are perceived as threatening the very foundations of the Christian faith (DeWitt, 2005a).

Modern American Evangelicalism has roots in a variety of 18th- and 19th-century renewal movements within Protestantism. The evangelical pattern of intense religious experience includes strong emphasis on conversionism (a stress on the new birth), biblicism (the Bible as ultimate religious authority), activism (energetic religious and social involvement with a strong focus on evangelism), and crucicentrism—an emphasis on Christ's redeeming work as the heart of essential Christianity (Noll, Bebbington, & Rawlyk, 1994, p. 6; Olson, 1998). Evangelicalism's emphasis on God's reconciliation with rebellious humans through salvation has tended to stress preparation for eternity and the eschatological rapture and the ensuing destruction of this Earth, as foretold in the Book of Revelation. This emphasis has had direct implications for the downgrading of nature: "We cannot expect to find nature untouched by human hands as in and of itself good or even neutral. We ought instead to find it under the Curse and in need of redemptive transformation" (Beisner quoted in Frame, 1996, p. 83).

Based on a literal reading of the Bible and congregational authority structure, with little influence from ecclesiastical tradition, evangelical leadership has centered on the person of the local pastor/evangelist. "Pastoral leadership" has been a major force behind the life and belief systems of every congregation—ranging from small rural congregations to "megachurches" in major metropolitan areas. In addition, evangelical leaders such as Jimmy Swaggart, Pat Robertson, James Dobson, Rick Warren, Jerry Falwell, and many others have assumed a national profile through the use of radio, television, and other media. Such leaders have provided guidance and engaged in adaptive work on a host of "modern" issues that are challenging to evangelicals, including (but not limited to) homosexuality, abortion and birth control, the teaching of the theory of evolution, political ideology, stem cell research, ecumenicalism, and, as it has become a salient public issue, the natural environment.

As to the latter, it is worth noting that evangelicals' response to the emergence of the modern environmental movement has been bound up with their widespread rejection of the theory of evolution. For evangelicals, it has been important to assert God's creation and dominion over the Earth, rather than seeing the Earth as a dynamic and self-sustaining system in its own right, with a much longer history than is implied in a literal reading of the Bible. Mainstream environmentalism is premised in large part on a deep understanding and affirmation of evolutionary processes; modern biology and ecology are grounded in evolutionary theory. To align oneself with "environmentalists" is to become aligned with an evolutionary understanding of nature and, very often, a secular humanist outlook and liberal politics. Thus the emergence of the term *creation care*: Richard Cizik, one of the key evangelical environmental leaders (profiled below) states that the reason for using this term rather than environmentalism is that it is "based not on politics or ideology, but in the scriptures" (Cizik, 2008). As an environmental movement within evangelicalism has emerged, evangelicals who wish to lead on this issue have needed to adapt evangelical terms and emphases to environmental concerns; even then, as we shall see, many conservatives have remained wary of environmental activism.

THE EMERGENCE OF AN EVANGELICAL ENVIRONMENTAL MOVEMENT

The call for a new evangelical commitment to environmental stewardship emerged from a number of quarters. The Au Sable Institute in Wisconsin launched the evangelical concern for nature by study institutes, policy conferences, and "creation care" publications and organizations, beginning in 1958 (DeWitt, 2005b, p. 129). The Christian Environmental Council (CEC), the Evangelical Environmental Network (EEN), and the Christian Society of the Green Cross were subsequently created to advance environmental issues among Christians, including evangelicals. A wide variety of groups joined the EEN in support of its activities, including the American Scientific Affiliation, Association of Evangelical Relief and Development Organizations, the Christian Camping Association, the Coalition of Christian Colleges and Universities, InterVarsity Christian Fellowship, World Vision, the Mission Society for United Methodists, and many others (Frame, 1996).

There is strong evidence that evangelicals at large are becoming concerned about the environment. A national poll conducted in 2007 found that 84 percent of evangelicals support legislation to reduce global warming pollution levels, and 54 percent were "more likely to support a candidate that works toward that end" (Creation Care, 2007, p. 21). Among the first politically oriented statements was the CEC's call on President Clinton and Vice President Gore to "exercise strong, just, and decisive leadership in addressing the challenge of Global Warming" at the Kyoto Conference in 1997. "An Evangelical Declaration of the Care of Creation" soon followed in 1999, signed by 290 academic, religious, and business leaders from across the United States (Creation Care, 2000, p. 6; see also Womersley, 2005, p. 1159).

In June, 2004, the "Sandy Cove Covenant" broadened the commitment among evangelicals to environmental care, and was signed by 29 active evangelical leaders concerned about the environment (Creation Care, 2004, pp. 10–11). In February 2006, "Climate Change: An Evangelical Call to Action" was signed by 98 pastors, presidents of denominations, colleges, universities, and other institutions, including leaders such as Jim Ball, Joel Hunter, Jim Wallis, Rick Warren, and Ron Sider (Signatories to Climate Change, n.d.). This statement was released immediately after the National Association of Evangelicals (NAE) decided *not* to take a stand on the human role in global warming, stating "global warming is not a consensus issue [among evangelicals]" (Goodstein, 2006).

Evangelicals have been divided on other environmental issues as well. For example, in 1995 the EEN passed a "Resolution on the Care and Keeping of Creation and its Living Species," which was presented to the U.S. Congress to support the Endangered Species Act. This action was publically opposed by conservative evangelicals, including James Dobson and Bill Bright (Kearns, 2005b, p. 1757). Some evangelicals claimed:

> The [evangelical environmental] movement has failed to maintain enough distance from a secular environmental movement laden with humanistic and pantheistic views. Isn't concern for the environment a part of New Age Religion? Why should we be anxious about environmental problems when God is in control? (Quoted in Frame, 1996, p. 83)

Soon after the "Statement of the Evangelical Climate Initiative" was released by leading figures in the NAE, a dissenting group, the Interfaith Stewardship Alliance, strenuously objected in "An Open Letter to the Signers of 'Climate Change: An Evangelical Call to Action' and Others Concerned about Global Warming." Theologian Wayne Grudem stated their position:

> It does not seem likely that God would set up the world to work in such a way that human beings would eventually destroy the earth by doing ordinary and morally good and necessary things as breathing, building a fire to cook or keep warm, burning fuel to travel, or using energy for a refrigerator to preserve food. (Cornwall Alliance, n.d.)

LEADERSHIP IN A CHALLENGING CONTEXT

Evangelicals showing leadership on the environment clearly face daunting adaptive challenges; indeed, without the strong leadership shown by self-selected individuals, it seems likely there would be no "evangelical" environmental movement to speak of. It is in ideologically challenging situations such as these that *leadership* becomes salient as a necessary condition for change. And, indeed, the radical changes in evangelical attitudes toward nature were instigated by a relatively small group of individuals who began to call for a reevaluation of evangelical attitudes toward, and relations with, nature. They were becoming aware of the negative reputation evangelicals were receiving for their neglect of nature in the larger religious and secular community and felt the need to do something about it. In what follows, five representative leaders are briefly profiled, with a focus on career trajectories, the strategies they used in becoming a leader, and how they overcame resistance by evangelicals and others. Unless otherwise indicated, interviews with each leader profiled serve as the primary source material for this section. These profiles illustrate how cognitive challenges resulted in adaptive work performed by such leaders.[1]

Calvin DeWitt (b.1935)

A Baptist, DeWitt majored in biology at Calvin College and earned a PhD in zoology at the University of Michigan. He taught at several colleges, then the University of Wisconsin. He became increasingly concerned that flora and fauna were threatened and rapidly disappearing. He pioneered a plethora of courses, majors, and conferences on conservation and preservation of nature. He became a leading consultant to various conservation organizations, was a co-founder of the EEN, and was a major architect of the Au Sable Institute, which has been a leader for evangelical colleges in environmental training and activism. DeWitt has "been one of the prime movers behind almost every significant collaboration between evangelicals, scientists, and politicians including the much discussed 'Evangelical Climate Initiative'" (Roberts, 2006).

DeWitt has thus been very influential, but his integration of theological principles with a scientific approach to environmental concerns has been questioned by conservative evangelicals.[2] Nevertheless, his status as a layman with scientific training, rather than a pastor or theologian, has allowed him to be relatively free of being "silenced" by the evangelical community and its theological leadership (DeWitt, 2009).

Ron Sider (b.1939)

A Brethren in Christ/Mennonite with an MA and PhD from Yale, Sider was employed at the Philadelphia campus of Messiah College. Confronted with the racial and economic injustices in the inner city, he became a prominent activist for social justice. He developed a conviction that biblical discipleship included care for the creation, and he built this conviction into his theology of redemption; his major theological goal is to heal the separation between the spiritual and the material world (the Platonic view) created by the Enlightenment (Sider, 2008). As a seminary professor, he has shown strong leadership in stressing the ethical side of Christian faith, which he feels has been neglected in evangelical Christianity. He was the founder of Evangelicals for Social Action (ESA), which seeks to develop biblical solutions to social and economic injustice, and he assisted in producing the "Chicago Declaration of Evangelical Social Concern." Sider was a founding member of the National Religious Partnership for the Environment, and a founding member of Christian Society of the Green Cross. Sider has written on poverty, abortion, capital punishment, and the environment in a wide variety of venues. He implemented his leadership by helping to create organizations that promote innovative causes as noted earlier. Sider is no "flaming" theological radical. Yet it would be hard to think of another evangelical who has been more ardently criticized for being "radical." Conservatives in the evangelical community have criticized his work as "bad theology and/or bad economics" (Stafford, 2000).

Richard Cizik (b.1942)

A member of the Evangelical Presbyterian Church, Cizik studied political science at Whitworth College and earned an MDiv at Denver Theological Seminary. Cizik was initially ensconced in conservative Evangelicalism. He was strongly opposed to environmentalism, was a "pro-Bush conservative" taking conservative positions on gay marriage, abortion, stem cell research, and related issues (Little, 2005). His activist style helped him become vice president of the NAE in charge of Governmental Affairs. He became widely known as one of the most prominent evangelical lobbyists in Washington DC. He advised the NAE to steer clear of environmental issues.

Cizik was "converted" to "care of creation" when he was invited to hear a presentation by evangelical Sir John Houghton in 2002. Cizik states, "I did not choose this role. The best scientific thinking [e.g., Houghton] converted me." Cizik subsequently became very active in promoting the importance of creation care, "the defining issue of our time" (Cizik, 2008). Cizik was a signer of the "Evangelical Climate Initiative," and at present is a strong advocate for a biblical view of creation care, and that the Bible and science can exist in harmony. "Climate change is real and human induced. It calls for action soon. If we are to be obedient to scriptures, there is no time to wait, no time to stall, no time to deliberate" (The Great Warming, n.d.). His greatest concern is failing "to become obedient to the command that God has given me and my role in Washington. God won't ask, 'Rich, how did I create the earth?' He'll [rather] say, 'Rich, what did you do to protect that which I created?'" (The Great Warming, n.d.). This aggressive approach caused him to come under attack by conservative evangelicals. In December 2008, he resigned from the NAE after some comments he made regarding gay marriage, although his support for environmental causes also appears to have played a role in his resignation (Eckstrom, 2008). Evangelical leaders agree that Cizik was highly influential in leading evangelicals toward environmental responsibility (Vu, 2008).

Jim Ball (b.1961)

Jim Ball attended Baylor University and Southern Baptist Seminary and has served as an ordained minister in various capacities. At Drew University, he met a peer who helped him to understand that "Christ's reconciliation included all creation." Subsequently he taught and researched environmental issues, publishing *Planting a Tree this Afternoon: Global Warming, Public Theology and Public Policy* (1998), a widely used primer for Christians on global warming and other environmental issues. He worked for the Union of Concerned Scientists and in January 2000 became executive director of EEN (EEN, n.d.)

Several years ago, Ball and his wife Kara drove across the United States in a Prius with a challenging placard: "What Would Jesus Drive?" Jim Ball has spent most of his energy and time as catalyst and liaison between various evangelical groups and institutions promoting an "Evangelical Call to Action" on climate change. As chairman of EEN, Ball has struggled to promote creation care in evangelical circles, and believes "the main reason many evangelicals have not been as engaged in caring for God's creation as the Bible calls them to be is because in their minds 'environmentalists' are liberals who hold beliefs [e.g., pantheism] that can be harmful and lead people astray." Environmentalists "who do not share our faith perspective will have to understand that we evangelicals will have some different reasons for addressing environmental concerns. But once committed, we can help make a difference" (Ball, 2005). Though mistrusted by some evangelicals, his moderate approach has allowed him to remain in an influential position.

Joel Hunter (b.1948)

Nurtured in an evangelical Methodist home and college, Hunter attained a Master of Divinity at Christian Theological Seminary before becoming pastor at Northland Community Church, north of Orlando, Florida. Hunter's numerous innovations expanded the effectiveness and outreach of the congregation. His dynamic persona soon made him a spokesman for evangelicals. But an invitation by fellow evangelical Rick Warren to sign the "Evangelical Climate Initiative" increased his awareness of the role of the Creation in God's plans. Hunter soon became known as one of the influential promoters of creation care among evangelicals. "Our approach would be to educate people and give them a theological basis for taking care of the environment as a biblical and moral mandate." He became a board member of EEN and has promoted an educational program that ties creation care with Christology. In his view, as a pastor, "If you have a vision, the people will follow" (Hunter, 2008). He characterizes himself as "a recent student [of environmentalism], but a very convinced student" (Roberts, 2006b). Because his approach involves working with interest groups and pastoral education, Hunter has been successful in communicating among evangelicals, and in 2006 he was asked to become president of the Christian Coalition, a conservative alliance of evangelicals formed by Pat Robertson in 1988. However, his attempts to broaden the theological base of the Coalition to include creation care produced opposition among conservative evangelicals, so he resigned in November 23, 2006, attracting considerable national attention.

CONCLUSION: EVANGELICAL ENVIRONMENTAL LEADERSHIP AS ADAPTIVE WORK

These selected evangelical leaders express a veritable "prophetic" appeal to evangelicals to awaken to the social, economic, and environmental degradations that are threatening the Earth. Though these five individuals accept the centrality of a biblically derived cosmology, all deviate from traditional evangelicalism by proposing that salvation involves caring for and restoring the natural world (creation) along with the individual soul. That is, all believe that the Bible's "salvation history" includes social, political, economic, and environmental healing and reconciliation. These leaders are furthermore involved in the "adaptive work" of reconciling ecological crisis with a belief system that is not inherently disposed towards concern for nature; their goal has been to challenge evangelicals to respond to "God's plan for nature." Their success in this endeavor is reflected in the growing number of evangelicals who express concern about the natural environment without fear of becoming stigmatized as "liberal" or worse.

Because Evangelicalism has a highly focused emphasis on a theistic understanding of natural and human history, leadership within this matrix cannot be easily regarded as a subtype of secular schemes of leadership. Unfortunately, conceptualization of religious leadership has not advanced much beyond Weber's famous discussion of "charismatic authority" (Weber, 1947), which needs to be developed further to be fully useful when analyzing religious leaders (McClymond, 2001). In this chapter I have offered an example of how Heifetz's notion of leadership as adaptive work can help to broaden our understanding of religious leadership and the role that evangelical leaders have played in steering evangelicals towards greater concern for the natural environment. As we have seen, they have worked hard to rally support for environmental causes from within the belief system of their co-religionists, by adapting religious terms and ideas (e.g., "creation care") to the issues at hand and framing environmental issues as faith issues. As Heifetz states, in cases like this "adaptive work [involves] utilizing both traditional values and the values represented by those who recognize . . . society's direct dependence on natural resources" (Heifetz, 1994, p. 34).

The example of these figures may be helpful and inspiring not only to other evangelicals interested in showing leadership on this issue, but to leaders at large, by demonstrating how important it is to adapt existing belief systems to the new reality of environmental crisis. An obvious extrapolation would be to suggest that political conservatives will likely respond more positively to leaders who frame environmentalism as an essentially *conservative* phenomenon: what could be more conservative than to keep things as they are, and prevent them from getting worse? (See Chapter 15 of this volume for discussion of the inherently "conservative" dimensions of sustainability.)

Evangelical eco-leaders may not only be working for the preservation of nature, but of their own faith tradition as well; for as Taylor (2005) suggests, "It is environments which decisively shape religions, not vice versa, and over the long run, the only religions that will endure will be those proving 'adaptive' within their earthly habitats" (p. 1376). Only time will tell if evangelical Christianity and other faith traditions will lead the way—or merely follow—towards environmental sustainability. The figures profiled in this chapter illustrate that the first steps have been taken by evangelical leaders in this direction. One can hope that in coming decades these figures will be remembered as some of the early founding figures in a much broader and deeper movement.

NOTES

1. These leaders were chosen on the basis of several criteria, including theological convictions, numerous publications regarding environmental care, and considerable achievements in organizing action in the evangelical community.
2. See, for example, the criticism in *Dossier*, a publication of The National Center for Public Policy Research, a conservative think tank (www.nationalcenter.org/dos31dewitt.html).

REFERENCES

Ball, J. (1998). *Planting a Tree this Afternoon: Global Warming, Public Theology, and Public Policy.* Wynnewood, PA: Evangelicals for Social Action.

Ball, J. (2005). Ungodly Distortions: Evangelical Christians Know that Caring for God's Creation Is a Scriptural Imperative. *Beliefnet.* Retrieved from http://www.beliefnet.com/News/2005/03/Ungodly-Distortions.aspx

Bass, B. (1990). *Bass & Stogdill's Handbook of Leadership: Theory, Research, and Managerial Applications.* New York: Free Press.

Chryssavgis, J. (2005). Christian Orthodoxy. In B. Taylor & J. Kaplan (Eds.), *The Encyclopedia of Religion and Nature* (pp. 333–337). London: Thoemmes Continuum

Cizik, R. (2008). October 3. Interview by telephone. Notes and recording in the author's possession.

Cornwall Alliance. (n.d.). An Open Letter to the Signers of "Climate Change: An Evangelical Call to Action" and Others Concerned about Global Warming. Retrieved from http://www.cornwallalliance.org/docs/an-open-letter-to-the-signers-of-climate-change-an-evangelical-call-to-action-and-others-concerned-about-global-warming.pdf

Creation Care. (2000). *Creation Care: A Christian Environmental Quarterly, 9*(Spring) 6–19.

Creation Care. (2004). *Creation Care: A Christian Environmental Quarterly, 26*(Fall) 10–11.

Creation Care. (2007). *Creation Care: A Christian Environmental Quarterly, 34*(Fall) 21.

DeWitt, C. (2005a). An Evangelical Perspective on Faith and Nature. In B. Taylor & J. Kaplan (Eds.), *The Encyclopedia of Religion and Nature* (pp. 369–371). London: Thoemmes Continuum.

DeWitt, C. (2005b). Au Sable Institute. In B. Taylor & J. Kaplan (Eds.), *The Encyclopedia of Religion and Nature* (p. 129). London: Thoemmes Continuum.

DeWitt, C. (2009). January 30. Interview by telephone. Notes and recording in the author's possession.

Eckstrom, K. (2008). Religion's Big and Unprecedented Role in '08 Politics. *Washington Post*, December 27.

Evangelical Environmental Network. (n.d.). Retrieved from http://www.creationcare.org/welcome.php

Frame, R. (1996). The Greening of the Gospel? *Christianity Today*, November 11, 82–86.

French, W. (2005). Roman Catholicism. In B. Taylor & J. Kaplan (Eds.), *The Encyclopedia of Religion and Nature* (328–333). London: Thoemmes Continuum.

Gallagher, E. (2004). Religion. In G. Goethals, G. Sorenson, & J. Burns (Eds.), *Encyclopedia of Leadership* (pp. 1307–1314). Thousand Oaks, CA: Sage Publications.

Goodstein, L. (2006). Evangelical Leaders Join Global Warming Initiative. *New York Times*, February 8.

Heifetz, R. (1994). *Leadership without Easy Answers.* Cambridge, MA: Harvard University Press.

———. (2004). Adaptive Work. In G. Goethals, G. Sorenson, & J. Burns (Eds.), *Encyclopedia of Leadership* (pp. 8-13). Thousand Oaks, CA: Sage Publications.

Hunter, R. (2008). September 5. Interview by telephone. Notes and recording in the author's possession.

Irons, P. (2007). *God on Trial: Dispatches from America's Religious Battlefields.* New York: Penguin Press.

Kalland, A. (2005). The Religious Environmentalist Paradigm. In B. Taylor & J. Kaplan (Eds.), *The Encyclopedia of Religion and Nature* (pp. 1367–1371). London: Thoemmes Continuum.

Kearns, L. (2005a). North American Conference on Christianity and Ecology. In B. Taylor & J. Kaplan (Eds.), *The Encyclopedia of Religion and Nature* (pp. 1212–1214). London: Thoemmes Continuum.

Kearns, L. (2005b). Wise Use Movement. In B. Taylor & J. Kaplan (Eds.), *The Encyclopedia of Religion and Nature* (pp. 1755–1758). London: Thoemmes Continuum.

Knopf, R. (1987). Human Behavior, Cognition, and Affect in the Natural Environment. In D. Stokols & I. Altman (Eds.), *Handbook of Environmental Psychology* (pp. 783–811). New York: John Wiley and Sons.

Lindt, G. (1986). Leadership. In M. Eliade (Ed.), *Encyclopedia of Religion Vol. 8* (pp. 485–490). New York: Macmillan.

Little, A. (2005). An Interview with Green Evangelical Leader Richard Cizik. *Grist*, October 5. Retrieved from http://www.grist.org/article/cizik

McClymond, M. (2001). Prophet or Loss? Reassessing Max Weber's Theory of Religious Leadership. In D. N. Freedman & M. J. McClymond, *The Rivers of Paradise: Moses, Buddha, Confucius, Jesus and Muhammad as Religious Founders* (pp. 613–658). Grand Rapids, MI: Wm. B. Eerdmans Publishing Company.

Nash, J. (2005). Christianity's Ecological Reformation. In B. Taylor & J. Kaplan (Eds.), *The Encyclopedia of Religion and Nature* (pp. 372–375). London: Thoemmes Continuum.

Noll, M., Bebbington, D., & Rawlyk, G. (1994). *Evangelicalism.* New York: Oxford University Press.

Oelschlaeger, M. (2005). Paleolithic Religions and the Future. In B. Taylor & J. Kaplan (Eds.), *The Encyclopedia of Religion and Nature* (pp. 1256–1257). London: Thoemmes Continuum.

Olson, R. (1998). Does Evangelical Theology have a Future? *Christianity Today*, February 9. Retrieved from http://ctlibrary.com/ct/1998/february9/8t2040.html

Roberts, D. (2006a). An Interview with Environmental Scientist and Evangelical Leader Calvin DeWitt. *Grist*, October 17. Retrieved from http://www.grist.org/article/dewitt

Roberts, D. (2006b). Rev. Joel Hunter Speaks out on Broadening the Evangelical Agenda. *Grist*, December 12. Retrieved from http://www.grist.org/article/hunter

Santmire, H. (2005). Christianity-Reformation Traditions: Lutheranism and Calvinism. In B. Taylor & J. Kaplan (Eds.), *The Encyclopedia of Religion and Nature* (pp. 341–344). London: Thoemmes Continuum.

Sider, R. (2008). September 8. Interview by telephone. Notes and recording in the author's possession.

Signatories to Climate Change. (n.d.). Signatories to Climate Change: An Evangelical Call to Action. Retrieved from http://christiansandclimate.org/ learn/call-to-action/signatories/

Sorenson, G., & Goethals, G. (2004). Leadership Theories: Overview. In G. Goethals, G. Sorenson, & J. Burns (Eds.), *Encyclopedia of Leadership* (pp. 867–874). Thousand Oaks, CA: Sage Publications.

Stafford, T. (2000). Ron Sider's Unsettling Crusade. *Christianity Today*, March 1. Retrieved from http://www.christianitytoday.com/ct/2000/marchweb-only/12.0a.html

Taylor, B. (2005). Critical Perspectives on "Religions of the World and Ecology." In B. Taylor & J. Kaplan (Eds.), *The Encyclopedia of Religion and Nature* (pp. 1375–1376). London: Thoemmes Continuum.

The Great Warming (n.d.). Interview with Richard Cizik. *The Great Warming.* Retrieved from http://www.thegreatwarming.com/revrichardcizik.html

Tillich, P. (1963). *Systematic Theology.* Chicago: University of Chicago Press.

Tucker, M. (2005). Teilhard de Chardin, Pierre (18811955). In B. Taylor & J. Kaplan (Eds.), *The Encyclopedia of Religion and Nature* (pp. 1627–1629). London: Thoemmes Continuum.

Van Wensveen, L. (2005). Theology and Ecology: Contemporary Introduction. In B. Taylor & J. Kaplan (Eds.), *The Encyclopedia of Religion and Nature* (pp. 354–355). London: Thoemmes Continuum.

Vu, M. (2008). Evangelical Cizik among *Time*'s 100 Most Influential People. *The Christian Post*, May 4.

Wach, J. (1942). *Sociology of Religion.* Chicago: University of Chicago Press.

Weber, M. (1947). *The Theory of Social and Economic Organization.* Glencoe, IL: Free Press.

Whitney, E. (2005). The Thesis of Lynn White. In B. Taylor & J. Kaplan (Eds.), *The Encyclopedia of Religion and Nature* (pp. 1735–1737). London: Thoemmes Continuum.

Wiebe, M. (2005). Creation's Fate in the New Testament. In B. Taylor & J. Kaplan (Eds.), *The Encyclopedia of Religion and Nature* (pp. 437–438). London: Thoemmes Continuum.

Womersley, M. (2005). National Religious Partnership for the Environment. In B. Taylor & J. Kaplan (Eds.), *The Encyclopedia of Religion and Nature* (pp. 1158–1159). London: Thoemmes Continuum.

York, R. (2005). Pantheism. In B. Taylor & J. Kaplan (Eds.), *The Encyclopedia of Religion and Nature* (pp. 1257–1261). London: Thoemmes Continuum.

14 The Turn to Spirituality and Environmental Leadership

Corné J. Bekker

INTRODUCTION

In the late 1960s, when the environmental movement was still an emerging cultural phenomenon, Lynn White, Jr., a history professor from the University of California, published a seminal article titled "The Historical Roots of Our Ecological Crises" (White, 1967). White's modest paper, which took contemporary western Christianity to task for contributing to the current ecological crises, marked a turning point in both the scholarly and public discussions of the roles of spirituality, religion, and religious leadership in the effort to construct sustainable models of environmental care (Santmire, 1985). White's thesis was that spirituality and theology shape leadership and behavior towards the environment. If this thesis is correct, then a better understanding of the dynamic relationship between diverse forms of spirituality and the natural world will be helpful in the ongoing efforts of environmental leaders to motivate and engage with a wide variety of people (Ivakhiv, 2007). This chapter seeks to explore the relationships between spiritualities and environmental leadership in order to open new avenues for dialogue between those who have concern for the "sacred" (Kourie, 2006) and those that have a "tender regard" for the Earth (Kelley, 1982). The possible convergence of the most deeply held values of lived spiritualities and environmental leadership might hold the theoretical and practical keys to construct and energize an integrated, contemporary approach to leadership that could address the growing environmental crises from deeper, spiritual perspectives.

The present age has been marked by an increasing interest in the phenomenon of spirituality (Kourie, 2006), and this interest has reached the field of organizational leadership (Singh-Sengupta, 2007) and the focused study of "religiously inspired conservation ethics" (Snodgrass & Tiedje, 2008, p. 6). Gottlieb (2007) argues that religious or spirituality-based environmentalism can make a positive contribution to environmental leadership for the following reasons: (a) religious environmentalism offers the secular world a particular language to describe the "depth of relationship" (p. 81) of humans to the rest of the world and the extent of the devastation of the damage done already to the environment; (b) environmentalists can draw on the religious traditions of their own cultures for positive values that in turn can provide critical assessment and thinking skills for their leaders; and (c) religious environmentalism at its "most moral and socially engaged" can offer "models of human and compassionate activist politics" (p. 83) that are of particular interest to environmental leaders.

The turn to spirituality comes at the same time that greater emphasis is being placed on the role of values in organizational leadership (Klenke, 2007). Schwartz (1992) highlights the transformative aspect of values when defining them as: "desirable states, objects, goals, or behaviors transcending specific situations" (p. 2). This chapter focuses on several core values of spiritualities that facilitate, empower, and sustain environmental leadership. I argue that these respective values work in religious and spiritual communities to form a conceptual and logical framework that facilitates the often radical and countercultural decisions and stances associated with environmentalism in these particular cultural and social contexts. At the same time, it is my conviction that such values at times transcend the religious and spiritual contexts described in this chapter, and that they can be observed in a diverse array of communities that seek to lead in the care of the Earth. It is the possible convergence of these values in both sets of communities that could assist environmental leaders in energizing and motivating spiritual leaders to consider the ethical demands of the growing environmental crisis. At the same time, observing the age-old values of concern for creation in these spiritualities could assist secular leaders to adopt leadership approaches and philosophies that take the spiritual dimensions of both humanity and the environment seriously.

Current phenomenological investigations in spirituality research distinguish three basic forms of spirituality:

established schools of spirituality
primordial spiritualities
counter-spirituality (Waaijman, 2006)

Established schools of spirituality have their origin in specific historical and sociocultural settings that over time give rise to discernable schools or ways of the "spirit." Primordial spiritualities are imbedded in ordinary human experiences such as birth, marriage, having children, experiencing death, and suffering. Countermovements in spirituality offer alternate solutions to existing social and religious power structures, and the research in these fields follows sociological descriptions of systems of liminality, inferiority, and marginality (Waaijman, 2002).

In this chapter I make use of this framework for defining spirituality to explore and discuss three examples of spiritualities that include a concern for the Earth and advocate ethical leadership behaviors as part of that concern. The medieval, kenotic, and nature mysticism of Francis of Assisi is discussed as an example of an established school of spirituality. The participatory mutuality of the southern African philosophy of ubuntu and its impact on environmental leadership is explored as an example of primordial spirituality. Finally, an example of a countermovement in spirituality and the implications for environmental leadership is presented through an examination of the frugal leadership of Quakerism.

ENVIRONMENTAL LEADERSHIP AND THE COSMOLOGICAL MYSTICISM OF FRANCIS OF ASSISI

The study of established schools of spirituality involve a "historical synthesis" (Waaijman, 2002, p. 117), often guided by hermeneutic research in the texts of the particular school, that describes progressive spiritual movements which begin in an original source-experience. For example, the formation of a Christian school of thought traces its origin to the source-experience of the birth, life, death, and resurrection of Jesus of Nazareth as recorded in the sacred texts of Christianity. These movements often open new ways of thinking about the past, present, and future. In time the movements are structured into an "organic whole" (Waaijman, 2002, p. 118) in order that a larger group of people can have access to the source-experience and new perspectives in thinking. As the movements grow through successive generations, access to the source-experience are sometimes blocked and thus a reformation of sorts becomes necessary (see Figure 14.1).

The medieval, penitent, and spiritual movement of Francis of Assisi (1181–1226) displays these kinds of historical structures and progressions. Despite its medieval roots, Franciscan spirituality continues to play an

1. A source-experience that gives birth to a spiritual way.
2. An inner circle of pupils takes shape around the spiritual way.
3. The spiritual way is situated within a specific sociocultural context.
4. The spiritual way opens a new, specific perspective on the future.
5. A second generation structures the spiritual way into an organic whole.
6. The spiritual way is shared with many people.
7. When the source-experience, the contextual relevance, and the power to open the future are blocked, a reformation is needed.

Figure 14.1 Waaijman's (2002) progressive description of established schools of spirituality.

important role in emerging Christian movements. The rise of several monastic movements that value voluntary social and environmental involvement amongst evangelical Christians, and cite the 13th-century Franciscan leader as their inspiration (Bessenecker, 2006), are examples of the vitality, resilience, and longevity of this 800-year-old school of spirituality.

Any effort to fully understand Francis of Assisi and his leadership must start with a focus on his view of the things of the spirit. Francis's spirituality was one of Christian mysticism (Delio, 2003). Ledoux (1997) defines Christian mysticism as "the experience of the interior and unifying encounter with the Divine Infinite that is the foundation of the Divine Being and of all existence" (p. 27). Franciscan mysticism has been described as (a) profoundly Christological, (b) affectionate, (c) biblical, (d) theological, (e) incarnational, (f) kenotic, and, finally, (g) cosmological (Kourie, 1993; Mueller, 2003; Ledoux, 1997; Karecki & Wroblewski, 2000b; Delio, 2003). Central to the original "source-experience" (Waaijman, 2002, p. 118) of Franciscan spirituality and leadership was the unique combination of the kenotic charisma of Francis and his particular understanding of the centrality of nature and the cosmos in the human efforts to love and lead.

The leadership of Francis was marked by a determined negation of the material trappings that are often perceived as the natural right of leaders. His radical practice of voluntary poverty was rooted in his desire to imitate the kenosis (self-emptying) of Jesus Christ (Teresa, 1995) as expressed within the Christological hymn of the Apostle's Paul's letter to the Philippians (Kourie, 1993). The theological concept of kenosis in Franciscan theology and leadership is seen as a "resolute divesting of the person of every claim of self interest so as to be ready to live the Gospel of Christ in every aspect of living, freed from the dictates of personal preference" (Cronin, 1992, p. 1). Francis's voluntary divesting of power, prestige, and possessions finds its theological context in his ardent desire to follow in the footsteps of the kenotic Christ who emptied Himself and embraced poverty as a way of leading for the sake of others. Poverty in leadership within Franciscan thought was a means to union with the Divine. Kourie (1993) describes this commitment to radical poverty as transformational: "[The] practice of poverty had as its aim the radical transformation of the person, the abolition of a narrow selfhood and the silencing of the all too natural tendency toward fragmentation and purely functional consciousness" (p. 124). The kenotic mysticism of Francis led to "human authentication" (Kourie, 1993, p. 125) that allowed for the leader to enter into the world of followers. Thus Francis's leadership of kenotic mysticism, through a radical commitment to poverty, linked mystical self-limiting and emptying with receptivity to the presence of the Divine and others around us.

Linking the "self-emptying and receptivity" of Christ in the Philippians hymn (2:5–11) and in Francis's leadership, and then seeing it as the "point of intersection where divinity and humanity meet" (Gau, 2000, p. 406), opens the door to explore the values of this radical stance of giving up of status, privilege, and possessions in leadership. The values of kenosis have been described as: (a) voluntary self-limitation, (b) vulnerability, (c) being present to the "other," (d) voluntary powerlessness, (e) continual purification from self-centeredness, (f) humility, (g) self-sacrifice, and (h) openness to the "other" (Barbour, 1990; Baker, 1970; Szabolcs, 2003; Papanikolaou, 2003). In this light, kenotic leadership as appropriated in the spirituality and leadership of Francis of Assisi was rooted in a mimetic reenactment of the self-emptying/kenotic leadership of Christ (Karecki and Wroblewski, 2000a). The missiologist Yves Raguin (1973), building on these precepts, argues that "kenosis, then, is the gateway to mutual understanding, and beyond this, to an intimate sharing that is the consummation of a relationship in union. . . . By dispossession of self we are able to absorb the amazing riches of others" (p. 112). The overcoming of the separation between leader and follower that this kind of radical practice facilitates finds its deepest dimension in kenotic love and self-sacrifice that negates the "dream of separateness" (Merton, 1966, p. 156).

The determined overcoming of separation in Franciscan spirituality goes beyond addressing mere human separation and leader–follower distance to bridging the conceptual gap between humans and the cosmos in medieval thought (Richstatter, 2001). Francis's theocratic and kenotic understanding of the Christian doctrine of the incarnation widened the scope and meaning of salvation and placed it within a cosmological context (Delio, 2003). For Francis, ecological conservation and the soteriological concern of the church became part of the same Divine thrust in the world (Hayes, 1996). As God emptied Himself to become fully human in Christ, so did creation bear witness of the original self emptying of God in creating this world to bear His own image. Delio (2003) illustrates the implications of combining the kenotic and the cosmological in Franciscan theology: "Redemption, therefore, is not being 'saved from' but rather being made 'whole for' the healing and the wholeness of God's creation, and this wholeness is ultimately the transformation of created reality through the unitive power of God's creative love" (p. 18). Franciscan leadership thus combines the proclamation of the truth and love of God with a central concern for the "healing and the wholeness of God's creation" (Delio, 2003, p. 18). To be in right relationship with God is to understand man's brotherhood with all creation and to participate in the Divine efforts to care for and heal the Earth. This vision of kenotic and cosmological spirituality has been obscured throughout the centuries of Christian history (Braybrooke, 1976; Powell, 2007), while efforts to foster a "greening" of the church (Warner, 2008, p. 113) have often included revisiting the original "source-experience" (Waaijman, 2002, p. 118) of the ecological vision of Francis of Assisi. Francis's unitive vision of human and cosmological salvation is perhaps best expressed in an excerpt from his most famous poem, "The Canticle of the Creatures":

> All praise be yours, my Lord, through all that you have made. And first, my Lord Brother Sun, who brings the day; and light you give to us through him. How beautiful is he, how radiant in all his splendor. Of you, Most High, he bears the likeness. All praise be yours, my Lord, through Sister Moon and Stars; In the heavens you have made them, bright, and precious and fair. All praise be yours, my Lord, through Sister Water, so useful, lowly, precious and pure. . . . Praise and bless my Lord, and give him thanks, and serve him with great humility. (Quoted in LeClerc, 1977, pp. 233–234)

ENVIRONMENTAL LEADERSHIP AND THE PRIMORDIAL SPIRITUALITY OF UBUNTU

There are forms of spirituality that do not belong to well-established schools of theological and philosophical reflection but rather are connected with lived experience. As Waaijman (2006) notes:

> They are closely related to life as it is directly lived, connected with realities such as birth, education, house, work, suffering, death. Of course, schools try to integrate this primordial spirituality, but by doing that, they admit that the primordial spirituality is originally independent, earlier than the school. (p. 7)

A synchronic study of primordial spiritualities (sometimes referred to as native spiritualities) identifies three universal characteristics: (a) a strong bond with the environment, mediated through the community; (b) the centrality of community that is structured around familial relationships; and (c) a personal life framed by birth and death, which connects with the community through service, love, and care (Waaijman, 2002, p. 7).

One such example of a primordial or native spirituality that has empowered and sustained acts of environmental leadership is the southern African social philosophy of ubuntu. The South African Nguni word *ubuntu* derives from the aphorism; "Umuntu Ngumuntu Ngabantu—A person is a person because/through others." It can be described as the capacity in African culture to express compassion, reciprocity, solidarity, dignity, humanity, and mutuality in the interest of building and maintaining communities with justice and mutual caring. More than a descriptor of African values, ubuntu should be seen as a social philosophy and a spirituality that is deeply embedded in African culture (Nama & Swartz, 2002). Mnyaka and Motlhabi (2005) describe ubuntu as the primary foundation of a South African religious and spiritual worldview.

A useful way of thinking about ubuntu is to consider it as a basic form of southern African spirituality that is manifested in mutuality and solidarity with all and the environment. It is part of the very fabric of indigenous southern African spiritual and intellectual identity (Mnyaka & Motlhabi, 2005). Ubuntu, seen in the spirit of participatory humanism and environmental concern, has the power to effect a revitalized commitment to environmental leadership by South Africans (Chivaura, 2006; Murove, 2004; Teffo, 1998). Leaders with the inherent values of ubuntu, as it might relate to environmental leadership, have been described as: (a) follower-centered, (b) humble, (c) ready to enter into dialogue, (d) caring, (e) polite, (f) tolerant, (g) considerate, (h) hospitable, (i) having an attitude of mutual acceptance or mutuality, and (j) recognizing an intimate bond between themselves and the environment (Teffo, 1998; Le Roux, 2000; Lorenzo, 2003; Mkabela, 2005; Murove, 2004).

Ubuntu-inspired leaders therefore see community rather than self-determination as the essential aspect of personhood. Thus the wealth of the individual is the wealth of the community. The South African Venda saying, "Muthu u bebelwa munwe—A person is born for the other," captures the spirit of this approach of interdependence between self and community. It is in locating, entering into honest dialogue, and taking steps to relocate the "self" in mutuality with the "other" that the self is enriched, formed, and defined. This relocation of the self in mutuality with others includes familial, economic, and ultimately environmental decisions. Building on this premise, Louw (2003) writes: "Ubuntu inspires us to expose ourselves to others, to encounter the difference of their humanness so as to inform and enrich our own" (p. 1). This broader, communal self-perception can form the basis for a renewed model of citizenship in African democracies (Enslin & Horsthemke, 2004) and a revitalized African commitment to ecological conservation (Murove, 2004).

The relocation of identify from "self" to "others" in southern African primordial spiritualities such as ubuntu also extends to locating the self within the natural environment (Van Schalkwyk, 2008). It is within this environmental self-understanding that traditional southern African leadership ethics, fueled by the spirituality of ubuntu, strongly recognize the "intimate bond between men and their environment" (Murove, 2004, p. 195). Ubuntu leadership, in its quest to ensure the radical mutuality of all, proposes that there is "no division between human society and other realities" (Murove, 2004, p. 207). It thus becomes an ideal philosophical and spiritual base to explore the unique nature and practice of an indigenous southern African form of environmental leadership. Indigenous southern African leadership is traditionally characterized by its emphasis on participation, responsibility, and spiritual authority (Lessem & Nussbaum, 1996). The unitive vision of ubuntu provides southern African leaders with the philosophical base of an authentic African leadership model that positions care of the environment as a spiritual value and the responsibility of all.

ENVIRONMENTAL LEADERSHIP AND THE COUNTER-SPIRITUALITY OF QUAKERISM

The phenomena of spiritual countermovements are described by Waaijman (2002) using the "structure–antistructure" matrix of Turner (1969):

> By structure he [Turner] means a coherent whole of social roles and positions which functions in accordance with legitimated norms and sanctions. Antistructure is the area outside of this: fruitful chaos, a place of incubation for new ideas and lifestyles, of resistance and creativity. Turner distinguishes three forms of antistructure: liminality, inferiority, and marginality. This three-part division can help us explore the field of spiritual counter-movements. (Waaijman, 2002, p. 214)

Liminal spiritualities are marked by being outside of the social structure in a state of indeterminacy; "inferior" spiritualities are cultivated by those that find themselves on the lowest ranks of society in positions of severe discrimination and disadvantage; and marginal spiritualities are constructed by those that stand on the margins of two opposing or differing social, religious, or philosophical contexts.

Quakerism's concern for the environment and its response of frugality is a good example of a marginal spirituality that willingly placed itself on the margins of society in order to bear an ethical witness marked by a "tender concern for the whole of creation" (Kelley, 1982, p. 69). Ethics of frugality have long been part of the economic norm of most Christian traditions (Nash, 1995). Weber (1958) notes that frugality combined with the values of industry, equity, generosity, and solidarity formed the core of an earlier Protestant ethic. But within the current western culture of "progressive plenty," frugality has been portrayed as "unfashionable, unpalatable, and even unpatriotic" (Nash 1995, p. 138). In contrast, Quakerism—a spiritual countermovement that had its start in the 17th century—always included the ethics of environmental concern and frugality as part of the movement's core values (Callen, 2001).

Over time, Quakerism has became known for the radical commitments and stances its adherents have embodied; such as resistance against slavery, complete commitment to nonviolence, radical environmental activism, and the values of frugality and experiential simplicity. It is important to note that the disciplines of frugality and simplicity in Quakerism are not limited to economic and environmental concern. The contemporary Quaker author Robert L. Smith (1998) summarizes the integrative role of simplicity in Quakerism: "Simplicity helps us to live to the point, to clear the way to the best, to keep first things first" (p. 63). Quaker spirituality has long influenced Christian and environmental proponents of a simpler lifestyle (Bittinger, 1978; Bush, 1999; Fager, 1971; Manno, 2006). The Christian ethicist James A. Nash (1995), deeply inspired by Quaker thought, argues that in order to facilitate an ecological reformation in contemporary Christian witness, one needs to not only bring back the Quaker value of frugality, but also that frugality must be seen as a "subversive virtue" (pp. 140–144). There is a strong countercultural tone inherent to Nash's language and proposals. Nash's work opens the door to constructing an ethical base on which the revitalized virtue of frugality can be integrated within a Quaker spirituality–based form of environmental leadership, here presented as frugal leadership. Frugal leadership: (a) rejects the popular assumption that humans are insatiable creatures, ceaselessly acquisitive for economic gains and goods and egoistically committed to pleasure maximization; (b) resists the temptations of consumer promotionalism—particularly the ubiquitous advertising that pressures us through sophisticated techniques to want more, bigger, better, faster, newer, more attractive, or state of the art; (c) struggles against the various psychological and sociological dynamics, beyond promotionalism, that stimulate overconsumption; and (d) rejects the prevailing ideology of indiscriminate, material economic growth in favor of an integrated environmental and human concern.

The transformative, witness-facilitating, countercultural, and environmentally focused values of Quakerism's frugal leadership have started to make something of a comeback in larger Christianity since the 17th century. At the International Consultation on Simple Lifestyle, sponsored by the Lausanne Committee on World Evangelization's Theology and Education Group (held at Hoddesdon, England, March 17–21, 1980), a statement was produced and endorsed, entitled "An Evangelical Commitment to Simple Lifestyle," which created a kind of Christian manifesto for simple living. Among the many statements concerning the need for ecological concern and practice of simplicity, the following commitments regarding personal witness were expressed:

> Our Christian obedience demands a simple lifestyle, irrespective of the needs of others. . . . While some of us have been called to live among the poor, and others to open our homes to the needy, all of us are determined to develop a simpler lifestyle. We intend to reexamine our income and expenditure, in order to manage on less and give more away. . . . Yet we resolve to renounce waste and oppose extravagance in personal living, clothing, and housing, travel and church buildings. We also accept the distinction between necessities and luxuries, creative hobbies and empty status symbols, modesty and vanity, occasional celebrations and normal routine, and between the service of God and slavery to fashion. (Stott & Sider, 1980, p. 178)

TOWARDS SPIRITUAL ENVIRONMENTAL LEADERSHIP

The current turn towards spirituality finds echoes in the rising phenomena of environmental leadership. A cursory overview of three spiritualities that support and facilitate spirituality-based, environmental leadership illustrates that these spiritualities all contain a concern for the environment as a part of their core spiritual values. These inner values operate as motivating and facilitating agents in these spiritualities to effect personal and communal transformation. In an established school of spirituality (Francis of Assisi), environmental concern is viewed as part of the overarching drama of human salvation and demands that spiritual leaders participate in the healing and restoration of all of creation. The southern African social and spiritual philosophy of ubuntu, as an example of a primordial spirituality, makes use of a deep and unitive regard for the environment as a way to express the African leadership values of radical mutuality and social respect. Quakcrism's call to simple living, frugality, and environmental activism are countercultural calls to authentic spiritual and humane leadership.

Concern for the Earth and the activist efforts of environmental leadership can be seen as spiritual phenomena and therefore part of the ongoing quest for the ultimate meaning of life (Kourie, 2006). They are part of ancient, spiritual wisdom that considers the environment as partaking of the sacred, and in turn facilitates mystical union with God, moral development, the formation of authentic witness, and mutuality and solidarity with all of humanity. It is a call to balance, integration, and fullness of life. But further work is needed to explore the possible points of congruence between the various emerging theories and models of religious, spiritual, and environmental leadership. This chapter is but a modest first step, and I encourage readers to explore further the topics and sources discussed here.

REFERENCES

Baker, J. (1970). *The Foolishness of God*. London: Darton, Longman and Todd.

Barbour, I. (1990). *Religion in an Age of Science*. San Francisco: HarperCollins.

Bessenecker, S. (2006). *The New Friars*. Downers Grove, IL: InterVarsity Press.

Bittinger, E. (1978). The Simple Life: A Chapter in the Evolution of a Doctrine. *Brethren Life and Thought, 23*(2), 104–114.

Braybrooke, N. (1976). Journey to Assisi. *The Christian Century,* October 27, 929–931.

Bush, T. (1999). Plain Living: The Search for Simplicity. *The Christian Century, 116*(30), 676–681.

Callen, B. (2001). *Authentic Spirituality*. Grand Rapids, MI: Baker Academic.

Chivaura, V. (2006). *Hunhu/Ubuntu: A Sustainable Approach to Endogenous Development, Bio-Cultural Diversity and Protection of the Environment in Africa*. Unpublished paper delivered at the International Conference on Endogenous Development and Bio-Cultural Diversity, Geneva, Switzerland, October 3–5.

Cronin, K. (1992). *Kenosis*. Rockport, MA: Element.

Delio, I. (2003). Revisiting the Franciscan Doctrine of Christ. *Theological Studies,* 64, 3–23.

Enslin, P., & Horsthemke, K. (2004). Can Ubuntu Provide a Model for

Citizenship Education in African Democracies? *Comparative Education, 40*(4), 545–558.

Fager, C. (1971). Experimenting With a Simpler Lifestyle. *The Christian Century, 88*(1), 9–13.
Gau, J. (2000). The Gestalt of Emptiness/Receptivity: Christian Spirituality and Psychotherapy. *Journal of Pastoral Care, 54*(4), 403–409.
Gottlieb, R. (2007). Religious Environmentalism: What It Is, Where It Is Heading and Why We Should Be Going in the Same Direction. *Journal for the Study of Religion, Nature and Culture, 1*(1), 81–91.
Hayes, Z. (1996). Christ, Word of God and Exemplar of Humanity. *Cord, 46*(1), 6.
Ivakhiv, A. (2007). Religion, Nature and Culture: Theorizing the Field. *Journal for the Study of Religion, Nature and Culture, 1*(1), 47–57.
Karecki, M., & Wroblewski, S. (2000a). *Franciscan Spirituality. Franciscan Study Guide Series: Volume I.* Jeppestown, South Africa: The Franciscan Institute of Southern Africa.
Karecki, M., & Wroblewski, S. (2000b). *Franciscan Spirituality. Franciscan Study Guide Series: Volume II.* Jeppestown, South Africa: The Franciscan Institute of Southern Africa.
Kelley, D. (1982). "A Tender Regard to the Whole Creation": Anthony Benezet and the Emergence of an Eighteenth-Century Quaker Ecology. *Pennsylvania Magazine of History and Biography, 160*(1), 69–88.
Klenke, K. (2007). Integrating Leadership, Spirituality, and Religion in the Workplace through Coalescing Values and Identity Transformations. In S. Sing-Sengupta & D. Fields (Eds.), *Integrating Spirituality and Organizational Leadership* (pp. 511–544). Delhi: Macmillan.
Kourie, C. (1993). The Kenotic Mysticism of Clare of Assisi in the Light of Inter-Religious Dialogue. *South African Journal of Medieval and Renaissance Studies, 3*(1), 124–140.
Kourie, C. (2006). The "Turn" to Spirituality. *Acta Theologica Supplementum, 8*, 19–38.
LeClerc, E. (1977). *The Canticle of Creatures, Symbols of Union: An Analysis of St. Francis of Assisi.* Chicago: Franciscan Herald Press.
Ledoux, C. (1997). *Clare of Assisi.* Cincinnati: St. Anthony Messenger Press.
Le Roux, J. (2000). The Concept of "Ubuntu": Africa's Most Important Contribution to Multicultural Education? *Multicultural Teaching, 18*(2), 43–46.
Lessem, J., & Nussbaum, B. (1996). *Sawubona Africa: Embracing Four Worlds in South African Management.* Johannesburg: Zebra Press.
Lorenzo, T. (2003). No African Renaissance without Disabled Women: A Communal Approach to Human Development in Cape Town, South Africa. *Disability & Society, 18*(6), 759–778.
Louw, D. (2003). *Ubuntu: An African Assessment of the Religious Other.* Unpublished manuscript, University of Limpopo, Medunsa, South Africa.
Manno, A. (2006). In Friendship with the Earth: Friend's Testimonies and Nuclear Energy. *Quaker Eco-Bulletin, 6*(5), 1–4.
Merton, T. (1966). *Conjectures of a Guilty Bystander.* New York: Doubleday.
Mkabela, Q. (2005). Using the Afrocentric Method in Researching Indigenous African Culture. *The Qualitative Report, 10*(1), 178–189.
Mnyaka, M., & Motlhabi, M. (2005). The African Concept of Ubuntu/Botho and its Socio-Moral Significance. *Black Theology, 3*(2), 215–237.
Mueller, J. (2003). *Clare of Assisi: The Letters to Agnes.* Collegeville, PA: Liturgical Press.
Murove, M. (2004). An African Commitment to Ecological Conservation: The Shona Concepts of Uhama and Ubuntu. *Mankind Quarterly, XLV*(2), 195–215.
Nama, N., & Swartz, L. (2002). Ethical and Social Dilemmas in Community-Based Controlled Trials in Situations of Poverty: A View from a South African Project. *Journal of Community & Applied Social Psychology, 12*, 286–297.

Nash, J. (1995). Toward the Revival and Reform of the Subversive Virtue. *Annual of the Society of Christian Ethics, 15*(1), 137–160.
Papanikolaou, A. (2003). Person, Kenosis and Abuse: Hans Urs von Balthasar and Feminist Theologies in Conversation. *Modern Theology, 19*(1), 1–26.
Powell, J. (2007). St. Francis of Assisi's Way of Peace. *Medieval Encounters, 13*, 271–280.
Raguin, Y. (1973). *I Am Sending You (John 22:21): Spirituality of the Missioner.* Manila: East Asian Pastoral Institute.
Richstatter, T. (2001). Franciscan Spirituality. *Liturgical Ministry*, Fall, 206–208.
Santmire, H. (1985). The Liberation of Nature: Lynn White's Challenge Anew. *The Christian Century*, May 22, 530–533.
Schwartz, S. (1992). Universals in the Content and Structure of Values: Theoretical Advances and Tests in 20 countries. *Advances in Experimental Psychology, 25*, 1–65.
Singh-Sengupta, S. (2007). Integrating Spirituality and Organizational Leadership: Towards an Integrative Human Framework for Organizations. In S. Sing-Sengupta & D. Fields (Eds.), *Integrating Spirituality and Organizational Leadership* (pp. 3–21). Delhi: Macmillan.
Smith, R. (1998). *A Quaker Book of Wisdom.* London: Orion.
Snodgrass, J., & Tiedje, K. (2008). Indigenous Nature Reverence and Conservation: Seven Ways of Transcending and Unnecessary Dichotomy. *Journal for the Study of Religion, Nature and Culture, 2*(1), 6–29.
Stott, J., & Sider, R. (1980). An Evangelical Commitment to Simple Lifestyle. *Occasional Bulletin of Missionary Research*, 4(4), 177–179.
Szabolcs, N. (2003). The Ministry of Reconciliation through Kenosis. *Mozaik, 1*, 8–10.
Teffo, L. (1998). Botho/Ubuntu as a Way Forward for Contemporary South Africa. *Word and Action, 38*(365), 3–5.
Teresa, F. (1995). *This Living Mirror: Reflections on Clare of Assisi.* London: Darton, Longman and Todd.
Turner, V. (1969). *The Ritual Process: Structure and Antistructure.* London: Ithaca.
Van Schalkwyk, A. (2008). Women, Ecofeminist Theology and Sustainability in a Post-Apartheid South Africa. *Journal of Theology for Southern Africa, 130*, 6–23.
Waaijman, K. (2002). *Spirituality: Forms, Foundations, Methods.* Leuven: Peeters.
Waaijman, K. (2006). What is Spirituality? *Acta Theologica Supplementum, 8*, 1–18.
Warner, K. (2008). The Greening of American Catholicism: Identity, Conversion, and Continuity. *Religion and American Culture: A Journal of Interpretation, 18*(1), 113–142.
Weber, M. (1958). *The Protestant Ethic and the Spirit of Capitalism.* New York: Charles Scribner's Press.
White, L. (1967). The Historical Roots of Our Ecological Crises. *Science, 155*, 1203–1207.

15 Deep Systems Leadership
A Model for the 21st Century

Rian Satterwhite

INTRODUCTION

Climate change is fast becoming one of the greatest challenges of our time. Amidst global conflict, economic dependency on limited resources, rapid technological development, the spread of open access to information, and other emerging characteristics of the 21st century, it is easy to lose sight of the environmental changes that are taking place all around us. The oceans are warming and their biochemistry is changing (Bindoff et al., 2007). Glaciers are melting, contributing to rising ocean levels, and snowfall has decreased in most places (Lemke et al., 2007). Average global surface temperatures are rising and average arctic temperatures are increasing at twice the global rate (Trenberth et al., 2007). These are markers of monumental changes that are taking place on our planet, which threaten the well-being of human as well as many plant and animal populations.

In order to address the challenges posed by climate change and other environmental problems, we first must do two things. We must begin to understand the causes of these changes, and we must reconceptualize our place in this world. In this chapter I propose a leadership model that represents a synthesis of four emerging fields of study: cultural biology, systems theory, Deep Ecology, and selected leadership models. This model is congruent with an emerging "eco-leadership paradigm" and may be seen as providing a conceptual foundation for leadership within that paradigm. It was assembled in an organic process over the past 10 years of my life. I humbly offer it up as an evolving philosophy that has profoundly affected the way I think and live my life and that may also resonate, in part or in whole, with others. I believe that once one absorbs this model, appropriate leadership behaviors will follow. Leaders must have a viable understanding of their place in the world if they are to lead effectively for sustainability.

I begin the chapter with an overview of relevant models proposed by leadership theorists as a starting point for my discussion. I then move into a discussion of cultural biology, as it lays the foundation for the model by clarifying the essential ties between the individual and their environment. This will be followed by systems theory, which will allow us to further extend our individual sphere of concern to large complex systems, and Deep Ecology, which will provide a road map for living in a manner that reflects what cultural biology and systems theory teach us. I conclude with a discussion of what I will call the Deep Systems Leadership Model and demonstrate the interconnectedness of its components. Each component tells us in a different way that we are linked in a fundamental manner, both to one another and to the environment around us. Taken together, they help build a view of leadership that is nonhierarchical and nonpositional; is a capacity rather than a position; and is more of a lifestyle adopted after deep reflection than a skill gained through specialized training. Any individual is capable of Deep Systems Leadership, and indeed it is the responsibility of everyone to exercise it if we are to successfully adapt to climate change and conserve what we value.

LEADERSHIP THEORIES

Within the past 50 years, the study of leadership has shifted focus from the individual to the group, and has recently begun to include systems approaches. Many leadership theories focus on personal leadership styles, characteristics, and qualifications, as well as organizational structure, efficiency, and cross-organizational collaboration. While these are all important considerations, we are now compelled to ask larger questions about our place in the world and our responsibility to it, the dynamics of living and working within complex systems, and our relationship with life around us. The issue of sustainability, now so obviously critical to our future, has just begun to come into focus in the leadership literature (see the literature review in the Introduction to this volume). In beginning to consider these larger questions, the study of leadership must now concern itself not only with bettering humans and their organizations, but also recognizing the care that we must nurture for the planet and the ways in which the systems that we are embedded in can better reflect the lessons learned from nature.

In leadership studies, efforts have already begun to link leadership with the natural environment. Allen, Stelzner, and Wielkiewicz (1998) call for examining the systemic processes from which leadership emerges and discuss four principles of an ecological approach to leadership: interdependence, open systems and feedback loops, cycling of resources, and adaptation (p. 68). Wielkiewicz and Stelzner (2005) convincingly conclude that "the ecological paradigm has the prerequisites of a complete theory of leadership" (p. 337), while perhaps the most comprehensive discussion so far is Western's (2008) chapter on eco-leadership and its three principles of connectivity, eco-ethics, and "leadership spirit" (for more, see Chapters 1 and 2 in this volume). Western (2008) describes eco-leadership as "a discourse, which creates self-organizing and emergent properties arising from dispersed leadership, which build into organizations the ability to be adaptive to fluctuations and constant change" (p. 186).

Wheatley (2006) talks eloquently about the lessons that leadership and human organizations can learn from complexity science and systems theory, suggesting, "Rather than building a rigid organization piece by stable piece, nature keeps things freely moving at all levels. These movements emerge into something new—an integrated system that can resist most demands for change at the global level because there is so much internal motion" (p. 167). A primary challenge of leadership in the 21st century will be to help guide the systems in which we live to become more like the complex and adaptive—yet generally stable—systems that we see around us in the natural environment.

Heifetz (2006) describes leadership in such a way, stating that "leadership generates new cultural norms that enable people to meet an ongoing stream of adaptive challenges, realities, and pressures likely to come . . . leadership develops an organization or community's adaptive capacity, or adaptability" (p. 76). As I will suggest in the following, cultural biology shows us that an autopoetic system (an informationally closed, self-generating system) can only respond to outside stimuli in ways that are consistent with its structure. The same principle can be extended to organizational and social systems. If the structure of an organization is not amenable to adaptation, then it will be unable to change in concert with the larger systems of which it is a part. Adaptive capacity and the ability to identify and utilize the interconnectedness of multiple systems are characteristics that many of our organizational and social systems do not currently have. Thus a crucial task of leadership within the Deep Systems Model is to assist the systems in which we are embedded to increase their adaptive capacity and ability to recognize the complex web of embedded systems that they operate within. A second task stipulated by the model is to engage the critical discussion of what is to be *conserved*, thereby shifting away from the idea that what leaders do is facilitate *change*. In this model, leaders facilitate conservation more than they seek to bring about change. Cultural biology helps to explain why this is so.

CULTURAL BIOLOGY: AUTOPOESIS, STRUCTURAL COUPLING, AND CONVERSATIONS OF CONSERVATION

I was exposed to cultural biology through the assistance of a friend and mentor, and it has since provided me with a foundational understanding of my own life. In August of 2008 I attended a five-day symposium in Boston sponsored by the Society for Organizational Learning and given by Dr. Humberto Maturana and Ximena Davila, founders of the Instituto de Formación Matriztica in Chile. Dr. Maturana received his PhD in biology at Harvard and has taught at MIT and the University of Chile. The symposium proved to be a profound awakening for me. The title was "Cultural Biology: The End of Leadership and the Beginning of Co-Inspirational Management," which was provocative, especially since the audience was primarily in the leadership development and organizational consulting fields. I was fortunate enough to spend those five days in the company of the likes of Peter Senge, Juanita Brown, and others whose work I am familiar with and whom I admire greatly, but it was the facilitators, Maturana and Davila, whose words resonated most strongly with my own evolving perspective.

For the purpose of this chapter, I will concentrate on only three aspects of cultural biology: autopoesis, structural coupling, and conversations of conservation. I highly encourage readers to pursue additional information on the topic, which extends well beyond the scope of its use here. In order to provide the reader with an overview of cultural biology before delving into the components to be used here, the following is a primer—a skeletal structure of sorts—for cultural biology shared by Maturana and Davila (2008) at the symposium proceedings:

> As we reflect [upon] ourselves as human beings, we find ourselves being molecular living systems (therefore dynamic, changing, living). We find that as molecular systems we are structurally determined systems. We also find that as structurally determined systems, we are systems such that anything external to us that impinges upon us only triggers in us structural changes that are determined in our system.
>
> Moreover, we find ourselves being living beings, and that as molecular systems we living beings are autopoetic systems. That is, we find ourselves being closed networks of molecular productions that exist in the continuous reproduction of themselves.
>
> We also find ourselves being bipedal primates that belong to a lineage that in its evolutionary drift existed by the gathering and sharing of food, and lived a particular history in which the hand became transformed from a foot into an instrument for delicate manipulation with the fingers and into a caressing organ.

In their seminal text, *The Tree of Knowledge: The Biological Roots of Human Understanding*, Maturana and Varela (1987) describe autopoesis as a defining characteristic of living beings, which are distinctive as organized systems in that "their organization is such that their only product is themselves, with no separation between producer and product. The being and doing of an autopoetic unity are inseparable, and this is their specific mode of organization" (pp. 48–49). Furthermore, "Every structural change occurs in a living being necessarily limited by the conservation of its autopoesis" (p. 100). In an instructive yet simple example, Maturana explains this by saying that the reason why we don't fly away from danger, even in some situations where that may be the best option, is because we are structurally incapable of flight. In other words, an autopoetic system's purpose is to continually renew or produce itself but it is only capable of acting in ways that are determined by its structure. Biologically, autopoesis is the *chief* process of a living system. Without it, the structural unity of an organism ceases to exist and the system (organism) perishes.

The second key concept to introduce is structural coupling, which is defined as "a history of recurrent interactions leading to the structural congruence between two (or more) systems" (Maturana & Varela, 1987, p. 75). Through the process of autopoesis, we are linked with our environment, and the interaction between autopoetic system and the environment consists of "reciprocal perturbations" in which the structure of the external environment:

> only *triggers* structural changes in the autopoetic unities (it does not specify or direct them), and vice versa for the environment. The result will be a history of mutual congruent structural changes as long as the autopoetic unity and its containing environment do not disintegrate: there will be a *structural coupling.* (Maturana & Varela, 1987, p. 75)

In other words, so long as the autopoetic being (you or me) and the environment that we are in are maintained, we will continue to interact and influence one another in a dynamic and fluid dance. Each party (the autopoetic system and the environment) influences the other, but does not dictate any change *in* the other; change in each is strictly determined by its internal structure.

For example, a cell is a relatively simple autopoetic entity—at least in comparison to you or me—structurally coupled to its environment. The primary purpose of a cell is to survive, to conserve its autopoesis. It is capable of gathering resources from its environment through its membrane, and utilizing those resources to sustain itself through metabolism and other internal processes. It is biologically distinct from its environment, but simultaneously dependent upon it. We too are autopoetic structures, drawing in resources from our environment, engaged in the singular (biological) purpose of continually producing ourselves. Our dance with our environment is a dynamic one; it effects changes in us that are consistent with our structure, and so too do we effect changes in our environment that are consistent with its structure.

We are thus inextricably linked to our environment and other autopoetic organisms within it through structural coupling. Think on this for a moment. I believe that each of us knows, deep down, that our fate is tied to that of our environment and other life that we share the world with. Perhaps we are tempted to forget it in the pace and priorities of our time, but we knew it at some point as we walked with bare feet through the grass or spent time staring at the vast ocean. Yet even if we do acknowledge this link, and feel a kinship for the life around us, it may be difficult to explain why we have this feeling. Cultural biology offers a sound framework for understanding our intimate connection to, dependence upon, feeling for, and place within the web of life. Autopoesis is a defining characteristic of life and a common link that we all share. Similarly, we are all structurally coupled to our environment and those around us.

With this in mind, Maturana and Davila (2008) state, "As human beings we find ourselves living in communities in recursive coordinations of doings, generating different worlds and realities as different manners of living together, in networks of conservation." This means that our social structures and histories conserve what has successfully enabled us to maintain our autopoetic processes. They further suggest that for all of our striving to manage, lead, create, or navigate change, what we should really be doing is *seeking what is most important to conserve* (Maturana & Davila, 2008). This becomes the most important question. Autopoesis is perhaps the fundamental act of conservation—the conservation of the self. In all else that we do, if we are to remain as a unity, an autopoetic system, we must conserve that which makes us whole. Yet the principle of structural coupling tells us that we are dependent upon our environment and those around us for this very basic act. Therefore, we must prevent changes in the external environment that threaten the finely tuned interaction between internal self and external world. We must conserve, in other words, the basic features of our relationship with nature or risk disrupting not only nature but the integrity of our own spiritual and biological selves.

In the leadership model I am proposing, these three components of cultural biology form the backdrop and foundation upon which the model rests. It can be no other way since both autopoesis and structural coupling speak directly to how we live and survive as biological entities. Autopoesis simultaneously establishes the self as distinct from environment and the essential relationship between the self and other. Structural coupling explains how we are tied to our immediate environment in an interdependent manner. Seeking to determine what to conserve, rather than fighting to bring about change, is a paradigm shift that leads us towards a sustainable future and forces deep, reflective questions. Systems theory, as we shall find, expands upon this foundation and suggests that we extend our concern not only to our immediate environment, but also to large and complex systems seemingly extraneous to our daily lives.

SYSTEMS THEORY

Over the past century, sciences as diverse as physics, biology, cognitive psychology, and chemistry have begun to understand the world in a more holistic manner, one that appreciates the complex and interconnected systems in which we live and depend upon. In physics, giants such as Einstein, Bohr, Dirac, Heisenberg, and Schrödinger revolutionized the way we see the world. The bizarre world of quantum mechanics is a prime example, where linear causality is exchanged for probability and where systems and relationships reign supreme rather than individual constituents (Prigogine, 1996). In biochemistry, Kauffman, Goodwin, and others have advanced the theory that the form of the organism may largely be a property of the system itself rather than of its genetic makeup (Lewin, 1999). In neurophysiology and the budding study of consciousness, Edelman, Tononi, Varela, and others have advanced remarkable theories where consciousness is understood as a dynamic information-processing system that can shift physical location in the brain in an incredibly complex manner (Edelman & Tononi, 2001; Tononi & Edelman, 1998). Ecology—coined by German biologist Ernst Haeckel in 1866 from the Greek word *oikos* ("household")—is perhaps best described as the study of biological systems and their relationships. It has become an increasingly important concept in recent years and continues to push us towards appreciating the importance of connections, relationships, and dynamic coupling in the world in which we live.

All of these diverse fields have led us to think in a more holistic, systemic manner. Together with new fields within mathematics, all have contributed to and drawn from what is called systems theory or complexity science. Capra (1996) suggests that this new way of thinking may be characterized as:

- the shift from the parts to the whole
- the ability to move attention back and forth between different systems levels
- recognizing emergent properties that can only be found when examining the whole and that are not found in the parts
- viewing life as a network of relationships

Systems theory allows us to begin to understand the highly complex world in which we live. The proverbial butterfly flapping its wings and causing a thunderstorm somewhere else in the world may seem a little far-fetched but serves as a vivid illustration of the dynamic web of connections in which we have always lived, but are only now learning (or relearning) to see.

The implications and applications of systems theory are profound. First, every thing is in constant and dynamic relation to every other thing. Seemingly separate entities are in fact related to, and often dependent upon, one another. An action that we take not only has far-reaching and often unanticipated implications, but was also influenced by a myriad of other effects upon us. Systems theory implies a deep and fundamental relationship between all things, and reflects closely the concepts from cultural biology of autopoesis and structural coupling. An organism is continually in a dynamic, structurally coupled relationship with its environment and other organisms around it; the moment that it is not, its system ceases to be sustainable and it perishes. We recognize this within an ecosystem when studying a rain forest or coral reef; why not apply it fully to our own experience?

While systems theory and cultural biology are complementary in many respects, they can also inform one another. The combination of autopoesis and structural coupling binds us to our immediate environment. But even with this tie, why should we care about what happens halfway around the world? Or even a few miles down the road? The application of systems theory allows us to begin to identify how seemingly distinct and separate locations and events are indeed related and interdependent. Cultural biology establishes for each of us a widening circle of care that includes other autopoetic systems that we are structurally coupled to as well as the environment that we are in. Systems theory, however, allows for the expansion of that circle to include the planet and all of its living systems. But what does a lifestyle that is congruent with this perspective look like and how does one become aware of these connections? Deep Ecology provides a compelling answer.

DEEP ECOLOGY

The father of Deep Ecology, Arne Naess, first coined the term in 1973 and offered as its philosophical underpinnings his *Ecosophy T* model, a type of biospheric egalitarianism where all life is allowed the same rights to exist (Naess, 1986). The central critique offered by the Deep Ecology movement, and the source of its name, is that more traditional environmental movements still maintain a human dominance over nature and that this "stewardship" approach ultimately falls short of recognizing humanity's place *within* nature. While there have been many Deep Ecology viewpoints put forward, Devall and Sessions (1985) in particular have popularized the idea within many environmentally conscious circles, especially in the United States. There are two common threads that link most Deep Ecology approaches: self-realization and identification. Diehm (2007) states that "most if not all of the thinkers who utilize the concepts of Self-realization and identification regard the latter as the means to the former: identification is the path to Self-realization, the process by which one develops one's 'ecological Self'" (p. 2). Therefore, understanding what is meant by "identification" is critical to understanding Deep Ecology.

Diehm (2007) distinguishes between two types of identification within the Deep Ecology literature. The first and most numerous type is "identification-as-belonging," meaning that in order for the individual to develop the ecological self and recognize the interconnectedness of his or her existence with the rest of the world, he or she must have a means to identify personally with nature and see oneself as a vital member of a natural community (p. 3). Despite human beings' innate affinity for nature and natural scenes (see Chapter 3 of this volume), this sense of belonging is not automatic and must be fostered through experience. For some, "identification-as-belonging" is the central aspect of a Deep Ecology perspective and once fully achieved all distinctions between the individual and environment quite literally dissolve (Fox, 1999).

A second type of identification that Diehm (2007) discusses resembles "the care-based perspectives adopted by some ecofeminists, [which] retain[s] the emphasis on relationships and interconnection that is so crucial to Deep Ecology theorists' accounts of the Self, while at the same time acknowledging distinctions between self and other" (p. 10). This approach, which Diehm calls "identification-as-kinship," is found almost exclusively in Naess's work (p. 11). For our purposes the kinship approach mirrors the viewpoint of cultural biology. Rather than an individual's identity being subsumed by the wider environment, something that cultural biology tells us is impossible or at best a misrepresentation of biological reality, "identification-as-kinship" allows for the distinction between self and others to be maintained:

> With this type of identification, and the empathy that flows from it, we experience others' well-being as intermingled with our own: we find that we are pained by their pain and uplifted by their flourishing; the 'hurt' they feel, we feel as well. As a result of identification, therefore, the self comes to 'include' others since the interests of others are discovered to be bound up with those of the self. (Diehm, 2007, p. 13)

This concept of identification, then, establishes a personal sense of interconnectedness with life just as cultural biology establishes and systems theory expands upon a biological interconnectedness. Therefore, it is Naess's concept of identification, "identification-as-kinship," that I suggest is compatible with the Deep Systems Leadership Model. Having established this, there is one critique of Deep Ecology that should be addressed, and it may be done so through this same "identification-as-kinship" approach.

Guha (1989) offers a strong critique of American Deep Ecology from a third world perspective, asserting that other environmentalist traditions "place a greater emphasis on equity and social justice . . . on the grounds that in the absence of social regeneration environmental regeneration has very little chance of succeeding" (p. 79). While Guha takes aim at the popularized American Deep Ecology perspective, Naess's conception of Deep Ecology is hardly mentioned. Nevertheless, it is precisely Naess's approach (as interpreted by Diehm) that addresses Guha's critique. The need for equity and social justice is undeniable as we pursue a better, more sustainable way of life; environmental justice alone will not allow for us to create a sustainable living environment. The empathy that flows from the "identification-as-kinship" approach necessitates the recognition of pain and suffering of people just as it does of other forms of life. For their part, cultural biology and systems theory establish fundamental ties between the individual and other surrounding organisms and tell us that our fate is irrevocably linked with theirs. In the end, the Deep Systems Leadership Model that I am proposing, based as it is on cultural biology, systems theory, and Deep Ecology, unavoidably includes the pursuit of social justice as a feature of leadership for sustainability.

CONCLUSION: DEEP SYSTEMS LEADERSHIP

"The separateness we thought we were creating melts into the unending dance of coadaptation and change as we become ever more aware of those from whom we cannot be separate" (Wheatley & Kellner-Rogers, 1996, p. 52).

Cultural biology helps establish our biological relationship and interdependence with our environment, as well as pushing us to consider what we choose to conserve together. Systems theory forces us to become aware of the complex systems in which we are embedded, and care for the systemic changes that, though distant or difficult to discern, threaten the web of connections that sustain us. Deep Ecology, through Naess and Diehm, suggests how we might identify with nature and see ourselves as a part of it, leading to a more ecocentric ethic, and also establishes the pursuit of social justice as parallel to ecological justice and sustainability. Systemic leadership disregards position and hierarchy, offering everyone a means by which to help organizations and social systems adapt while reinforcing the call to social, as well as ecological, sustainability (see Figure 15.1).

The threat of climate change offers us a chance to recognize our interconnectedness with, and draw greater inspiration from, complex natural systems. Deep Systems Leadership begins with this realization of interdependence, and is a means of living our daily lives in congruence with natural systems while fostering greater adaptive capacity in our social systems. We must learn to be mindful of the multiple overlapping systems in which we are embedded as well as our common biology that informs how we relate to our environment. In truth, Deep Systems Leadership can be extended to a great many problems. Cultural biology helps us learn how to relate to one another in a loving manner, while systems theory can be applied to a myriad of social ills. Yet in climate change we have unwittingly created one of the greatest systemic challenges that we have ever known. We must make the most of the opportunity and come together, recognizing our common biology and interdependence, and conserve what we most deeply value. We no longer have the excuse of ignorance. We know, more and more every day, the far-reaching impact of our decisions and have begun to see ourselves as a part of the world rather than stewards of it.

Deep Systems Leadership requires first a deep recognition of our place within natural systems and the common interdependence and future that we share with life around us. From this flow four core principles. First, both anthropocentric ethics and eco-ethics demand that we live in a more

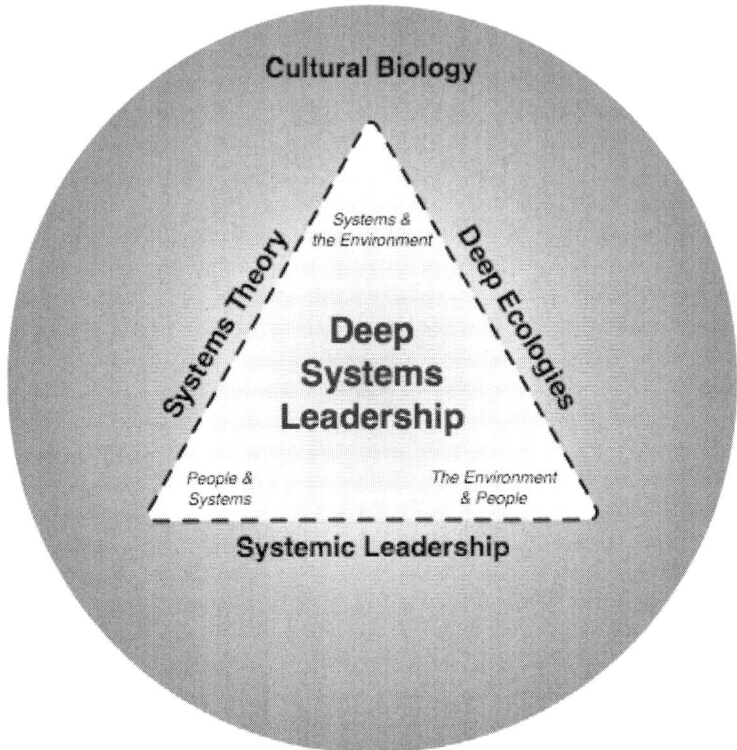

Figure 15.1 Model of Deep Systems Leadership.

sustainable manner. We have a responsibility both to our own future generations and the life with which they will share the world to create a sustainable manner of living; one that does not threaten to inalterably change the natural climate or destroy habitat. Second, that this is a shared responsibility that is blind to hierarchy, position, influence, power, or structure. Deep Systems Leadership is a lifestyle that infuses action and daily living with the awareness of complex systems while increasing the adaptive capacity of our own organizations. Third, while we must pursue a sustainable relationship with the natural world, we must also pursue sustainable relationships with one another. The pursuit of social justice and equity is unequivocal in Deep Systems Leadership and necessary for a balanced relationship with the world around us. Fourth, perhaps the most important frame of reference may now be "conservation." In recognizing that all things are in a state of constant flux, the most important question becomes what we seek to conserve. In choosing to conserve a sustainable lifestyle congruent with complex adaptive systems and deeply respectful of our interdependence, we allow everything else to shift and change around that central focus.

Deep Systems Leadership is exercised whenever any individual or group lives and acts according to the principles outlined here. It represents a decisive move away from thinking about leadership in terms of the traditional "leader–follower" relationship working towards a particular goal, and instead conceives of leadership as a "systemic capacity" (Drath, 2001), that is, a property of social systems that draws in increasingly more participants and addresses collective challenges. It provides a different and I would suggest healthier way of thinking about what it is that makes a person a leader. Drath (2001) argues that "leadership effectiveness is related more to the sharing of meaning in a community than it is to any particular style or approach to leadership" (p. 28). Leaders help make meaning of adaptive challenges. While we are simultaneously members of multiple communities, we are all members of a singular global community—life on Earth—and we share a common challenge. We must come together and begin to make common meaning of the threats that we face, and collectively work towards sustainable solutions. Once one adopts this awareness, and understands that we are all structurally distinct but deeply interdependent beings, the "way forward" becomes clear.

Leadership becomes a capacity of social systems that obviates the need for traditional "command and control" forms of leadership and functions in line with the principles of complex, adaptive systems. Leaders become meaning-makers within the systems in which they are embedded, mindful of their interdependence with systems around them, facilitating conversations of what we choose to conserve. Deep Systems Leadership offers a language and set of principles relevant, and perhaps common, to us all. As we become more aware of our shared history and future, it is increasingly the responsibility of *everyone* to ensure that we live sustainable lifestyles, embedded within sustainable systems.

REFERENCES

Allen, K., Stelzner, S., & Wielkiewicz, R. (1998). The Ecology of Leadership: Adapting to the Challenges of a Changing World. *Journal of Leadership Studies, 5*(2), 62–82.

Bindoff, N., Willebrand, J., Artale, V., Cazenave, A., Gregory, J., & Gulev, S. (2007). Observations: Oceanic Climate Change and Sea Level. In S. Solomon, D. Qin, M. Manning, Z. Chen, M. Maquis, & K. Avery (Eds.), *Climate Change 2007: The Physical Science Basis* (pp. 385–432). Cambridge & New York: Cambridge University Press.

Capra, F. (1996). *The Web of Life*. New York: Anchor Books.

Devall, B., & Sessions, G. (1985). *Deep Ecology: Living as if Nature Mattered*. Salt Lake City: Gibbs Smith.

Diehm, C. (2007). Identification with Nature: What It Is and Why It Matters. *Ethics and the Environment, 12*(2), 1–22.

Drath, W. (2001). *The Deep Blue Sea: Rethinking the Source of Leadership*. San Francisco: Jossey-Bass.

Edelman, G., & Tononi, G. (2001). *A Universe of Consciousness: How Matter Becomes Imagination*. New York: Basic Books.

Fox, W. (1999). Deep Ecology: A New Philosophy of Our Time? In N. Witoszek & A. Brennan (Eds.), *Philosophical Dialogues: Arne Naess and the Progress of Ecophilosophy* (pp. 153–163). Lanham: Rowman and Littlefield.

Guha, R. (1989). Radical American Environmentalism and Wilderness Preservation: A Third World Critique. *Environmental Ethics, 11*(1), 71–83.

Heifetz, R. (2006). Anchoring Leadership in the Work of Adaptive Progress. In F. Hesselbein & M. Goldsmith (Eds.), *The Leader of the Future 2: Visions, Strategies, and Practices for the New Era* (pp. 73–84). San Francisco: Jossey-Bass.

Lemke, P., Ren, J., Alley, R., Allison, I., Carrasco, J., & Flato, G. (2007). Observations: Changes in Snow, Ice and Frozen Ground. In S. Solomon, D. Qin, M. Manning, Z. Chen, M. Maquis, & K. Avery (Eds.), *Climate Change 2007: The Physical Science Basis* (pp. 337–383). Cambridge & New York: Cambridge University Press.

Lewin, R. (1999). *Complexity: Life at the Edge of Chaos* (2nd ed.). Chicago: University of Chicago Press.

Maturana, H., & Davila, X. (2008). *Symposium Proceedings*. Presented at the Cultural Biology: The End of Leadership and the Beginning of Co-Inspirational Management symposium, August, Boston, MA.

Maturana, H., & Varela, F. (1987). *The Tree of Knowledge: The Biological Roots of Human Understanding*. Boston: Shambhala Publications.

Naess, A. (1986). The Deep Ecology Movement. In G. Sessions (Ed.), *Deep Ecology for the 21st Century* (pp. 64–84). Boston: Shambhala Publications.

Prigogine, I. (1996). *The End of Certainty: Time, Chaos, and the New Laws of Nature*. New York: Free Press.

Tononi, G., & Edelman, G. (1998). Consciousness and Complexity. *Science, 282*(5295), 1846–1851.

Trenberth, K., Jones, P., Ambenje, P., Bojariu, R., Easterling, D., & Klien Tank, A. (2007). Observations: Surface and Atmospheric Climate Change. In S. Solomon, D. Qin, M. Manning, Z. Chen, M. Maquis, & K. Avery (Eds.), *Climate Change 2007: The Physical Science Basis* (pp. 235–336). Cambridge & New York: Cambridge University Press.

Western, S. (2008). *Leadership: A Critical Text*. Los Angeles: Sage Publications.

Wheatley, M. (2006). *Leadership and the New Science* (2nd ed.). San Francisco: Berrett-Koehler Publishers.

Wheatley, M., & Kellner-Rogers, M. (1996). *A Simpler Way*. San Francisco: Barrett-Koehler Publishers.

Wielkiewicz, R., & Stelzner, S. (2005). An Ecological Perspective on Leadership Theory, Research, and Practice. *Review of General Psychology, 9*(4), 326–341.

Conclusion

Towards a New General Theory of Leadership

Benjamin W. Redekop

The chapters collected in this volume approach the topic of leadership for sustainability from a variety of perspectives, yet there is a great deal of coherence and commonality in ideas and approach. That is likely due at least in part to the fact that the book was conceived from the start as a response to a particular problem—the unsustainable human treatment of the biosphere. As stated in the Introduction, "leadership" is conditioned by the requirements of time and place, by context. Thus in any one situation a general understanding of leadership is bound to emerge that seems most likely to meet the challenges posed by that situation, even if variation remains depending on the particularities of time and place. But although context shapes our understanding of leadership, the context is often obscured in general treatises on leadership, with the implication that the sort of "leadership" being espoused is universal. It seems likely that only by explicitly focusing on a universal context does a truly "general theory of leadership" (Goethals & Sorenson, 2006) become possible, because the main starting points and assumptions are in principle shared by everyone.

As many of the chapters in this volume demonstrate, such a conception is grounded in the process and workings of nature itself. Attentive readers will notice that Heifetz's (1994) theory of adaptive leadership informs a number of the chapters, and for good reason: it is the most fully developed modern theory of leadership that incorporates the perspectives of both Freud and Darwin. Leadership scholars may have shied away from the latter because of the excesses of Social Darwinism, furthering as it did the dominance of the rich and powerful and underwriting dictatorial philosophies and social movements (Hofstadter, 1992; Hawkins, 1997). Yet it seems increasingly obvious that any leadership approach that aims to be responsive to the natural world must take modern biology—and by extension evolutionary theory—into account. And if, as we maintain, "leadership" now entails concern for nature *by definition*, it is difficult to see how any truly important and useful theory of leadership will not be informed by evolutionary approaches, including evolutionary psychology (see Wright, 1995; Hedrick-Wong, 1998; Gaulin & McBurney, 2003; Buss, 2007).

Chaos and complexity theory have become more popular "scientific" approaches taken by leadership scholars, and indeed the influence of Margaret Wheatley (2006) is apparent in some of the chapters in this volume. Yet going back to the 1950s, thinkers have been rightly skeptical of too-literal applications of the insights and mysteries of modern physics to everyday human affairs (e.g., Oppenheimer, 1954). It may be true that quantum physics can tell us something interesting and perhaps useful about human behavior and organizational dynamics, but the world inhabited by human beings and other forms of life is quite different than the strange world of subatomic particles. Causality in the human world is not always perfectly linear, but it is much more so than at the level of electrons. If we are going to draw analogies from nature—and our current situation requires that we work *with* rather than against nature—Darwin is more pertinent than Heisenberg, and the relatively frequent discussion of "adaptive leadership" in the present volume substantiates this point.

Chaos/complexity and evolutionary approaches join together in their emphasis on systems thinking, and nearly every chapter in this volume takes a systems perspective in one form or another. Clearly, achieving environmental sustainability will require a fundamental shift towards systems thinking and behavior at all levels of society. Leaders must recognize that they are merely parts in complex systems and act accordingly, even if that means giving up on the idea that they alone can control the systems of which they are a part. It may in fact mean giving up control altogether, when doing so helps to move the system that they are "leading" in a useful direction. It may mean recognizing that they are leaders in name only, and that the system contains more than enough leadership within itself, if only allowed to be expressed in a useful fashion. This suggests that leaders will increasingly need to see themselves—and act—more as facilitators and designers of systems than controllers; they will need to become, in effect, "leaders by design" (for discussion of sustainability as a design problem, see McDonough & Braungart, 2002). A primary question will be, "How can we design an organization or system to produce leadership that sustains it as well as the larger systems of which it is a part?"

Doing so may require a fundamental reordering of values and/or culture, and it is here that positional leaders will play a crucial role. Although much has already been written on the general requirements and dimensions of sustainability, much less has been written on the particular processes by which leaders can help make it happen. Founders play a large role in establishing organizational cultures (Schein 1983/2004), and it normally falls to positional leaders to initiate changes in culture. A number of the chapters in the present volume provide insights on how to begin moving organizational cultures in a sustainable direction, and in most cases it first involves a change in mind-set of the leader herself. Leaders must first begin to see themselves (Chapter 15)—and their organizations (Chapters 1 and 2)—differently, and find ways to convey a more sustainable organizational vision to their constituents, whether it be through agrarian metaphors (Chapter 9), inspired storytelling (Chapters 5 and 6), an understanding of environmental psychology (Chapter 3), or holistic rhetorical practices (Chapter 7). They will need to understand and work within the dynamics of existing political systems (Chapter 12) as well as religious belief systems (Chapter 13), and they may draw strength and insight from existing spiritualities that provide deep and meaningful connections to nature (Chapter 14). They will do well to pay attention to historical precedent (Chapter 11) and the potentiality of "leadership from below" when it comes to solving complex adaptive problems (Chapter 10). And finally, they will want to bring all forms of creativity to the table (Chapter 8), as they seek to "lead by design."

Cooperation and collaboration also emerge as central themes in this collection; words that are easy to say but much more difficult to enact, as demonstrated at length in Chapter 4. This is particularly the case in economic and political systems that make individual rights, freedoms, and behaviors the fundamental values and units of analysis. One of the great unsolved questions of the new millennium is really one of the oldest: how to reconcile individual rights and freedoms with the needs and requirements of "the group" and by extension its shared resources and habitat. The difficulty of "solving" this problem is compounded by the failure of communist and other utopian ideologies to produce a just and workable socioeconomic system, and the attendant revulsion by many segments of the western body politic (particularly in America) to any sort of collectivist thinking. If it is true that collaboration and cooperation are some of the main avenues leading towards a sustainable world-system, then much work remains to be done by political and social thinkers—and leaders—to continue groping towards a reconciliation of individual freedom with collective good that is acceptable to ardent individualists and amenable to a market-based economic system that harnesses self-interest as its most fundamental driver.

Some of the chapters in the present volume contain at least signposts for further thinking on this fundamental question. The chapters by Wielkiewicz and Stelzner (Chapter 1) and Western (Chapter 2) articulate models of organizational leadership that work *within* rather than against a market system. What is new and different is that self-interest is analyzed at a systemic level and put within a much longer time frame. Leaders in this conception are those people who enact one of the most fundamental and widely agreed-upon functions of leadership, which is to have at least one foot in the future (see the Introduction). They must not only "see" what is coming, they have to help their constituents understand how present behaviors connect to future outcomes (Chapter 3). They must redefine "enlightened self-interest" to include the self-interest of the organization or system of which they are but a part (Chapter 15), and they must frame stories of organizational success in ways that go beyond the current fixation on quarterly profits (Chapter 5). To do so requires leaders who themselves inhabit a time frame that is both longer and shorter than is the norm in the west;

one that sees the world in "geological time" (see Anderson, 1999) as well as in the moment, when one takes satisfaction in simply being present to what is happening in the here and now (see Senge, Scharmer, Jaworski, & Flowers, 2004).

Yet as Western (Chapter 2) points out, before we get too caught up in such philosophical reveries, we need to confront the very real power dynamics that lie at the root of significant transformation. Postmodern critical theory, with its focus on the subterranean workings of power and the plight of the poor and marginalized, has an important role to play in this discussion, yet has been, until very recently, largely absent in the leadership discourse. More often than not it is the poor and powerless who suffer the effects of unsustainable practices (even if it is also the poor who are often driven to destroy natural habitats just to survive); thus the more that *everyone* on the planet can be involved in deciding how we are going to live, the more likely the path chosen will be a sustainable one. As discussed in Chapter 3, people are motivated to act when issues are framed in terms of justice and human rights, and leaders are thus well advised to link the current move towards sustainability with ongoing movements for civil rights and self-determination.

Doing so will also help to reframe the more negative (but realistic) "avoidance goal" of environmental collapse with a more positive "approach goal" of universal justice and human rights. Other possible approach goals include: achieving a way of life that is more integrated, harmonious, and affordable than present modes of living (Chapters 5 and 9); the creation of more aesthetically pleasing urban environments (Chapter 8); the creation of political parties that are eco-friendly, inclusive, and empowering of women (Chapter 12), and the creation of organizations that contain within themselves the capacity to adapt to the larger systems that contain them (Chapters 1 and 2); and spiritual fulfillment (Chapter 14) and belief systems that are in harmony with their surroundings (Chapters 13 and 15). These are tasks and opportunities for leadership, and as in the past, the most influential leaders for sustainability will be those figures who "embody" a new and compelling story about who we are and where we are going (Gardner, 1995; Chapters 6 and 12 of this volume).

Finally, it is worth noting that if the underlying premises of this book are correct, then the emerging "eco-leader" paradigm evident in its pages presents our best hope for success, both environmentally and as a civilization. As many of the chapters in this volume suggest, an ecological perspective on leadership is more than just good for the natural environment, but also for the human organizations that inhabit it. Either we adapt to the exigencies of our habitat or we suffer the consequences—it's not like we really have a choice. Probably the greatest impediment to our facing up to this fact is our technological proficiency, which has done more to make us forget our dependence on natural processes than anything else. The eco-leader paradigm, as Western (Chapter 2) suggests, does not reject technology, but it puts it in its place, which is that of a servant of people and systems rather than their master. That is to say, the enlightened eco-leader understands that technological "solutions" to our problems are provisional and temporary; as Heifetz (1994) might say, they are keen to treat the illness and not just its symptoms. The greatest leaders are those who, like Mohandas Gandhi, have a vision that is both cosmic and individual, universal and yet pragmatic, highly spiritual but rooted in time and place. It is our hope that this book contributes to the broadening and deepening of vision that will be required of leaders and their constituents if we are to achieve a truly sustainable relationship with our world.

REFERENCES

Anderson, R. (1999) *Mid-Course Correction: Toward a Sustainable Enterprise—The Interface Model.* White River Junction, VT: Chelsea Green Publishing Co.

Buss, D. (2007). *Evolutionary Psychology: The New Science of the Mind.* Upper Saddle River, NJ: Allyn and Bacon.

Gardner, H. (1995). *Leading Minds.* New York: Basic Books.

Gaulin, S., & McBurney, D. (2003). *Evolutionary Psychology 2nd Edition.* Upper Saddle River, NJ: Prentice Hall.

Goethals, G., & Sorenson, G. (2006). *The Quest for a General Theory of Leadership.* Northampton: Edward Elgar.

Hawkins, M. (1997). *Social Darwinism in European and American Thought, 1860–1945: Nature as Model and Nature as Threat.* Cambridge: Cambridge University Press.

Hedrick-Wong, Y. (1998). The Global Environmental Crisis and State Behavior: An Evolutionary Perspective. In C. Crawford & D. Krebs (Eds.), *Handbook of Evolutionary Psychology: Ideas, Issues, and Applications* (pp. 573–594). Mahwah, NJ: Lawrence Erlbaum Associates.

Heifetz, R. (1994). *Leadership without Easy Answers.* Boston: Harvard University Press.

Hofstadter, R. (1992). *Social Darwinism in American Thought.* Boston: Beacon Press.

McDonough, W., & Braungart, M. (2002). *Cradle to Cradle: Remaking the Way We Make Things.* New York: North Point Press.

Oppenheimer, R. (1954). *Science and the Common Understanding.* New York: Simon and Schuster.

Schein, E. (1983/2004). The Role of the Founder in Creating Organizational Culture. In T. Wren, D. Hicks, & T. Price (Eds.), *Modern Classics on Leadership* (pp. 443–458). Northampton: Edward Elgar.

Senge, P., Scharmer, C., Jaworski, J., & Flowers, B. (2004). *Presence: An Exploration of Profound Change in People, Organizations, and Society.* New York: Doubleday.

Wheatley, M. (2006). *Leadership and the New Science: Discovering Order in a Chaotic World.* San Francisco: Berrett-Koehler Publishers.

Wright, R. (1995). *The Moral Animal: Why We Are the Way We Are.* New York: Vintage.

Contributors

Corné J. Bekker previously served as the Associate Dean for a theological seminary in Johannesburg, South Africa, and is currently an Associate Professor in the School of Global Leadership and Entrepreneurship at Regent University. His interest in spirituality, leadership, and the environment stems from the ecological challenges he observed growing up in southern Africa. He is also the editor of the *Journal of Biblical Perspectives in Leadership* (JBPL) and the co-editor of *Inner Resources for Leaders* (IRL).

Beth Birmingham is Associate Professor of Leadership and Change at Eastern University teaching in both the PhD in Organizational Leadership program and graduate programs of the School of Leadership and Development (SLD). At Eastern she created a graduate degree in organizational leadership serving international NGOs and was responsible for a number of international partnerships that make up the SLD including World Vision International, Habitat for Humanity International, and Cornerstone Christian College in Cape Town where she lived from 2006 to 2008. Her dissertation and recent research and writing are focused on partnerships in the international development sector.

Michael D. Callahan is Francis Willson Thompson Professor of Leadership Studies at Kettering University, Michigan. He is author of *Mandates and Empire: The League of Nations and Africa, 1914–1931* (Sussex: Academic Press, 1999) and *A Sacred Trust: The League of Nations and Africa, 1929–1946* (Sussex: Academic Press, 2004). In addition to courses on the history of international relations and American foreign relations, he teaches seminars on leadership, ethics, and contemporary issues.

Ezekiel Gebissa (PhD Michigan State University) is Associate Professor of History at Kettering University. He is the author of *Leaf of Allah: Khat and Agricultural Transformation in Harerge Ethiopia, 1875–1991* (Athens: Ohio University Press, 2004), and editor of *Contested Terrain:*

Essays on Oromo Studies, Ethiopianist Discourses, and Politically Engaged Scholarship (Trenton, NJ: Red Sea Press, 2008) and *Taking the Place of Food: Khat in Ethiopia* (Trenton, NJ: Red Sea Press, 2010). He is the current editor of the *Journal of Oromo Studies*. His research focuses on agricultural transformation, livelihood sustainability, and religious leadership, and he teaches courses on leadership and sustainable development.

Jill B. Jacoby is founder and Executive Director of Sweetwater Alliance, a nonprofit organization with a mission to raise water literacy through the arts and science. She has a PhD in Leadership and Change from Antioch University, a Master's of Study in Environmental Law from Vermont Law School, an MSc in water resources from the University of Minnesota, and a bachelor's degree in Agriculture and Environmental Education from the Pennsylvania State University.

Xia Ji is Assistant Professor of Science and Environmental Education at the University of Regina in Canada, and co-coordinator for the "Reconnecting with Native Prairie Ecosystems" Working Group of the Regional Centre of Expertise in Education for Sustainable Development (RCE -ESD), Saskatchewan. Her work focuses on civic discourse in science and environmental education, and deep pedagogy. She has a master's degree in Environmental Learning and Leadership and a PhD in Environmental Education and Teacher Education from the University of Minnesota (Twin Cities).

Paul Kaak has a PhD in Leadership from Andrews University (2005) and is currently Associate Professor of Leadership at Azusa Pacific University. His primary assignments include teaching graduate and undergraduate leadership courses. In addition, he teaches a course on sustainable societies in APU's Global Studies program. Paul is board chairman for the Southern California Agricultural Land Foundation (SCALF—www.agrariansolutions.org), a nonprofit organization focused on land preservation, community supported agriculture, agri-eco-culinary education, and food justice. In Paul's courses, Wendell Berry is often given an opportunity to speak to the students through selections from his essays and poetry.

Stan L. LeQuire is an instructional designer and adjunct faculty member at Eastern University. While he is often seen teaching graduate courses, behind the scenes LeQuire spends a great deal of time investigating the viability of community-based ecological tourism (ecotourism) and its impact on economic development, environmental preservation, and the support of cultures. Through Eastern University's School of Leadership and Development, LeQuire works to conserve creation by promoting sensible tourism that, in turn, improves the well-being of the local community.

Heather R. McDougall is Associate Dean of the Global Leadership Program, Prague, Czech Republic, and Founder/Executive Director of the Global Institute for Leadership and Civic Development (GILCD), Bloomington, Indiana. Dr. McDougall teaches courses on leadership, global citizenship, political philosophy, and women in leadership. Her teaching and research interests focus on training future leaders and responsible global citizens. She has worked with students from more than 65 different countries and hosted leadership study trips in the Czech Republic, Germany, United States, Italy, Argentina, Cuba, United Arab Emirates, and India.

Martin Melaver has served for the past 17 years as CEO of Melaver, Inc., a third-generation family-owned real estate business focused on sustainable principles and practices. He is the author of *Living above the Store: Building a Business that Creates Values, Inspires Change, and Restores Land and Community* (White River Junction, VT: Chelsea Green, 2009) as well as *The Green Building Bottom Line* (New York: McGraw-Hill, 2008). Martin holds a BA from Amherst College, an MA and PhD from Harvard University, and an MBA from the Kellogg School of Management at Northwestern University. He divides his time between Savannah, Georgia (work), and Tel Aviv, Israel (family).

Benjamin W. Redekop is Associate Professor of Leadership Studies at Christopher Newport University in Newport News, Virginia. His publications include *Enlightenment and Community* (Montreal: McGill-Queen's University Press, 2000), *Power, Authority, and the Anabaptist Tradition* (Baltimore, MD: The Johns Hopkins University Press, 2001), and articles in *The Leadership Quarterly*, *Management Decision*, *The Encyclopedia of Sustainability*, *Building Leadership Bridges*, and *Journal of Practical Consulting*. He teaches courses in leadership to students in the President's Leadership Program at CNU.

Calvin W. Redekop is Professor Emeritus of Conrad Grebel University College, Waterloo, Ontario. A longtime advocate of environmental conservation, Redekop has promoted environmental sustainability in a variety of business ventures while pursuing a career in academia. He earned a PhD in Sociology from the University of Chicago in 1959. His many publications include *Mennonite Society* (Baltimore, MD: The Johns Hopkins University Press, 1989) and *Creation and Environment: An Anabaptist Perspective on a Sustainable World* (Baltimore, MD: The Johns Hopkins University Press, 2000).

Rian Satterwhite is Assistant Director for Leadership Programs in the Center for Student Leadership at Kennesaw State University. In addition to coordinating multiple extra- and co-curricular leadership development programs, he teaches a course on Leadership and Sustainability. Rian grew up in the Pacific Northwest and has had a deep and abiding love for the diversity of our natural world from an early age. As an amateur photographer he strives to document common human experience, especially our relationship with the environment and delicate place within it.

Stephen P. Stelzner obtained his PhD from the University of Illinois at Chicago in 1989. He is a Professor of Psychology at the College of Saint Benedict and Saint John's University in central Minnesota. His background is in organizational psychology, community psychology, and developmental psychology, with an emphasis on the ecological contexts of organizations, communities, and human development. His scholarly work has focused on using ecological principles to change social systems, including the development of leadership processes that emphasize ethical and sustainable approaches for organizations and communities.

Denise Stodola earned her PhD at the University of Missouri-Columbia, with two areas of specialization: rhetoric and composition, and medieval literature. Her research focuses on the rhetoric of didacticism and pedagogy in the Middle Ages and the modern day. She is an Assistant Professor of Communication at Kettering University, where she teaches courses in communication, humanities, and literature.

Simon Western worked as a nurse, family therapist, and clinical manager in public health before turning to leadership development and organizational consultancy work. As an academic he has taught leadership and coaching and has worked internationally at leading business schools and with leaders in all sectors. A Quaker and social activist, Western is currently principal consultant at the Tavistock Centre London, where he directs the master's program in Organizational Consultancy. His recent book *Leadership: A Critical Text* (Los Angeles: Sage Publications, 2008) offers a novel approach to leadership, aligning organizational leadership with sustainability and the environmental agenda.

Richard M. Wielkiewicz obtained his PhD from the University of Hawai'i in 1977. He is a Professor of Psychology at the College of Saint Benedict and Saint John's University in central Minnesota. He infuses a sustainability perspective into teaching statistics, principles of learning, and a writing seminar for first-year students. Most of his scholarly work has focused on development and validation of the Leadership Attitudes and Behavior Scales (LABS) and promoting the idea that leadership theories need to focus on sustainable models of leadership processes instead of positional leaders and the drive for corporate profit.

Robert L. Williams is a Senior Fellow at the Fanning Institute at the University of Georgia where he is responsible for leadership education, including the Institute for Georgia Environmental Leaders, the Fuld Fellows for Leadership in Academic Nursing, and LEAD21, a national program for academic leaders. He was formerly a managing partner for Triangle Associates, a national consulting firm in health care and higher education and Associate Director for the Pew Center for the Health Professions. His research and writing have focused on American social advocates, the social psychology of too much leadership, and group dynamics and collaboration.

Index

G

H

I

J

K

L

M

N

P

Q

R